100 Questions -

MW00961545

Volume I
Second Edition

100 Questions Every Social Worker Should Know: ASWB-LCSW Exam Preparation Guide

Volume I

Questions 1-100
Second Edition

100 Questions Every Social Worker Should Know:
ASWB-LCSW Exam Preparation Guide

Harvey Norris, MSW, LCSW

TURTLE PRESS

All effort has been made to proof-read this text and make sure grammar and spelling are flawless. However, 43,000+ words leaves room for possible error. If you find an error, please bring it to my attention at harveynorris@yahoo.com

Any help is sincerely appreciated

What is new in the second Edition.

1. Five new questions were added to replace the 5 duplicate questions which snuck in

2. Spelling errors and Typos were corrected.

3. Font is increased to 12 pt for easier reading and less eye-strain.

Library of Congress Cataloging in Publication Data

Norris, Harvey S.

ACKNOWLEDGEMENTS

Many people helped me in the creation of this book. I want to especially thank my wife Marguerite, who has stood by me for 20 years, my children, Aidan, Bryannah, Liam, Deaglan and Ciaran for keeping me involved and engaged during the entire process.

Extra special thanks goes to my mother, Alice, who (while not a social worker) provided feedback and insight on every question. And to my father, David, who taught me to always fight for your principles, and to never "sell-out".

I would also like to thank my friends and interns who provided me with feedback and support during this process. Special thanks to Anthony Scott, Dan Knippel, Erica Miller, Akiela Anderson, Heather Lincicome and Cathy Wortham.

To my FIRST and BEST clinical Supervisor, Pesula Faulkner, MSSW, I say thank you.

To Sam Phifer, LCSW for always being available, to Mike Mates for teaching me about friendship, and John Cooper for showing me a different way.

To all the other friends, clients and professionals who have touched my life and made me who I am today!

CONTENTS

1) symptoms of depression
2) Diagnosing with the DSM
3) with a client in crisis
4) severe anxiety and paranoia
5) coming to you for marriage counseling
6) a report to the child welfare agency
7) assess a 15 year old female client
8) who has made two attempts at suicide
9) on 65 year old male client
10) Committing an ethical violation
11) Of the following drugs
12) Relates a history of drug use
13) to learn Rational Emotive Therapy
14) an initial session with a battered woman
15) and they arrive 22 minutes late
16) She is preoccupied with her "large" jaw, "small" breasts and "uneven" skin
17) is known as "synergistic articulation and awareness"
18) They have elected to pay in cash
19) counseling strategies with Native American populations
20) been assigned an elderly client
21) working with an African-American client
22) You are assigned a gay teen-age client
23) plan a program to be presented to your client base
24) whose live has been turned upside down due to Agoraphobia
25) to cope with a traumatic event
26) with an agency that does community organization
27) Libido is described as
28) stages of dying include all of the following
29) use a very primitive defense mechanism
30) several theories of understanding human behavior
31) T o observe you completing an interview

[7]

32) diagnosis of Schizophreniform Disorder

33) In an indigent care psychiatric receiving hospital

34) history of incestuous relationships

35) you need to be more confrontational

36) assesses the needs of the client

37) works with the HIV/AIDS population

38) management philosophy reflects a "Theory Y" approach

39) primary classes of medications prescribed for

40) medications prescribed for the relief of depressive symptoms

41) one WOULD NOT lend itself to family therapy

42) your supervisor throws out some impromptu questions

43) and is obviously in acute mental distress

44) Carl Roger's theory of personality development

45) technique of sitting in a room with two chairs

46) about his sexual desires and feels they are disgusting

47) survivor of childhood sexual abuse

48) anxiety is caused by

49) only serve to increase the child's misbehavior

50) client is a survivor of childhood sexual abuse

51) the teacher's reprimands only serve to increase the child's misbehavior

52) asked to see a child who is withdrawn

53) provide therapy towards "Stress inoculation"

54) "you must eat your string beans before you can go watch TV"

55) she asks for advice on a specific area of her current situation

56) impulsive use of obscene language

57) cigarette smoking as a behavioral fixation

58) Crisis is a process

59) The ecological approach is a favorite approach

60) asked to set up a program to assist a family

61) questions about depressogenic schemas
62) place an emphasis on coaching, giving immediate feedback
63) help because he has intense anxiety and panic attacks
64) asks detailed questions about the specific sexual abuse incidents
65) clients who are survivors of sexual child abuse
66) problems addressing the resistance a client
67) The consultant starts tell what needs to change
68) offers you a free catered event
69) Task centered treatment model contains
70) agency uses the functional model of intervention
71) Xanax (Alprazolam) is
72) upon reviewing his medications you find he has been prescribed
73) appear to be homeless, as they have an unpleasant body odor
74) primary problem associated with criminals and addicts as
75) talking about the client's "life script"
76) client in terms unconditional positive regard
77) current diagnosis of Borderline Personality Disorder
78) who is currently complaining about how her brother treats her
79) During your assessment of a 7 year old child
80) black social worker receives a new client on their caseload who is white
81) stumble upon an area where the client believes something that could not be true
82) begin yelling at each other in a loud, threatening manner
83) You receive a voicemail from the guidance department
84) complain about therapy and state they are not happy with it
85) working at a rural mental health clinic near the coast

86) Social workers treat each person in a caring and respectful fashion

87) Social workers' primary goal is to

88) Social workers continually strive to increase their professional knowledge

89) Social workers should use clear and understandable language

90) Social workers should not solicit a private fee or

91) responsibility to serve the broader public good

92) our social safety-net bureaucracy

93) lists ten personality disorders

94) At an office party for your agency

95) Food Stamps and Medicaid are examples

96) United States Supreme Court ruled that a juvenile has a right to

97) A major problem with managed care (HMO) mental health services

98) the risk of eventually dying from suicide is 10 times greater

99) who are in treatment for substance abuse disorders

100)   Social workers who function in case management positions

100+   clients in terms of their conscious motivation

100++   identifies himself as a reality therapist

Question 1   **Section: Clinical**

While interviewing a new client referred for some symptoms of depression, the client reports the following issues of concern, (1) weight gain over the past 2 weeks of more than 5 pounds (2) difficulty with concentration, (3) headaches (4) disrupted sleep patterns and (5) suicidal thoughts. Upon questioning, the client states they have no idea why these things have occurred and that they are unusual. A short time later, the client mentions in an off-handed fashion that their Primary Care Doctor placed them on a new medication 3-4 weeks ago for a new medical condition.

A) arrange for an involuntary commitment in reference to client's suicidal thoughts
B) refer for a consultation with a psychiatrist for possible anti-depressant medications
C) complete a thorough Biopsychosocial Assessment to complete treatment planning
D) determine the prescribed medication, gather information on side-effects and if necessary refer to Primary Care for medication evaluation.

Answer on Page: 65

Question 2   **Section: Clinical**

Diagnosing with the DSM allows certain diagnoses for mental disorders to be made, even though there is not enough information available or gathered to complete the criterion. When using the DSM in this manner, the diagnosis should have which word following it.

A) Latent

B) Temporary
C) Provisional
D) Revised

Answer on Page: 66

Question 3 Section: Clinical

On your initial session with a client in crisis, you should focus on which of the following FIRST:

A) any underlying personality issues you perceive
B) client's immediate or stated presenting problem
C) general day-to-day problems in functioning
D) client's possible substance use

Answer on Page: 67

Question 4   Section: Assessment

A patient arrives at a walk-in clinic and is obviously in acute mental distress: The patient presents with severe anxiety and paranoia. A chart review indicates the patient has a history of polysubstance abuse and suffers from chronic liver disease. You are unable to determine if the patient is currently using drugs due to the presenting symptoms. The most likely DSM IV diagnosis you would assign is:

A) Anxiety Disorder, NOS
B) Anxiety Disorder, provisional
C) Anxiety Disorder, without general malaise
D) Anxiety Disorder, undifferentiated type

[12]

Answer on Page: 68

Question 5 Section: Clinical

On your first session with a husband and wife, coming to you for marriage counseling, the wife begins the session by saying the biggest problem in their marriage is her husband's nasty temper. Your best first response should be to say...

A) Have you done anything that might provoke his anger?
B) Can you tell me more about this problem?
C) ...at our session today he doesn't seem to have a problem with self control.
D) to ask the husband if he wishes to discuss his problems with his temper.

Answer on Page: 70

Question 6   Section: Assessment

In Florida, and in most states, social workers, and all other human service professionals, are required to make a report to the child welfare agency or law enforcement in which of the following situations:

A) imminent threats to a child
B) evidence of child sexual abuse
C) suspicion of child abuse
D) child custody battles

Answer on Page: 72

Question 7   Section: Assessment

You are asked to assess a 15-year old female client who has recently arrived at a mental health center with the following complaints: For the past 4 weeks she has been uncharacteristically angry and irritable. She states she has difficulty concentrating on her schoolwork and her after-school activities. When asked how she feels she says she feels "Blah...you know...like YUCK". She relates she has been eating less, skipping breakfast and has lost 9 pounds in the last 4 weeks. She relates a serious decrease in appetite. She relates she has difficulty sleeping and has dropped out of several school activities she was very involved with. During your assessment her hands are in constant nervous motion and she gets up from her seat several times and restlessly paces the room. Your most probable diagnosis would be:

A) a drug induced depression
B) a somatoform disorder
C) a depressive episode
D) an anxiety disorder

Answer on Page: 73

Question 8   Section: Clinical

You have been providing therapy for a teenage boy who has made two attempts at suicide over the past 6   months. The first attempt involved taking his grandfather's pills. He was rushed to the ER but was not admitted to the behavioral health unit. The second attempt, two months after the first, involved an attempted suffocation, for which you had the client involuntarily committed. He was held for 24 hours, then, released. During the past three

[14]

months, he has been anxious and depressed, but has stopped talking about suicide.

You receive a phone call from his mother on Monday morning stating that he succeeded in committing suicide over the weekend. She is upset and stated she is going to sue you and your agency supervisor for malpractice. Which statement best reflects the supervisor's legal status in this lawsuit?

Do not assess a suicidal person unless you have received special training from an expert and they are comfortable with your skill level!

A) The direct clinician bears total responsibility. The supervisor, never personally treated the youth, and are not liable for   any negligent actions committed by a supervisee.

B) The agency is the only legally liable party because they employ the social worker and the social work supervisor. They have promulgated policies, rules and a malpractice   policy,   so the workers are not individually responsible.

C) The social worker is legally liable and the supervisor shares vicarious legal liability due to their responsibility for   carefully monitoring and evaluating every case under   treatment by their supervisees, and for reviewing   supervisee's case notes.

D) There is no liability because of the earlier involuntary commitment. The social worker acknowledged the   severity of the case, by going forward with the   commitment   and   has lifted liability from themselves for future   suicidal   threats   and actions.

Answer on Page: 75

Question 9   **Section: Clinical**

You accept a referral from an agency on 65-year old male client. During the initial interview you learn he has been physically abusive to his wife of 40 years and he appears very depressed.

He relates that two of his children will not talk to him and did not call him for his birthday this year. You quickly find you dislike this client intensely and have difficulty feeling any empathy for this client and his situation. That evening after the session you realize he reminds you of your spouse's step-father who was abusive to your spouse during their childhood. You should…

A) Share your feelings with the client
B) Talk to your supervisor about your reactions toward this client
C) Accept your feelings as part of the therapeutic process when working with abusers
D) Continue your sessions with the client and ignore your feelings

Answer on Page: 77

Question 10   **Section: Ethics**

Committing an ethical violation in Social Work can occur very quickly if you are not clear on the NASW Code. Which of the following situations create the greatest opportunity for a breach of ethics?

A) Using the client's first name during therapy without asking permission.
B) Giving the client several personal books you have for pleasure reading.
C) Discussing the progress of the local or college sports team with the client
D) Exchanging lawn care services at your home for therapy time instead of cash.

Answer on Page: 78

Question 11   Section: Assessment

Of the following drugs prescribed by a psychiatrist, which would be most likely prescribed for a diagnosis which included psychosis?

A) Wellbutrin (Bupropion)
B) Risperdol (Risperidone).
C) Prozac (Fluoxetine Hydrochloride)
D) Lithobid (Lithium Carbonate)

Answer on Page: 80

Question 12   Section: Clinical

A 31-year-old female client is referred to you by her uncle. During your initial evaluation the client relates a history of drug use since age 15, and states that she is currently using cocaine several times a week and Marijuana daily, but does not feel this is a major problem because she has held her same job for 4 years without problems. She denies a history of arrest or legal involvement. Your first action should be to:

A) talk with the client about a referral for substance abuse treatment and assist them in scheduling and arranging the assessment.
B) complete the assessment, create a treatment plan and enter into an agreement with the client to NOT use drugs during her time in therapy.
C) Bring in the client's family for the next session and complete a family interview and assessment to determine intergenerational issues.
D) determine the client's motivation for change and discuss different treatment options.

Answer on Page: 82

Question 13   Section: Clinical

As a social worker in a clinic, you are studying with a clinician to learn Rational Emotive Therapy. When interacting with a client, as a RET Therapist you would be MOST interested in therapeutic techniques, which help to modify which of the following:

A) behaviors
B) emotions
C) beliefs
D) events

Answer on Page: 83

Question 14   Section: Assessment

[18]

You have just begun an initial session with a battered woman who is just starting to tell you about the story and history of abuse. The BEST thing you can do as a therapist is...

A) during her disclosure ask her leading questions as a method of eliciting as much information as possible and to let her know you are supportive of her situation.
B) Simply listen to her story and do not offer advice or suggestions.
C) Stop her at different times during, her discussion and provide her with an interpretation of her nonverbal behavior and statements to assist her in becoming more self-aware.
D) Provide her with information about other domestic violence victims you have worked with in order to help her understand you are empathetic to her situation.

Answer on Page: 85

Question 15   Section: Clinical

It is your fourth session with a client and they arrive 22 minutes late. Upon seating themselves on the couch they say, "I know I am late, I got stuck at work today and could not get away from my desk. This is the third time they are late to a session. Your decide it is time to address this situation. Your BEST response is to say:

A) Can you think of any reason why you want to avoid talking today?
B) Maybe we need to explore what it means to you to come here for our sessions.

[19]

C) I know that your work is important, but we will just have less time together today

D) You seem to expect me to be angry with you. Let's talk about how you feel.

Answer on Page: 86

Question 16   Section: Assessment

You have been asked to consult with another social worker who is working with a 15 year-old girl. During her first visit the youth stated "I wish I could convince my parents to take me to a plastic surgeon". She presented with the following issues. She is preoccupied with her "large" jaw, "small" breasts and "uneven" skin and will ask her mother whether she looks okay at least a dozen times per day. She has begun to use heavy makeup and has also started wearing long sleeves and pants at all times in order to cover her skin. Her appearance concerns are so time-consuming and distressing that she has ceased to spend time with her friends and has dropped her extracurricular activities. What is her probable diagnosis according to DSM-IV or DSM-IV-TR symptoms?

A) Schizophreniform Disorder
B) Obsessive-Compulsive Disorder
C) Body Dysmorphic Disorder
D) Post Traumatic Stress Disorder

Answer on Page: 87

[20]

Question 17   Section: Assessment

You have recently begun working in a rural southern mental health clinic and are assigned a male client who you determine has reached the fifth and final stage of the Minority Identity Development Model proposed by Atkinson, Morten, and Sue in 1993.   This stage is known as "synergistic articulation and awareness". You are the same race and ethnicity of the client, and you are aware that they would probably prefer a counselor ...
A) who challenges his attitudes, beliefs and world views.
B) who is from a racial or ethnic minority group.
C) who is from the majority group.
D) who shares his attitudes, beliefs and world views.

Answer on Page: 91

Question 18   Section: Behavior

You have been working with a client for six sessions and they are covered by BCBS Insurance. They have elected to pay in cash rather than use their insurance benefits.   Their insurance company sent you a letter requesting information about the client's progress and the current focus of therapy.   Your best response is to...

A) throw the letter in the trash and forget about it.
B) send the insurance company a complete copy of the file.
C) verify the validity of the letter and then copy and send the file.
D) Send the requested information only with the client's written authorization.

Answer on Page: 92

Question 19   Section: Clinical

[21]

According to LaFromboise, Teresa D., Joseph E. Trimble, Gerald V. Mohatt, effective counseling strategies with Native American populations include all of the following EXCEPT:

A) Assess level of acculturation
B) Include families in interventions
C) Providing therapy in a "value-free" environment
D) Acknowledge the client's tribal and familial affiliation

Answer on Page: 93

Question 20   Section: Clinical

You have been assigned an elderly client.   Of the following interventions, which is *LEAST* likely to be useful during therapy?

A) insight-oriented therapy
B) relying on a multidisciplinary team using a
        Multimodal approach
C) letting the client to set the pace and agenda
        in a non-directive therapy modality
D) supportive therapy

Answer on Page: 95

Question 21   Section: Clinical

You are working with an African-American client in an agency setting. Your review of current research would indicate that the MOST effective counseling approach would be:

A) non-directive, exploratory therapy

[22]

B) directive, problem-solving therapy that is time-limited,

C) individual therapy that is short-term and has an emphasis on problem-solving

D) non-directive family therapy

Answer on Page: 96

Question 22   Section: Clinical

You have been assigned a gay teen-age client. Of the many roles you play as a therapist, which one is the MOST important role for you in this situation?

A) helping the client prepare to tell his or her family that he or she is gay

B) helping the client unlearn maladaptive self-protective behaviors

C) exposing the client to gay role models

D) providing the client with relevant information and resources

Answer on Page: 97

Question 23   Section: Behavior

You have been approached by your director and asked to plan a program to be presented to your client base. First thing to do is to clearly define the problem you are seeking to resolve, the next step would be...

A) review all available resources and existing programs

B) order resources that are available for a similar issue.

C) detail the goals of your program and determine the action steps needed.

[23]

D) deciding who will be eligible for your program.

Answer on Page: 98

Question 24   Section: Assessment

You receive a client whose life has been turned upside down due to Agoraphobia. She relates that it is affecting her relationship with her husband and her ability to lead a normal life. Agoraphobia is ...

A) Fear of heights
B) Fear of snakes
C) Fear of closed places
D) Fear of open spaces

Answer on Page: 99

Question 25   Section: Clinical

Young children, trying to cope with a traumatic event can use a very primitive defense mechanism, the results of which can lead them to view people as un-integrated. They have a tendency to perceive people as either innately good or innately evil, rather than a whole, continuous being. This defense mechanism is known as...

A) Denial
B) Splitting
C) Sublimation
D) Projection

[24]

Definition: A defense mechanism is a strategy used to cover up or change unconscious desires and wishes that may be inappropriate or difficult to express.

Answer on Page: 100

Question 26   Section: Behavior

You have taken a job with an agency that does community organization. You will use all of the following interventions EXCEPT:

A) Provide mental health services
B) Hold work training sessions with groups
C) Hold community empowerment meetings
D) Organize neighborhood improvement groups

Answer on Page: 102

Question 27   Section: Clinical

You are in our second session with a client and are deeply engaged in rapport building. In developing this trust and alliance you should...

A) help the client understand that the agency's treatment goals are best for the client.
B) help the client understand that confidentiality is complete.
C) help the client understand that you are experienced and can help them.
D) help her understand her needs are important and they will be in the treatment plan.

Answer on Page: 102

[25]

Question 28   Section: Clinical

Elisabeth Kübler-Ross, the Swiss-born psychiatrist, a pioneer in near-death studies and the author of the groundbreaking book "On Death and Dying" (1969) postulated five stages of dying. These stages have become the cornerstone of palliative care. The Kübler-Ross's stages of dying include all of the following EXCEPT:

A) Anger
B) Denial
C) Peace
D) Acceptance

Answer on Page: 103

Question 29   Section: Assessment

You have accepted a job working with habitual sex offenders who seek out young children. What is the primary type of therapy you will be doing with them?

A) Psychotropic Drugs
B) Long-term treatment groups.
C) Individual treatment.
D) Family therapy.

Answer on Page: 105

Question 30   Section: Clinical

Libido, is defined, as the force or psychic energy behind human action. It plays a large role in several theories of understanding human behavior. Which theorist believed that libido was general psychic energy?

A) Carl Rogers
B) Sigmund Freud
C) Carl Gustav Jung
D) Aaron Beck

Answer on Page: 106

Question 31   Section: Ethics

Your supervisor wants to observe you completing an interview with a new client. The observation will take place in a room equipped with a two-way mirror. The supervisor is a qualified clinical professional who has supervisory responsibility over all cases under treatment by the agency. Your supervisor should inform you that ...

A) You are not required to notify the client they that will be observed during the interview because they signed a "consent for treatment" which indicates they might be   observed.
B) You do not need get informed consent because the observation is for your clinical supervision and not directly related to treatment issues. Also the observation is not being recorded so there will be no record of the session.
C) You need to obtain the client's informed consent at the beginning of the session and give the client the opportunity to decline to be observed.

D) You should notify the client they are being observed but you are not required to obtain their specific permission.

Answer on Page: 107

Question 32   Section: Assessment

You receive a client with a diagnosis of Schizophreniform Disorder. You immediately understand that this client displays psychotic symptoms at various times. These symptoms are reported as disorganized speech and grossly disorganized behavior. The PRIMARY thing you should know about this diagnosis is that it is ...

A) related to very long term symptoms
B) related to substance abuse and dependency
C) related to a marked decline in functional behavior that has lasted for more than 1 year and less than 5 years.
D) related to symptoms of schizophrenia with symptoms lasting less than 6 months and more than 1 month.

Answer on Page: 109

Question 33   Section: Assessment

You are working the night shift in an indigent care psychiatric receiving hospital and the sheriff shows up with a 27-year-old male. The client is disheveled, with bloodshot eyes and slurred speech. Multiple attempts to question the client have been met with rambling statements and an inability to stay focused. The Sheriff gives you the following information. The client has been stopping every hundred miles or so and has been calling the

[28]

highway patrol to state that the "truckers" are spying on him and he can hear them talking to each other as they pass his car. He also related to the sheriff that when he stops at Truck Refilling Stations, the "prostitutes talk about him and tell lies about him to each other. He is from San Diego and is Active Duty Navy and has driven all the way to Florida in 37 hours. An empty bottle of NO-DOZ was found on the floor of his car. You realize that he is suffering from caffeine overdose. His "paranoid-like" statements are a manifestation of....

A) Depersonalization
B) ideas of reference
C) conversion symptoms
D) Delusions of reference

Answer on Page: 111

Question 34   Section: Clinical

You have begun working with a family in which there is a verified history of incestuous relationships. Of the following characteristics, which one is MOST often found in families in which incestuous relationships have occurred?

A) Enmeshment of family members
B) Relaxed attitude toward sexuality
C) Symbiotic mother-child relationships
D) Distorted communication patterns

Answer on Page: 113

Question 35   Section: Clinical

As a new clinical social worker you find yourself being told by your supervisor you need to be more confrontational. This seems at odds with the social work mission, until you supervisor explains the primary purpose of confrontation is to:

A) demonstrate accurate understanding
B) help a client change her view of a problem
C) make a client aware of inconsistencies
D) provide a client with information to identify alternatives to her present behavior

Answer on Page: 114

Question 36   Section: Behavior

You have been hired as a social work case manager for an urban based agency. Your mission is to assess the needs of the client, the needs of the client's family, and to arrange for, coordinate, monitor, evaluate and advocate for a package of multiple services to meet the specific client's complex needs. Social work case management is distinct from other forms of case management because it addresses all of the following EXCEPT:

A) the client's Biopsychosocial status and the state of the social system in which the client operates.
B) intervention occurs at both the client (micro) and system (macro) levels.
C) the need for the social worker to develop and maintain a therapeutic relationship with the client.

[30]

D) the need for the client to accept the services provided because they are identified as necessary by the social work case manager.

Answer on Page: 115

Question 37   Section: Behavior

You have been hired, by a private, non-profit agency, which works with the HIV/AIDS population. The primary function of your unit is to educate sexually active individuals about the disease and to help them understand the importance of testing, life-style changes and treatment if necessary. Your unit is involved in the provision of:

A) primary prevention
B) secondary prevention
C) tertiary prevention
D) crisis intervention

Answer on Page: 116

Question 38   Section: Behavior

You are new to an agency and the Executive Director left during your first month on the job. The agency has just hired a new Executive Director. You overhear one of the supervisors state that the new director's management philosophy reflects a "Theory Y" approach. You know that over the next six months, you should be able to watch the agency change, in which of the following ways?

A) Highly cohesive and effective work groups

B) a high degree of employee self-direction and self-control
C) the use of pay and bonuses as the primary mechanisms of reward
D) promotion and selection based on technical competence

Answer on Page: 118

Question 39   **Section: Clinical**

There are three primary classes of medications prescribed for the relief of depressive symptoms. They are MAOI's (Monoamine Oxidase Inhibitors), Tricyclics, and SSRI's (Serotonin Selective Reuptake Inhibitors). Chose the answer that lists them in length of time they have been on the market (from oldest to newest).

A) Tricyclics then MAOI's then SSRI's
B) MAOI's then SSRI's then Tricyclics
C) SSRI's then MAOI's then Tricyclics
D) MOAI's then Tricyclics then SSRI's

Answer on Page: 120

Question 40   **Section: Clinical**

There are three primary classes of medications prescribed for the relief of depressive symptoms. They are MAOI's (Monoamine Oxidase Inhibitors), Tricyclics, and SSRI's (Serotonin Selective Reuptake Inhibitors). Each answer contains the names of 5-6 common antidepressants. Choose the answer where all of the antidepressants named belong to the class known as SSRI's.

[32]

A. Procarbazine (Matulane), Safrazine (Safra), Phenelzine (Nardil, Nardelzine), Pheniprazine (Catron), Iproniazid (Iprozid)

B. Citalopram (Celexa), Escitalopram (Lexapro), Fluoxetine (Prozac), Fluvoxamine (Luvox),Paroxetine (Paxil), Sertraline (Zoloft)

C. Amitriptyline (Elavil), Clomipramine (Anafranil), Desipramine (Norpramin), Doxepin (Sinequan), Imipramine (Tofranil), Nortriptyline (Pamelor)

D. Citalopram (Celexa), Fluoxetine (Prozac), Nortriptyline (Pamelor), Phenelzine (Nardil, Nardelzine), Amitriptyline (Elavil)

Answer on Page: 121

Question 41   Section: Clinical

You are sitting in a case staffing meeting at your agency while several other social workers are discussing their new cases and receiving feedback and suggestions. Of the four following situations, which one WOULD NOT lend itself to family therapy…

A) An enmeshed family, improvement in one member is likely to cause distress in the other members

B) A separated couple with two children, one child in the family has an eating disorder

C) A 17 year-old son who needs to separate psychologically from his family

D) A couple with two children that has decided to divorce.

Answer on Page: 122

Question 42   Section: Assessment

During a staff meeting, your supervisor throws out some impromptu questions. He asks you; "When should discussions, with your client, about termination of therapy begin?" In order to impress them, you should answer:

A) at the end of every session during the wrap up process.
B) only during the last two or three sessions.
C) at the beginning of therapy when goals are set and then again at the end of therapy
D) throughout the course of therapy at different times during the process

Answer on Page: 123

Question 43   Section: Behavior

You have reached an agreement, with a 75-year-old woman, who lives on public assistance. She is willing to move into an assisted living facility for the elderly. She talks about her fear of moving into a facility where she does not know anyone and feels she will be all alone. Your BEST response to help her adjust is to say...

A) "Don't worry, you'll make new friends."
B) "I guess you'd rather stay where you are."
C) "It seems like part of you wants to move to a more comfortable place and another part feels scared and wants to stay with people you know."
D) "Most older people feel just like you, but then feel better after they move."

Answer on Page: 124

Question 44   Section: Clinical

[34]

You and two colleagues attend a seminar on Carl Roger's theory of personality development. The presenter, a Rogerian therapist, discusses the need for unconditional positive regard and continues by stating that, according to Carl Rogers, a DYSFUNCTIONAL behavior is caused by…

A) disturbances of the ego boundary
B) incongruence between self and experience
C) the client's lack of awareness of their surroundings and/or environment
D) irresponsibility of actions

Answer on Page: 125

Question 45   Section: Clinical

You are introduced to a colleague who begins talking about the therapy technique of sitting in a room with two chairs… you are on one chair and try to imagine what it would be like to experience the world as if you were the other chair. You realize they are talking about the highly experiential intervention known as Gestalt Therapy (Fritz Perls). The colleague then asks you what a Gestalt therapist would think about the concept of INTROJECTION. Because you are a true social worker, you know it …

(Introjection is usually defined as "the process whereby the client replicates behaviors, attributes or other fragments of the surrounding environment into themselves. This is especially true in regards to the behavior of other people.)

A) is a type of defense mechanism

[35]

B) increases awareness
C) is necessary for healthy growth
D) can lead to neurosis

Answer on Page: 128

Question 46   Section: Clinical

John has deep concerns about his sexual desires and feels they are disgusting. In response to these feelings, he becomes an active crusader against pornography. What ego defense mechanism did he use?

A) Projection
B) Transference
C) Reaction formation
D) Sublimation

Answer on Page: 130

Question 47   Section: Clinical

You have been seeing a court-ordered adolescent client for 10 weeks when he says to you, "I see no reason to keep coming. I have not been in trouble over the past 10 weeks and you should trust me and know I have changed so I won't get in trouble again." Your BEST response is to say …

A) "It is frustrating to have to do something you don't want to do. Have you had other experiences like this before?"
B) "Two months isn't long enough to judge your trustworthiness."
C) "You broke the law and now must suffer the consequences."
D) "Sometimes we have to do things we don't want to do."

[36]

Answer on Page: 132

Question 48   Section: Clinical

According to Sigmund Freud, anxiety is caused by:

A) excitation due to internal or external stimulation or stimulus
B) consequences due to being unable to construe or understand an event
C) a signal that the "self" is in danger of "splitting"
D) an indication that the "unified self" is being threatened.

Answer on Page: 133

Question 49   Section: Assessment

You have been asked to help a teacher with a child. The child has been exhibiting misbehavior and you has been noticed that the teacher's reprimands only serve to increase the child's misbehavior. The behavior is disrupting the entire class. The reprimands given by the teacher are acting as which type of reinforcer...

A) secondary
B) negative
C) positive
D) primary

Answer on Page: 135

Question 50   Section: Assessment

[37]

Your client is a survivor of childhood sexual abuse who has been doing rather well in therapy. She revealed that she always believed her mother knew about the abuse by a family friend, yet did not intervene to protect her. She described her mother as cold, a harsh disciplinarian, and stated she is currently living four states away. She has not seen her mother for eight years, but talks monthly to her on the phone. She has just informed you her mother called her three nights ago and told her she was coming to visit at the end of the month. She also tells you in a rather embarrassed tone that she "found" herself drinking from her two year old son's "Sippy Cup" last night, after he was asleep, and does not remember filling it up. She reports feeling "very strange" about this behavior. The client is most likely experiencing the unconscious onset of the ego defense mechanism known as...

A) Repression
B) Splitting
C) Regression
D) Introjection

Answer on Page: 136

Question 51   Section: Assessment

You are in a staffing and the supervisor asks you to state the characteristics of fetal alcohol syndrome. You BEST response is to respond with...

A) albino coloration.
B) aggressive and acting-out behavior.
C) slow moral development.

[38]

D)mental retardation, slow or reduced growth, and abnormalities in the shape and size of the head.

Answer on Page: 138

Question 52   Section: Assessment

You are seeing a child, who is withdrawn. You have been asked if you can increase his social behaviors and help him become more interactive with peers and social situations. The technique you would LEAST likely use would be...

A) time-out
B) problem-solving skills training
C) Premack Principle
D) negative reinforcement

Answer on Page: 138

Question 53   Section: Behavior

A colleague has asked you to see a client to provide therapy towards "Stress inoculation". The process of "stress inoculation" involves:

A) training in interpersonal effectiveness
B) the acquisition of coping skills
C) eliminating obsessive ruminations
D) the use of stimulus control techniques

Answer on Page: 140

Question 54   Section: Assessment

[39]

A new social worker is discussing a case with you in which they have seen the grandmother say "you must eat your string beans before you can go watch TV". They think this is a great behavioral technique. You realize this is a variation of the ...
A) punishment
B) Premack Principle
C) extinction
D) response cost

Answer on Page: 144

Question 55   Section: Clinical

As you are beginning your second session with a client, she asks for advice on a specific area of her current situation. The time to give advice, which would be MOST appropriate, would be:

A) When she is clearly resistant to making her own decision
B) When she needs additional information regarding her options
C) when she states she is not able to figure out the problem on her own
D) when she is clearly too overwhelmed to be able to chose her own direction.

Answer on Page: 145

Question 56   Section: Clinical

The impulsive use of obscene language, sometimes associated with symptoms of Tourette's disorder is known as...

A) Kelptomania

B) Coprolalia
C) Ornithophobia
D) Trichotillomania

Answer on Page: 147

Question 57   Section: Clinical

A psychodynamic social worker may view addiction to cigarette smoking as a behavioral fixation, designed to recreate the needs of which, developmental phase in Freudian Theory?

A) Anal
B) Phallic
C) Latency
D) Oral

Answer on Page: 148

Question 58   Section: Clinical

Crisis is a process. There is a start and end. People in crisis typically experience all of the following stages except…

A) Increased tension
B) Reintegration
C) Reflective
D) Precipitating event

Answer on Page: 149

Question 59   Section: Clinical

[41]

The ecological approach is a favorite approach for social workers. Which of the following concepts, is NOT GENERALLY associated with the ecological approach:

A) cultural norms
B) stress
C) ego state
D) neighborhood/habitat

Answer on Page: 151

Question 60   **Section: Behavior**

You have been asked to set up a program to assist a family with a therapeutic objective. Your first step would be to define the problem the family the family faces in objective terms. Your next step in this process would be...

A) helping the family set goals and plan actions
B) helping the family exam necessary resources
C) helping the family apply for needed resources
D) deciding how to monitor the program's success

Answer on Page: 152

Question 61   **Section: Behavior**

A fellow social worker asks you questions about depressogenic schemas. You know this is a part of Aaron Beck's Cognitive Behavioral Therapy. When asked to explain more about depressogenic schemas you explain they...

[42]

A) often assist the client in functional reality testing
B) affect the client's behavior all the time.
C) are never dormant after they are activated.
D) they are dormant until stress levels increase too much.

Answer on Page: 153

Question 62   Section: Behavior

If a social worker follows a model of practice where they place an emphasis on coaching, giving immediate feedback, and setting clear, explicit, therapeutic goals, they are practicing which of the following:

A) the Life Model method
B) the functional model
C) psychosocial model
D) brief task-centered treatment

Answer on Page: 155

Question 63   Section: Behavior

You meet a new client.   He is 38-years-old, a white-collar professional and has stated that he is seeking help because he has intense anxiety and panic attacks.   He has never been diagnosed with a panic disorder and tells you he got the "diagnosis" from his neighbor, a school teacher. He describes the following symptoms: nausea, waves of dizziness and intense feelings of fear with no recognizable source of a threat. *Your first step in the therapeutic process would be to:*

A) Arrange for a psychiatric consultation

[43]

B) Recommend books and reading material on relaxation techniques

C) Assess the client's current situation and environment.

D) Develop specific goals for managing anxiety and panic

Answer on Page: 163

Question 64   Section: Behavior

You are working with a client who is a member of a Health Maintenance Organization (HMO). You have reached the final authorized session and need to call the utilization review manager to request more sessions. During the utilization review, the manager, who is a social worker, asks detailed questions about the specific sexual abuse incidents endured by the client. While the questions seem innocuous, the level of detail requested seems excessive. You should...

A) put the reviewer on hold and review the HMO release of information

B) call the reviewer back and review the HMO contract with a supervisor before re-contacting the reviewer

C) provide the reviewer with all information requested.

D) provide only general information about the client and refuse to give specific details of the abuse.

Answer on Page: 157

Question 65   Section: Behavior

You have been working with adult clients who are survivors of sexual child abuse. You have noticed that they use a number of ego defense mechanisms to protect themselves during

[44]

disclosure. A colleague asks which ego defense mechanism do you encounter the most...and why?

A) suppression
B) denial
C) intellectualization
D) reaction formation

Answer on Page: 158

Question 66   Section: Behavior

A social work colleague is having problems addressing the resistance a client (who was referred by the court system) is giving them during therapy. They ask you for help. Your BEST response is to tell them...

A) Explore the feelings underlying the resistance
B) Confront the client on their resistance
C) Point out the client's resistance and work out a behavioral contract to change this resistance
D) Help the client re-order the resistance as an opportunity to grow.

Answer on Page: 160

Question 67   Section: Assessment

Your agency has just brought in a consultant to help adjust to some new Medicaid and Medicare regulations. After their initial review, the consultant starts telling you what needs to change in your documentation style. You go to your supervisor and ask them what you should do? Compared to the administrative authority your supervisor has over you, the consultant...

A) has greater authority over you than your supervisor
B) has the same authority over you than your supervisor
C) has no authority over you
D) has limited authority over you

Answer on Page: 161

Question 68   Section: Ethics

A former client who owns a catering service offers you a free catered event for your next family reunion. How should you respond to the client's offer?

A) Turn down the catering as a conflict of interest.
B) Turn down the catering as an unethical bartering for services.
C) Accept the catering event
D) Ask the client if they can cater a friend's event instead.

Answer on Page: 162

Question 69   Section: Behavior

The Task centered treatment model contains all of the following elements except...

A) understanding ego functions and ego states
B) reframing distorted perceptions
C) role-play and rehearsal
D) feedback and giving advice

Answer on Page: 163

Question 70 **Section: Diversity**

Your supervisor tells you that the agency uses the functional model of intervention. You know this means that when dealing with your clients, WHICH of the following are is of primary importance...

A) the environment is emphasized
B) problem-solving skills are emphasized
C) the social agency's purpose is emphasized
D) diagnosis is emphasized

Answer on Page: 164

Question 71 **Section: Clinical**

Xanax (Alprazolam) is a/an _____ and is primarily used to treat _____:

A) analgesic / chronic fatigue
B) anxiolytic / panic disorders
C) metabolic interferant / Alcohol Abuse
D) stimulant / Attention Deficit

Answer on Page: 165

Question 72 **Section: Assessment**

You begin an intake on a juvenile and upon reviewing his medications you find he has been prescribed Lamictal in the morning (po AM) and Clonidine at bedtime (po HS). You ask him

[47]

what the medications are for and he just shrugs. Without access to his medical records you could assume he has been diagnosed with a mood disorder (Lamictal is a new ANTI-MANIC used to treat Bipolar Disorder). What reason(s) could you conclude that he had been given the prescription for Clonidine?

A) Panic Attacks
B) Anger and aggression
C) sleep disturbance
D) hypertension
E) Answers A & B
F) Answers B & C & D

Answer on Page: 166

Question 73   **Section: Clinical**

You are working at an emergency neighborhood walk-in mental health center and a client drops in. They appear to be homeless, as they have an unpleasant body odor and while they seem sober, they have a heavy alcohol smell on their breath. They have been sitting in the lobby for about half-an-hour when they begin exhibiting the following symptoms: 1) uncontrollable eye movements, 2) slow and/or slurred speech, 3) uncontrollable shaking of the upper body and 4) vomiting. You look in their chart as the receptionist calls 911 and you see a list of medications including fluoxentine, Catapres, Phenytoin, and ibuprofen PRN. Which of these medications should be of greatest concern to you at that moment and when the EMT's arrive to take the client to the hospital?

A) Fluoxentine
B) Catapres

[48]

C) Phenytoin
D) ibuprofen

Answer on Page: 168

Question 74 Section: Diversity

According to Adlerian Psychology, Alfred Adler would have defined the primary problem associated with criminals and addicts as having

A) no personal responsibility
B) poorly developed social interest
C) a failure identity
D) incongruence between experience and self-concept

Answer on Page: 169

Question 75 Section: Clinical

Your new supervisor begins discussing a case by talking about the client's "life script" and how the most important overall intervention is to get the client to begin revising their "life script". You know your supervisor is trained in ....

A) Transactional analysis
B) Gestalt Therapy
C) Adlerian Psychotherapy
D) Reality therapy

Answer on Page: 170

Question 76   **Section: Clinical**

A new social worker on your staff has been discussing a client in terms of unconditional positive regard. You know they are a Rogerian, person-centered, therapist. They then start talking about "incongruence" and the client's need to overcome this. What specific aspect of person –centered therapy coincides with incongruence?

A) Conflict perspective
B) Factor analysis
C) Oedipus complex
D) conditions of worth

Answer on Page: 171

Question 77   **Section: Clinical**

The current diagnosis of Borderline Personality Disorder is related to which of the following theorists?
(Borderline personality disorder is a condition in which a person makes impulsive actions, and has an unstable mood and chaotic relationships.)

A) Erikson
B) Mahler
C) Bowen
D) Freud

Answer on Page: 172

Question 78   Section: Assessment

You are seeing a 30-year-old female client who is currently complaining about how her brother treats her. You ask the client; "Is this is another brother or if it is the same brother they described last week as the 'most kind, caring and loving brother ever.' " They confirm they only have one brother and it is the same one. After about 30 seconds of silence, you state, "Wow, this is a complete reversal of where you were with your brother just last week!" Then you fall silent again to let your statement 'sink in.' You are using the therapeutic technique known as...

A) unconditional regard
B) paradoxical intent
C) controlled confrontation
D) analytic redress

Answer on Page: 174

Question 79   Section: Assessment

During your assessment of a 7 year old child, you ask the child "Do you like the rules in your family?" Then you ask them, "If I were to ask your mother and father how they would describe you, what do you think they would say?" With this second question, you are seeking to discover the child's...

A) ability to do reality testing
B) reliance on their parents
C) self-concept
D) level of conscious awareness

Answer on Page: 175

[51]

Question 80   **Section: Diversity**

A black social worker receives a new client on their caseload who is white. Because of the difference in racial backgrounds, the most important item for the social worker, in order to increase the success of therapy, is...

A) The social worker's ability to identify with the client
B) The client's ability to experience transference toward the social worker
C) The social worker's awareness of self
D) The client's ability to communicate openly

Answer on Page: 177

Question 81   **Section: Clinical**

You are talking to a client during a session and you stumble upon an area where the client believes something that could not be true, and is not a cultural norm. After several minutes you come to understand that, despite abundant evidence to the contrary, they feel they are being controlled by an external source and do not have any control over the direction of their life. This believe appears unshakeable. They may be suffering from...

A)   Delirium
B)   Delusion
C)   Dissociation
D)   Dysphoria

Answer on Page: 178

Question 82   **Section: Clinical**

[52]

During your fourth marital session with a young couple who have only been married for about 3 years, they begin yelling at each other in a loud, threatening manner. This is the third session they have yelled at each other. You stop them and then say, "You two don't listen to each other, your situation is hopeless, you just need to go home and fight as often as you like." You have just used the technique known as...

A)   Reframing
B)   Coaching
C)   Disengagement
D)   Paradoxical directive

Answer on Page: 181

Question 83   Section: Assessment

You are seeing a 14-year-old boy in therapy at his parent's request. You have had 5 sessions with him. You receive a voicemail from the guidance department of his school asking you to call Mr. Smith, the boy's guidance counselor. Upon contacting Mr. Smith, he tells you that the boy is having some problems at school with another peer group and wants to talk with you about the current course of your client's treatment to try to 'brainstorm' ideas to help the youth at school. Your ethical duty requires that you …

A) refuse to talk to Mr. Smith because he is not a clinician.
B) should give Mr. Smith information only related to issues with the youth and his peer group problems at school, because   that is the only information you two have in common.

C) should provide Mr. Smith with any necessary information because you are both working with the youth and both want what is best for him.

D) Tell Mr. Smith that you will be able to talk to him after you have contacted your client's parents, as he is a juvenile,   and received their permission to discuss their son's issues with the guidance counselor.

Answer on Page: 181

Question 84   Section: Ethical

Seven months ago, you were assigned a client, who you have seen weekly since. The client keeps appointments with you for about 6 weeks and then stops coming for several weeks. They show up again at their appointment and during the new session and complain about how they are not happy with therapy. Each time you have discussed treatment goals and modified them as the client see fit.   They have been seeing you for 6 weeks straight and have again begun to complain about therapy and state they are not happy with it. You feel you may be in an ethical challenge. The ethical response in this situation is….

A) Understand this behavior as a sign of resistance, discuss it with the client and continue therapy.

B) Notify the client that you don't think they are benefiting from therapy and that you are going to terminate the relationship and stop therapy.

C) Discuss the client's feeling and acknowledge their ideas. Offer to continue therapy if they choose, and if they don't offer to help them locate another therapist to meet their   needs.

D) Discuss the situation with your supervisor and ask them for advice.

Answer on Page: 183

Question 85   Section: Ethics

Your have been working at a rural mental health clinic near the coast. There are three other professionals working in the clinic. One is a psychiatrist, one is a psychologist and one is a marriage and family therapist. You are the only licensed social worker in the clinic. You have received a job offer from a larger facility and are going to accept it. What action should you take with regard to your client files.

A) Take the files home when you leave the job because they are your clients and you need to keep their information confidential.
B) Give the files to the client's during their final visit
C) Shred all the files on your last day
D) Lock the files in a filing cabinet at the mental health clinic and turn your file cabinet key over to the director on your last day.

Answer on Page: 184

Question 86   Section: Ethics

According to the NASW Ethical Code: Social workers treat each person in a caring and respectful fashion, mindful of individual differences and cultural and ethnic diversity. Social workers promote clients' socially responsible self-determination. This is an example of the value of…

A) Dignity and Worth of the Person
B) Importance of Human Relationships
C) Integrity
D) Competence

Answer on Page: 185

Question 87   **Section: Ethics**

According to the NASW Ethical Code: Social workers' primary goal is to help people in need and to address social problems. This principle encourages social workers to …

A) Social workers are encouraged to volunteer some portion of their professional skills with no expectation of significant financial return (pro bono service).
B) … social work's core values of service, social justice, dignity and worth of the person, importance of human relationships, integrity…
C) Social workers promote clients' socially responsible self-determination.
D) Social workers engage people as partners in the helping process.

Answer on Page: 187

Question 88   **Section: Ethics**

According to the NASW Ethical Code: Social workers continually strive to increase their professional knowledge and skills and to apply them in practice. This is an example of …

A)   Integrity
B)   Competence
C)   Service
D)   Social Justice

Answer on Page: 188

Question 89 **Section: Ethics**

According to the NASW Code of Ethics: Social workers should use clear and understandable language to inform clients of the purpose of the services, risks related to the services, limits to services because of the requirements of a third party payer, relevant costs, reasonable alternatives, clients' right to refuse or withdraw consent, and the time frame covered by the consent, is a clear statement of…

A) 1.03 Informed Consent
B) 1.04 Competence
C) 1.05 Cultural Competence and Social Diversity
D) 1.06 Conflicts of Interest

Answer on Page: 189

Question 90 **Section: Ethics**

According to the NASW Code of Ethics: Social workers should not solicit a private fee or other remuneration for providing services to clients who are entitled to such available services through the social workers' employer or agency. This is an example of the principle of …

A) 2.01 Respect
B) 1.15 Interruption of Services
C) 2.02 Confidentiality
D) 1.13 Payment for Services

Answer on Page: 190

Question 91   **Section: Ethics**

According to the NASW Code of Ethics: Social workers have a special responsibility to serve the broader public good. In order to carry out this mandate, which of the following are prescribed by the code of ethics? Social workers should:

A) advocate for living conditions conducive to the fulfillment of basic human needs
B) should provide appropriate professional services in public emergencies
C) Social workers should act to expand choice and opportunity for all people
D) All of the above

Answer on Page: 191

Question 92   **Section: Diversity**

Currently, our social safety-net bureaucracy works on the principle that local agencies have the primary responsibility for provision of services for the poor in the local area. This is much like the legal concept of jurisdiction. This concept has its roots in the ..

A) Reform Act of 1911
B) Poor Law of 1662
C) Reform Act of 1834
D) Poor Law of 1601

Answer on Page: 192

[58]

Question 93   **Section: Clinical**

The DSM-IV (Our current Diagnostic Manual) lists ten personality disorders. This was not always the case! Currently the ten categories are split into three specific, separate clusters (groups of similar content). These clusters are labeled A, B, and C.
Cluster B (dramatic, emotional or erratic disorders) is made up of four personality disorders. Chose the answer with the correct four disorders (for cluster B).

A) Avoidant Personality Disorder (DSM-IV code 301.82)
   Paranoid Personality Disorder (DSM-IV code 301.0)
   Histrionic Personality Disorder (DSM-IV code 301.50)
   Schizotypal personality disorder (DSM-IV code 301.22)

B) Paranoid personality disorder (DSM-IV code 301.0)
   Dependent personality disorder (DSM-IV code 301.6)
   Schizoid personality disorder (DSM-IV code 301.20)
   Schizotypal personality disorder (DSM-IV code 301.22)

C) Borderline personality disorder (DSM-IV code 301.83)
   Histrionic personality disorder (DSM-IV code 301.50)
   Narcissistic personality disorder (DSM-IV code 301.81)
   Antisocial personality disorder (DSM-IV code 301.7

D) Avoidant personality disorder (DSM-IV code 301.82)
   Dependent personality disorder (DSM-IV code 301.6)
   Obsessive-compulsive personality disorder (DSM-IV code 301.4)
   Paranoid personality disorder (DSM-IV code 301.0)

Answer on Page: 194

[59]

Question 94   **Section: Ethics**

At an office party for your agency, a relatively new secretary comes over to you and starts talking to you about trouble they are having with their teenage son. It is clear they respect you and value your opinion. You should...

A) Try to talk about something that happened at work earlier in the week as a way of sidetracking her request, so she will   get the "picture" regarding dual relationships.
B) Let the secretary know that she is asking for professional information and it would be inappropriate for you to   comment on her situation.
C) Tell them know they probably need a therapist and offer a referral.
D) Listen to her issues politely with an open mind

Answer on Page: 197

Question 95   **Section: Diversity**

Food Stamps and Medicaid are examples of

A) block grants
B) in-kind assistance.
C) categorical grants
D)   grants-in-aid.

Answer on Page: 198

Question 96   **Section: Legal**

[60]

In 1967, the United States Supreme Court ruled that a juvenile has a right to cross examine complainants and a right to counsel and protection against self-incrimination in the

A) Gault Decision
B) Kelly v. Goldberg.
C) Ginsberg v. New York.
D) District of Columbia v. Heller

Answer on Page: 199

Question 97   Section: Clinical

A major problem with managed care (HMO) mental health services for chronically ill patients is that

A) HMOs do not provide mental health services
B) HMOs can provide excellent case management, but poor clinical services.
C) clients needing longer term supportive services are rarely able to access those services in managed care organizations.
D) payment for services is slow and inadequate.

Answer on Page: 203

Question 98   Section: Clinical

Compared to the general population the risk of eventually dying from suicide is 10 times greater for which group of substance abusers?

A) Individuals treated for alcohol abuse and dependence

B) Individuals being treated for the abuse of Injectable drugs (Heroin, Etc)
C) Individuals who have completed a detoxification program and are working on long-term stability.
D) Individuals just entering treatment for substance abuse disorders

Answer on Page: 203

Question 99   Section: Clinical

Individuals who are in treatment for substance abuse disorders are at a very high risk of suicide because of which of the following factors:

A) They tend to enter treatment at a time in their addiction when their substance abuse is out of control.
B) They enter treatment with a number of co-occurring life crises, including marital problems, legal difficulties and job problems.
C) They tend to enter substance abuse treatment at the point when their depression symptoms are at their highest.
D) All of the above
E) A and C only

Answer on Page: 205

Question 100   Section: Clinical

Social workers who function in case management positions are usually interacting with which of the Freudian Personality Structures?

A) Conscious motivation

B) Ego
C) Superego
D) Id

Answer on Page: 205

Question 100+   **Section: Clinical**

You are working with a newly hired clinical social worker who discusses his clients in terms of their conscious motivation. You can conclude that their training and/or theoretical orientation is

A) Behavioral
B) structural
C) psychoanalytic
D) Bowenian

Answer on Page: 207

Question 100++   **Section: Clinical**

You work for an agency who has hired a new clinical social work therapist. He identifies himself as a reality therapist. Given his theoretical beliefs, he would most likely be INTERESTED in increasing a client's:

A) social interest
B) awareness
C) responsibility
D) Self-Esteem

Answer on Page: 207

Why are there 102 questions in a book that is supposed to have 100 questions?

One of the great answers of life...

Always give someone more than they pay for!

Others to think about...

Justice, Justice, thou shall pursue!

Innocent until proven Guilty!

and said unto them, He that is without sin among you, let him first cast a stone at her. John 8:7

No one understands Quantum Mechanics
    Richard Phillips Feynman, PhD.

Question 1   Section: Clinical

The correct answer is D
Always eliminate the medical and pharmacological factors first. Many prescription drugs have very strong side effects. Refer the client back to her Primary Care Physician for an immediate medication evaluation. From a liability standpoint, you should also get the number and name of the Primary Care and make contact in order to explain your concerns about possible side effects of the medication.

There is not a need for a psychiatric consult and the headaches, depression, difficulty concentrating and disrupted sleep patterns could make the client a poor historian for current events for Biopsychosocial Assessment.

 Also, you need to focus on the issues of immediate concern and leave the history for after the current medical and safety needs are met.
Suicidal thoughts are not enough to determine danger at a level that would support an involuntary commitment. A complete suicide assessment should be provided by a competent and properly trained professional.

S - Male sex
A - Older Age
D - Depression
P - Previous Attempt
E - Ethanol Abuse (Alcohol)
R - Rational Thinking Loss
S - Social Supports Lacking
O - Organized Plan
N - No Spouse
S - Sickness

Question 2   **Section: Clinical**

Multi-Axial Diagnosis

Axis I:	Clinical Disorders & V-Codes	V61.10 Partner Relational Problem
Axis II:	Personality Disorders & Mental Retardation	301.83 Borderline Personality Disorder
Axis III:	General Medical Conditions	Diabetes Type II
Axis IV:	Psychosocial & Environmental Problems	Economic Problems
Axis V:	Global Assessment of Functioning (GAF)	75

C is CORRECT.

The DSM-IV, Page 3, indicates that "the specifier provisional when there is a strong presumption that the fill criteria will ultimately be met for the disorder." Sometimes you will see the term "Rule-Out" or "R/O" used in the same manner. This is an older way of saying 'I see most of the criteria but not enough to make the diagnosis, so I will flag the disorder and let someone more experienced or more specialized rule it out." Either way the disorder should be documented as such:

301.83 Borderline Personality Disorder, Provisional

A is INCORRECT
Latent is a psychological term usually used for learning, where the learning takes place without any evidence and "what" is learned exhibits itself when the time or reinforcement is right.

B is INCORRECT
Temporary is not a term that is used in clinical practice unless it is used by an insurance company, when they tell you there is a temporary delay in your reimbursement for a claim because they do not intend to pay you. (SMILE)

D is INCORRECT
Revised is not a term used in differential diagnosing. If you revise a diagnosis, you simply remove the prior diagnosis from the axial diagram and put in the newer diagnosis.

Question 3   Section: Clinical

The correct answer is B
The client's immediate presenting problem is the most important issue for the client at that time. It is important to understand that for a social worker, the client's needs drive the intervention. Clients always have the right to decide their course of treatment. If you respond to something that is not important to the client, they can perceive you as not interested in their concerns and may not continue to seek help.

A is INCORRECT
Many clients will have underlying personality issues which may or may not affect their functioning and their situation, however personality issues are usually long-standing in duration and do not lend themselves to 'quick fixes'.

PS: They may also be very functional behaviors in their own world.

C is INCORRECT
Everyone has day-to-day problems in functioning. It is entirely likely that you will be able to identify several problems your client has that they are unaware of. The client's right and desire to drive treatment is always respected.

D is INCORRECT
This one seems like a good answer and would be if the question was phrased *... client in crisis due to their substance use...* Substance use may be an integral part of your client's life and not be perceived of as being a problem. In fact, they may actually see their 'use' as a benefit and a way to cope with a world they consider – "Hostile". As the social worker, you should become aware of your biases toward substance use, what your culture taught you, about substance abuse, and how your perceptions affect your clients.

Example: *Early in my career I was involved in an assessment with another social worker where the father admitted to drinking "a beer or two" every night upon coming home from work. He was from Wisconsin (think Pabst Blue Ribbon and Milwaukee's Best) and had worked in a factory for most of his adult life. The social worker wrote in their report that the father had an alcohol problem and needed treatment. When asked to defend their position, it came out that their parents were heavy drinkers during their childhood and now were "DRY". They viewed any alcohol use as a problem, which needed treatment.*

Question 4　　　　Section: Assessment

The correct answer is A
NOS is the proper abbreviation for (Not Otherwise Specified.) It is used when you are sure of a larger disorder category but do not have specifics. Remember the basic diagnostic criteria for an Anxiety disorder is:

[68]

A) At least 6 months of "excessive anxiety and worry" about a variety of events and situations.

B) There is significant difficulty in controlling the anxiety and worry.

C) The presence of 3 or more (1 for children) over the previous six months for most days:

>1. Feeling wound-up, tense, or restless

>2. Easily becoming fatigued or worn-out

>3. Concentration problems

>4. Irritability

>5. Significant tension in muscles

>6. Difficulty with sleep

D) The symptoms are not part of another mental disorder.

E) The symptoms cause "clinically significant distress"   **or** problems functioning in daily life.

F) The condition is not due to a substance or medical issue

B is INCORRECT

There is enough information to diagnosis, just not enough to be specific. Provisional is used when you don't know enough to diagnose but you believe the information will be discovered if enough history is obtained. NOS is used when the client meets the general conditions but may not meet all of the criteria in section "C)" either due to lack of history or the client being a poor or manipulative historian. However, if you used this diagnosis on a chart you would be able to argue your decision and would probably be forgiven.

C is INCORRECT

Malaise is a generalized feeling of discomfort, illness, or lack of well-being. There is no particular category with a modifier of malaise. Unfortunately, we cannot go around making up our own diagnoses, even though it might better fit the situation. (smile)

D is INCORRECT

Undifferentiated type is only used when diagnosing Schizophrenia. One of the common 'quick' diagnoses you may see in a chart, given to a client with schizophrenia is SCUT (sometimes abbreviated S.C.U.T.) It stands for Schizophrenia Chronic Undifferentiated Type.

Clinical Pearl:

You may also hear a clinician call a patient a SCUT. If you do, please take time to gently remind them that clients may have a mental illness, but they are NOT A MENTAL ILLNESS. We are all guilty of objectifying our clients from time to time.

Diagnosing Schizophrenia
www.MyMSW.info/Diagnosis.html

Question 5   Section: Clinical

B is CORRECT

This is the wife's initial problem and it is clearly stated. Asking the client to expand on the issue not only allows the wife to feel she has been heard, but that you are taking her seriously. Also, you want ask open-ended questions to elicit as much information as you can to determine the cause and severity of the problem as it relates to the couple.

Domestic Violence Screen:

S = Stress
A = Afraid
F = Friends
E = Emergency Plan

Stress and safety
Do you feel safe in your relationship?
Afraid or Abused
- Has your partner ever threatened you or your children
- Has your partner ever abused you or your children

Friends and Family
- If you were hurt, would your friends or family know?
- Would they be able to help you?

Emergency Plan
- Do you have a safe place to go in an emergency?
- Do you need help in locating a shelter?
- Would you like to talk to a counselor about this?

Ref: Guth (2000) Am J Surgery 179:134-40

A is INCORRECT

This statement, would probably be perceived as 'blaming the victim'. In this statement, there is the inherent idea that 'he has a right to vent his temper on her' and that her actions are a 'primary influence for the way he treats her.' A response like this may well shut down the wife from further participation in therapy.

C is INCORRECT

Therapy sessions are notoriously contrived interactions. Especially the first session where each of the clients are trying to make the best impression.   Also, you don't have enough information to know if the husband's current state is his usual or even angry state.

D is INCORRECT
This response not only ignores the relevance of the wife's statement, it concedes power over decision making to the husband. It indicates that as the therapist, you are willing to let one or the other control the session. You must always be in control of how the session should be steered.

Question 6   Section: Assessment

The correct answer is C.
In order to report abuse or neglect in good faith, the reporter need only suspect that child abuse has occurred. This may come from statements the child has made, reactions and responses the child may have had to therapy or interview questions, and/or observance of injury, behaviors or interactions which raise suspicion. **YOU DO NOT NEED PROOF.** Gathering proof is the job of the child welfare agency.

Florida Statute 39.201
Mandatory reports of child abuse, abandonment, or neglect; mandatory reports of death; central abuse hotline.-- (1)A Any person who knows, or has reasonable cause to suspect, that a child is abused, abandoned, or neglected by a parent, legal custodian, caregiver, or other person responsible for the child's welfare, as defined in this chapter, or that a child is in need of supervision and care and has no parent, legal custodian, or responsible adult relative immediately known and available to provide supervision and care shall report such knowledge or

suspicion to the department in the manner prescribed in subsection (2).

A is INCORRECT.

This statement is far too broad to be effectively used. How would the professional determine the nature or level of a threat which could be imminent? You would have to gather information in order to determine the level, severity and dangerousness of the threat, as well as the level of access that would be required for the threat to be carried out. All of these functions are the role of the Department of Children and Families.

B is INCORRECT.

There are two glaring errors with this answer. First, this answer would require a complete knowledge of the rules of evidence for Florida Law, as well as knowledge of the proper procedures for gathering evidence in an appropriate and lawful manner. Secondly, it would simply require the gathering of information, which is the function of DCF. Evidence is a very high bar to set for a decision to report.

D is INCORRECT.

These battles often result in multiple complaint of child abuse or neglect. When a marriage is falling apart and/or child custody is at stake, the roles of the individuals have been damaged and there is a natural desire to regain control of "the situation" by all parties. The hurt, blame, anger, resentment and guilt can run very deep and children can be used against the other spouse. It should also be noted that child abuse and neglect occur in situations where there is no custody issues involved.

Question 7   Section: Assessment

The correct answer is C
These are all classic signs of depression

A is INCORRECT.
While she shows all of the classic signs of depression and a depressive disorder, there is no indication of substance use and/or abuse. If you were seeing this client in real life it would be a good idea to ask questions about past and current possible drug use.

B is INCORRECT.
Somatoform disorder is the name for a group of conditions in which the physical pain and symptoms a person feels are related to psychological factors. These symptoms can't be traced to a specific physical cause. In people who have a somatoform disorder, medical test results are either normal or don't explain the person's symptoms.
http://familydoctor.org/online/famdocen/home/common/pain/disor ders/162.html

> PS: 'soma' refers to 'body' and the hand movement and restless pacing might throw off a clinician who is not familiar with this class of disorders.

D is INCORRECT.
...uncharacteristically   angry   and   irritable...difficulty concentrating...   eating   less...   difficulty   sleeping...constant nervous motion...restlessly pacing...
These are all characteristic behaviors that may been seen in an anxiety disorder, but they are not a cluster of symptoms that are always seen in an anxiety disorder. Also the ... feels "Blah...you know...like YUCK" and the ... dropping out of several school

[74]

activities she was very involved in...all relate to a depressive diagnosis.

Depression Screens

www.MyMSW.info/clinicaltools.html

Question 8   Section: Clinical

The correct answer is C

A clinical supervisor and the agency are both responsible for the actions of their employees. This is a legal concept known as Vicarious Liability*. People or entities typically charged with vicarious liability include supervisors or companies since they bear responsibility for the actions of their employees.

For the supervisee, this is where accurate and timely note-writing will do more to cover yourself than a bullet-proof vest. Nothing is worse than a supervisor asking for your notes in a situation like this and you having to tell them you are 'about 3 weeks behind' on getting them completed. Writing notes more than 24 hours after the contact make it difficult to be accurate and detailed. You may also misremember something in your panic to get caught up which could be contradictory to the rest of your services. In the situation above they lawyers will have hours to pick apart your notes, and will certainly find inconsistencies.

(Vicarious liability is a legal concept, which refers to one party being held liable for the injury or damage sustained by another party, despite the fact that they had no active involvement in the incident.)

A is INCORRECT.

[75]

Your supervisor will probably feel this way for the first five minutes after they are notified. They also may use a variety of expletives. Truthfully a clinical supervisor is responsible for all the actions committed by their supervisee's during their job performance. As a supervisor, you should keep very accurate records of every supervision and conversation with a supervisee. This information should include date, time, client, the information given by the supervisee and your response. Nothing looks worse that being asked by an administrator "When was the last time you staffed this case with your supervisee?" and your response is..."I don't know"

B is INCORRECT.
This is a great fantasy and one you may cling to for a while. Being involved in a lawsuit is horrible. Questioning yourself on whether you could have stopped a client's death is even worse. Unfortunate, due to human nature, it is very likely the agency will blame the supervisor for not being involved enough and the supervisor will blame the supervisee for not providing enough or the proper information for the supervisor to do their job.

> PS: The supervisor blaming the supervisee for not providing enough information is really a red herring. The supervisor should know more than the supervisee, and is responsible for asking questions during supervision. Experience counts when working with people. Often the supervisor will see patterns developing that the supervisee lacks the experience to see. If a supervisor is not getting enough information, the fault is not yours.

D is INCORRECT.
Mostly NO...with a little YES. The social worker lifted liability from themselves and the agency for the specific event which caused the need for the Baker Act, but not for all events in the

client's life. Sometimes client's must be Baker Acted multiple times simply because of their responses. The most important liability shield for a social worker is the depth and detail of their notes. What the client said and how you responded. If you ask a client "Do you want to hurt yourself?" and they respond with 'NO' and then you follow-up with "Are you feeling suicidal or feeling like you want to die?" and they respond with a 'NO' and you document this in your notes, your liability is drastically reduced.

DOCUMENTATION NUGGET: *The simple phrase <u>"Client denied suicidal/homicidal ideations"</u> goes a long way towards liability reduction, as long as you have asked the questions.*

Question 9   Section: Clinical

The correct answer is B

Let your supervisor know how you feel, why you feel the way you do and how it might affect your interactions. Then, work with your supervisor on how you can either use this awareness to help the interactions with your client or whether you need to be replaced by another social worker. There will be clients you can work with and clients that 'trigger you' in ways that make therapeutic interactions impossible. This type of a reaction is due to *the human condition.* Don't run from it.

A is INCORRECT.

This answer falls under the category "Nothing good will come of this…" The best you can hope for, is the client will understand your feelings and agree with you, but it will not establish any rapport and will probably build up a rather severe adverse reaction to you and your attempts at therapy. It would also bring up ethical issues, as the client is not responsible for how you feel and it is inappropriate to burden them with your issues.

C is INCORRECT.
While you have to accept your feelings as part of any therapeutic process, the key ingredient is the level of consciousness you maintain in relation to your issues. You must be aware of your feelings as it will guide you during therapy, but you cannot let them control you. This type of situation was custom made for a clinical supervision staffing or a discussion with a colleague.

D is INCORRECT.
The old **'bury your head in the sand and hope it goes away'** trick. Not very useful, although you will see it used by many of your clients. NEVER ignore your feelings. This is the short path to malpractice, ethical violations and worse. Always have someone you can talk to. No one is strong enough to handle all situations alone.

Question 10   Section: Ethics

The correct answer is D
Just a short list of problems with this idea. 1) the client will know where you live and may feel they can drop by for a visit in hard times (Boundaries), 2) There may not be an agreement on the exact types and amounts of services traded and one or both parties could feel slighted or used. 3) Etc, Etc, ... This could definitely impact the therapeutic process. The relationship between a client and a therapist should be very strict and specific. Anything that blurs the boundaries of that relationship should be avoided at all cost.

** Always remember there is a power difference between the therapist and the client. This power inequity is one of the ideas that allow change to occur in therapy.

NASW CODE OF ETHICS --- 1.13 Payment for Services
B Social workers should avoid accepting goods or services from clients as payment for professional services. Bartering arrangements, particularly involving services, create the potential for conflicts of interest, exploitation, and inappropriate boundaries in social workers' relationships with clients. **http://www.socialworkers.org/pubs/code/code.asp**

A is INCORRECT

Generally it is polite to ask the client what they would like to be called. "Can I call you….?" Without this pleasantry client might feel there is an arrogance in the relationship. During therapy all conflict should be directed towards problem resolution and be controlled by the therapist. Adding unnecessary conflict can slow the healing process

B is INCORRECT

While this type of behavior would not necessarily involve a breach of ethics, the possibility is out there…lurking. Always remember that the power dynamic in a therapeutic relationship is skewed towards the therapist. The client may perceive the books in a different manner than you intended. They may feel compelled to read them even if they do not like the books. They may not want to disappoint the therapist if they are asked about the books in the next session. Some examples:

BAD IDEA: Therapist "Have you read the latest Stephen King novel? I just finished it and it was great, here take my copy home and enjoy it!"

NOT SO BAD AN IDEA: Client "I see you are just finishing the latest novel by James Patterson. When you get done with it, can I borrow it?"

BETTER IDEA: Therapist, "You know you can get any of these books from the public library."

C is INCORRECT

Nothing is overtly wrong with this action, although it would be best to use this interaction only as a rapport buiiding tool. The client is not coming to see you to talk about sports and this negative side of this is they may feel more familiar with you than would be good for therapy.

Question 11   Section: Assessment

The correct answer is B

Risperidone is used to treat the symptoms of schizophrenia (a mental illness that causes disturbed or unusual thinking, loss of interest in life, and strong or inappropriate emotions) in adults and teenagers 13 years of age and older. It is also used to treat episodes of mania (frenzied, abnormally excited, or irritated mood) or mixed episodes (symptoms of mania and depression that happen together) in adults and in teenagers and children 10 years of age and older with bipolar disorder (manic depressive disorder; a disease that causes episodes of depression, episodes of mania, and other abnormal moods). Risperidone is also used to treat behavior problems such as aggression, self-injury, and sudden mood changes in teenagers and children 5-16 years of age who have autism (a condition that causes repetitive behavior, difficulty interacting with others, and problems with communication). Risperidone is in a class of medications called atypical antipsychotics. It works by changing the activity of certain natural substances in the brain.

Reference:

http://www.ncbi.nlm.nih.gov/pubmedhealth/PMH0000944

A is INCORRECT.

Bupropion (Aplenzin, Wellbutrin, Wellbutrin SR, Wellbutrin XL) is used to treat depression. Bupropion (Wellbutrin XL) is also used to treat seasonal affective disorder (SAD; episodes of depression that occur in the fall and winter each year). Bupropion (Zyban) is used to help people stop smoking. Bupropion is in a class of medications called antidepressants. It works by increasing certain types of activity in the brain.

Reference:

http://www.ncbi.nlm.nih.gov/pubmedhealth/PMH0000970

C is INCORRECT.

Fluoxentine (Prozac) is used to treat depression, obsessive-compulsive disorder (bothersome thoughts that won't go away and the need to perform certain actions over and over), some eating disorders, and panic attacks (sudden, unexpected attacks of extreme fear and worry about these attacks). Fluoxentine (Sarafem) is used to relieve the symptoms of premenstrual dysphoric disorder, including mood swings, irritability, bloating, and breast tenderness. Fluoxentine is in a class of medications called selective serotonin reuptake inhibitors (SSRIs). It works by increasing the amount of serotonin, a natural substance in the brain that helps maintain mental balance.

Reference:

http://www.ncbi.nlm.nih.gov/pubmedhealth/PMH0000885

D is INCORRECT.

Lithium is used to treat and prevent episodes of mania (frenzied, abnormally excited mood) in people with bipolar disorder (manic-

depressive disorder; a disease that causes episodes of depression, episodes of mania, and other abnormal moods). Lithium is in a class of medications called anti-manic agents. It works by decreasing abnormal activity in the brain.
Reference:
http://www.ncbi.nlm.nih.gov/pubmedhealth/PMH0000531

Question 12   Section: Clinical

The correct answer is A
Client's with a long history of substance abuse are generally very good at using the ego defense mechanisms of rationalization and denial. They often engage in a circuitous pattern of self-talk that allows them to continue their drug use even in the face of serious consequences. They are also excellent manipulators and should be assessed and treated by someone trained to deal with their issues. It is generally accepted that psychotherapy is ineffective with clients until they are "Clean and sober."

B is INCORRECT.
Therapy requires the development of trust, and the ability of the transference, counter-transference relationship to occur. Current use of illegal substances, especially substance which can be very addictive (Cocaine), make establishing this rapport all but impossible.

C is INCORRECT.
Once the client is 'clean and sober' this would probably be an excellent idea. Gathering information about the client's social support system and developmental history is always a good idea when trying to determine the causes of a set of behaviors.

D is INCORRECT.

Generally when a client is actively involved in their addiction there is no motivations for change. Their use of drugs meets many of their internal needs, and the ability to meet these needs is often stronger and more compelling than the conflict with family and friends , caused by the drug use. As with answer C, Once the client is 'clean and sober' this would probably be an excellent idea.

Question 13   Section: Clinical

The correct answer is C
Albert Ellis' approach to cognitive therapy, which sees emotional disturbances as the result of irrational beliefs that guide people's interpretation of events. Clients are helped to appraise their situations realistically and develop new ways of interpreting experience.

REBT has a simple exercise to help us make this adjustment, called "the ABCs".   It is used to analyze the situation and change our thinking about it so that without trying to change external reality, we can feel better about it.

This doesn't mean that we should never try to change external reality- sometimes it is appropriate- it's when it isn't an appropriate or effective response that we can choose to have a different response instead in order to feel better. While the ABCs are for use to help with any emotional upset, anger is the example we'll use here.

To use this ABC exercise for yourself, just pick any situation where you were angry about someone's behavior and take a look and see what it is you are thinking about it that is DEMAND-ing and irrational, and change it into something more rational- a PREFERENCE.

It is irrational to demand that people behave in the way we want them to! Here is an example using drunken people making a lot of noise late at night as they pass by outside on the street.

• A. (Activating event) Drunk people outside, making some noise.
• B. (irrational Belief (iB) I have about A) They MUST NOT make any noise.
• C. (Consequences of having those beliefs about A) When noisy drunk people pass in the street outside late at night and wake me up. I Feel angry. It feels bad. I lie awake feeling angry and upset and don't get back to sleep for a long time.
• D. (Dispute the irrational Beliefs (iB's) in B by turning them into questions and answers) WHY shouldn't they make any noise-where is that commandment written in stone? Where is the evidence? Again, who made you Supreme Ruler of the Universe dictating how people Should or Must act?
• E. (Effective new thinking- substitute something rational instead of B) Drunk people are often noisy, but it's no BIG deal. I don't like it, but I can deal with what I don't like. Maybe I will touch base with them in the morning (when they are sober).
        Reference:
http://www.stressgroup.com/abcscrashcourse.html

A is INCORRECT.
IN RET / REBT behaviors are a response to our emotions and are derived from our beliefs. Focus should always start on the beliefs.

B is INCORRECT.
IN RET / REBT emotions are controlled by our beliefs. Change the belief and the emotion changes.

D is INCORRECT.

IN RET / REBT events are beyond the client's control. Events are interpreted through our beliefs filter, which then control our emotional responses and are precursors to our behaviors.

Question 14   Section: Assessment

The correct answer is B
Listening empathically, with total attention, is probably the most powerful tool you have in your toolbox. Clients need to be HEARD. They need to feel they can communicate. When you have heard the entire situation you are then in a position to ask the question: "What can I do to help you get what you need?"

A is INCORRECT.
It is never a good idea to ask a client "leading questions". With any therapeutic relationship there is a power structure in which the clinician holds more power than the client. It is possible, when asking leading questions, to give the client the idea that you are looking only for specific information and they may alter their story to please you. Leading questions are almost always bad.

C is INCORRECT.
Providing clients with an interpretation of their thoughts, statements and non-verbal behaviors is an aspect of psychoanalysis that occurs AFTER A VERY LONG TIME IN THERAPY. Psychoanalytic psychotherapy can last for 3-5 years and the interpretive phase is only during the last couple of sessions. Anytime you provide an interpretation of a client's behavior or thoughts, it should be with their direct permission after a clear discussion of informed consent. (So they know what they are getting into.) Without a deep trust built over a long time this method will backfire and probably drive the client away.

PS: Psychoanalysis takes years to learn and is a rather rigorous discipline. If you are interested in providing this type of therapy, there are PhD programs in psychoanalysis which take approximately 5 years to complete and usually require you to undergo psychoanalysis personally for several years.

D is INCORRECT.
The best way to show empathy is to listen carefully, ask questions which allow the client to provide you with clarity and allow them to be in control. The fact that the client has come to you places you in the expert role, you do not need to prove it.

Clinical Pearl: When seeking to gather trust with a client, especially in a situation where they have been victimized, and excellent statement to make in response to any questions they have about your ability to understand their situation is: "I am not sure I completely understand, could you explain more to help me learn?" Remember, the client is the expert of their situation and you are simply a visitor. Let them guide you.
Anthony, thanks for reminding me of this principle!

Question 15   Section: Clinical

The correct answer is B
This approach allows them to open up and explain themselves. It is accepting and non-judgmental. It also gives you the chance to clarify roles and to ask the client to explain in to you, in more detail, what they are expecting from this process.

A is INCORRECT.
This is a very confrontational approach and requires the client to agree to the fact that they don't want to work with you (Which may or may not be an accurate assumption). If they have been

late to 3 of their four sessions, it is entirely likely that they are not completely invested in the therapeutic process and this type of confrontation may drive them away.

C is INCORRECT.
This is a statement of the obvious and may be taken as a rebuke. If a client is wavering in relation to their investment in therapy, they may use this as an excuse to terminate and avoid working with their issues.

D is INCORRECT.
This is definitely confrontation and assumes anger, for which there is no indication in the above information. Reluctance is not anger.

It is entirely possible that the resistance is due to an upcoming breakthrough with the client and they are concerned that something they want to reveal may offend you or cause you to dislike them. They are the expert of their life, but you are the expert in psychotherapy.

Question 16   Section: Assessment

The correct answer is C
Body Dysmorphic Disorder is a serious illness where a person is preoccupied with minor or imaginary physical flaws, usually of the skin, hair, and nose. Persons with BDD tend to have cosmetic surgery. Even if the surgery is successful, they do not think they have changed and are unhappy with the outcome. What are the symptoms of BDD?

Being preoccupied with minor or imaginary physical flaws, usually of the skin, hair, and nose, such as acne, scarring, facial lines, marks, pale skin, thinning hair, excessive body hair, large nose, or crooked nose.

Having a lot of anxiety and stress about the perceived flaw and spending a lot of time focusing on it, such as frequently picking at skin, excessively checking appearance in a mirror, hiding the imperfection, comparing appearance with others, excessively grooming, seeking reassurance from others about how they look, and getting cosmetic surgery.
Reference:
www.medicinenet.com/body_dysmorphic_disorder/article.htm

A is INCORRECT

Schizophreniform disorder (SFD) is a time-limited illness wherein the sufferer has experienced at least two of the major symptoms of psychosis for longer than one month but fewer than six months. Hallucinations, delusions, and strange bodily movements or lack of movements (catatonic behavior) are all symptoms that may be observed. Additionally, minimal or peculiar speech, lack of drive to act on one's own behalf, bizarre behavior, a wooden quality to one's emotions or near-absent emotionality are all typical psychotic symptoms that may occur in SFD.

<u>Delusions are a fairly common psychotic feature.</u> Delusions are strongly held irrational and unrealistic beliefs that are highly resistant to alteration. Even when the person encounters evidence that would invalidate the delusion, the unjustified and improbable belief remains a conviction. Often, delusions are paranoid or persecutory in tone. In these types of delusions, the person is excessively suspicious and continually feels at the mercy of conspirators believed to be determined to cause harm to the sufferer. However, delusions can also take on other overtones. Some delusions are grandiose, or involve elaborate

[88]

love fantasies (erotomanic delusions). Delusions may involve somatic content, or may revolve around extreme irrational jealousy.

Reference:www.minddisorders.com/PyZ/Schizophreniform-disorder.html

B is INCORRECT.

Obsessive-Compulsive Disorder is characterized by obsessive thoughts and compulsive actions, such as cleaning, checking, counting, or hoarding. Obsessive-compulsive disorder (OCD), one of the anxiety disorders, is a potentially disabling condition that can persist throughout a person's life. The individual who suffers from OCD becomes trapped in a pattern of repetitive thoughts and behaviors that are senseless and distressing but extremely difficult to overcome. OCD occurs in a spectrum from mild to severe, but if severe and left untreated, can destroy a person's capacity to function at work, at school, or even in the home.

Treatment is by cognitive behavioral therapy and/or medication. One patient may benefit significantly from behavior therapy, while another will benefit from pharmacotherapy. Some others may use both medication and behavior therapy. Others may begin with medication to gain control over their symptoms and then continue with behavior therapy. The neurotransmitter serotonin can significantly decrease the symptoms of OCD. The first serotonin reuptake inhibitor (SRI) specifically approved for the use in the treatment of OCD was the tricyclic antidepressant clomipramine (AnafranilR). It was followed by fluoxetine (ProzacR), fluvoxamine (LuvoxR), and paroxetine (PaxilR). Large studies have shown that more than three-quarters of patients are helped by these medications. And in more than half of patients, medications relieve symptoms of OCD by diminishing the frequency and intensity of the obsessions and compulsions.

Improvement usually takes at least three weeks or longer. If a patient does not respond well to one of these medications, or has unacceptable side effects, another SRI may give a better response. Medications are of help in controlling the symptoms of OCD, but often, if the medication is discontinued, relapse will follow. Indeed, even after symptoms have subsided, most people will need to continue with medication indefinitely, perhaps with a lowered dosage.
Reference:
www.medterms.com/script/main/art.asp?articlekey=4610

D is INCORRECT.

Post Traumatic Stress Disorder is a common anxiety disorder that develops after exposure to a terrifying event or ordeal in which grave physical harm occurred or was threatened. Family members of victims also can develop the disorder. PTSD can occur in people of any age, including children and adolescents. More than twice as many women as men experience PTSD following exposure to trauma. Depression, alcohol or other substance abuse, or other anxiety disorders frequently co-occur with PTSD.

The diagnosis of PTSD requires that one or more symptoms from each of the following categories be present for at least a month and that symptom or symptoms must seriously interfere with leading a normal life:

* Reliving the event through upsetting thoughts, nightmares or flashbacks, or having very strong mental and physical reactions if something reminds the person of the event.

* Avoiding activities, thoughts, feelings or conversations that remind the person of the event; feeling numb to one's

surroundings; or being unable to remember details of the event.

* Having a loss of interest in important activities, feeling all alone, being unable to have normal emotions or feeling that there is nothing to look forward to in the future may also be experienced.

* Feeling that one can never relax and must be on guard all the time to protect oneself, trouble sleeping, feeling irritable, overreacting when startled, angry outbursts or trouble concentrating.

Reference:

www.medterms.com/script/main/art.asp?articlekey=18779

Question 17   Section: Assessment

The correct answer is D

Stage 5, permits greater individual control and flexibility. The individual accepts and rejects the views, values and attitudes of minority groups and the dominant group based on experience. At this point in time the client has processed all there is the process and will be more comfortable with an individual who "see's things their way!"

A is INCORRECT.

This would be more indicative of stage 2 where the client begins to develop conflict between their cultural views and the dominate culture view.

B is INCORRECT.

This answer would be accurate for an individual in Stage 3, Resistance and Immersion. In this stage the individual accepts and endorses minority views and culture, then rejects the view of the dominant party.

C is INCORRECT
This answer would be more likely for a person in Stage 1, Conformity. Individuals in this stage often show a preference for the dominant cultural values over their own values.

Minority Identity Development (MID) Model
The theory defines 5 stages of development that oppressed people may experience as they struggle to understand themselves in terms of their own minority culture, and the oppressive relationship between the two cultures (minority and White). Note: not all individuals will experience all stages. Some may begin at later stages, some may begin and end in the final stage. Family influences play a prominent role on the developmental process and where the process begins.

Stage 1: Conformity
Stage 2: Dissonance
Stage 3: Resistance and Immersion
Stage 4: Introspection
Stage 5: Synergetic Articulation and Awareness

Source: Atkinson, D.R. Morten, G. & Sue, D.W. (Editors) (1998). Counseling American Minorities: A Cross Cultural Perspective (5th Edition). McGraw. Hill Company.

Question 18   **Section: Behavior**

The correct answer is D
 While you could send the information with the client's verbal authorization, it would not be wise to do so. If the client later denied giving you authorization, it is a hearsay issue and cannot be resolved. A piece of paper with a client's original signature on

it, in your file is a tremendous stress reducer in the event of litigation or complaint. I usually ask my clients to sign in BLUE INK, because it does not photocopy well and is easier to prove as genuine. Even if the client signs a release at the beginning of therapy, I would encourage discussing it with them prior to release and then letting them determine if release is still their preferred choice.

A is INCORRECT.
Personally, I like this answer the best even though it is wrong. Perhaps is goes to my dislike of insurance companies. You must respond because the letter could have consequences for the client's continued insurance coverage and /or liability. However, you can never release information on a client without their express consent. I make it a practice to always talk to my client before I take any action on a release of Information request.

B is INCORRECT.
Only if you enjoy being the focus of lawsuits and complaints against your license. The client has the ultimate control over the release of their information.

C is INCORRECT.
Nope! Even if the letter is valid and the request for information form is appropriate, legal and binding, and your opportunity for payment is involved, the client always reserves the right to refuse to allow you to release information that does not comply with mandatory reporting requirements.

Question 19   Section: Clinical

The correct answer is C

Native American culture exists in a tightly knit web of values that bind the community and the individual. Their culture emphasizes the needs
of the community over the needs of the individual and even the needs of the family over the needs of the individual. To live in a "value-free" environment would be similar to renouncing your heritage.

A is INCORRECT.

This is very important when counseling the Native American client. American Indians and other ethnic minorities have been socialized to interpret their experiences in the world much differently than in the larger westernized culture. The greater the level of acculturation, the greater the need for sensitivity and treatment planning that includes
the family and the community.

B is INCORRECT.

The family is the primary base unit for Native American Culture. Native American socialization teaches the needs of the family and conformity to family values and tribal customs are more important than individual needs. The individual is completely connected to family and counseling would not be effective without this aspect being considered in treatment planning and at the beginning of every session.

D is INCORRECT.

Without tribal and familial affiliation, the individual ceases to exist. Unlike Western Culture where our socialization teaches that the individual must break free of family and be able to live on their own, independent of background and upbringing, Native American culture uses tribal and family affiliations as the backbone of its existence.

Question 20   Section: Clinical

The correct answer is C

Most of the elderly client's I have worked with, that are not in the end stages of dementia, are very aware that their time is limited. As a culture we do not like to talk about death. As a profession bent on healing, we don't like to delve into palliative care. An elderly client would probably not accept this 'healing' intervention and may well feel that you are wasting their time.

> *Personal Note: I believe this is because our culture deals with "action" and "doing" as a way of proving our worth. When faced with an impossible situation, we are out of our depths and generally feel inadequate.*

A is INCORRECT.   (THIS IS MORE EFFECTIVE THAN C)

This (insight-oriented technique) is almost always a good approach to therapy. The exception may be trauma debriefing and severe crisis intervention where your immediate goal is to stabilize the client and reduce stress level quickly.   Insight oriented therapy is, at its simplest, bringing actions, behaviors and beliefs into the open air (read: consciousness) and allowing the client to acknowledge and work towards accepting, modifying or rejecting them.

B is INCORRECT.   (THIS IS MORE EFFECTIVE THAN C)

Multidisciplinary teams are almost always good when working with an elderly client because the client is more likely to have physical limitations or concerns, health issues and has a higher probability of being on medication to control any number of physical conditions. Having a cooperative, sharing team that will allow all members access to information and insight is a very powerful intervention.

D is INCORRECT.   (THIS IS MORE EFFECTIVE THAN C)
As human beings we all need and crave support. This is one of the basic hierarchy of needs as defined by Abraham Maslow, BELONGING.   Sometime, simply being there and not saying anything is enough support to help someone find their way.

Question 21   Section: Clinical

The correct answer is A
In Working with African American Clients, Dr. Thomas A. Parham demonstrates an African-centered, culturally based approach that can augment any therapy with African American clients.

Dr. Parham's approach honors spirituality, interconnectedness, and self-knowledge, and is aimed at treating the client holistically—that is, without dividing a client's issues into affective, cognitive, and behavioral factors. Dr. Thomas A. Parham, PhD is the Assistant Vice Chancellor of University of California - Irvine

B is INCORRECT.
While this approach is the one pushed most frequently by HMO, insurance companies and agencies, it is a short-term solution to many problems.   The issues that are at the root of many problems with African-American clients are systemic and socially based in a culture, which has a long history of exploitation of minorities. What seems like a rather simple short-term problem, may be linked to decades of abuse, mistreatment, dehumanization and feelings of futility at trying to live the "American Dream."

Janis Sanchez-Hucles :

Therapists need to be able to do "perspective taking": that is, how might I look at the world differently or respond to this situation if I were black? How are my cultural and political beliefs shaped by my family and my personal experiences? To what extent have I been assuming that my values or the values of the majority culture are correct and normative for all individuals?

C is INCORRECT

Once again we are plagued with the concept of short-term therapy. This model is highly effective for driving down reimbursement rates and limiting services but lacks many of the necessary characteristics to create change in a client's life. Problems facing the African-American community, family and individual in America are neither short-term nor are they brief.

D is INCORRECT

This is the second best answer. The non-directive approach assists the client by honoring their cultural heritage and showing respect for the issues they face daily, however, you are involved with individual therapy, not family counseling.

Question 22   Section: Clinical

The correct answer is D

This is one of those questions where several of the answers appear to be very good, and in fact are good depending in the amount of information you are given. In this case the only information you are given is that the client is a teenager and gay. There is no listing of problems and we have no way of knowing what this client needs. However, referrals and education are always an essential to therapy and a great place to start.

Depending on the feedback you can learn a great deal about how a person perceives their current environment.

A is INCORRECT.
If he was having problems with his family this would be great, but we have no idea what kind of relationship he has with his family and whether it is causing him distress. In fact, his family could have been the one to send him to you to help him accept himself and his orientation.

B is INCORRECT.
There are no maladaptive behaviors noted in the information given, therefore, nothing to work with.

C is INCORRECT.
Also a good idea if this is a presenting problem or comes up in your assessment. However, we do not know if this is an issue for him.

In conclusion, when a person is dealing with a difficult issue and you feel like a full structured assessment might not be appropriate, it is always useful to take the stance that the client requires more information. This is a non-biased and non-judgmental approach. As the client accepts, declines or counters your information you will be able to assess the depth and level of their understanding and the amount of consciousness they bring to the situation.

Question 23   Section: Behavior

The correct answer is C
Before you start anything, you should always define your goals. Otherwise, you will tend to wander. A lot of people get

discouraged with goal planning because after putting effort into it, you find the goals you have created do not clearly fit your idea. It is important to understand that goal setting is a process and your goals will be fluid and flexible until you achieve the perfect mix. Also, when working in an agency, your supervisor and director may have to approve your goals. Don't get to emotionally attached to them, as they may not make it into the final cut. Once you determine your goals, the writing of action steps (What will I specifically need to do in order to achieve each goal) comes next.

A is INCORRECT.
Until you have determined the goals of your program, you have no idea what resources you will need because you have no idea about the specifics you will need.

B is INCORRECT.
If you do not have goals, you cannot order material. Most projects have a limited budget. It would be very bad to order $250 worth of materials only to find that your focus is different and not you have no more money to purchase the proper materials.

D is INCORRECT.
The cart before the horse: Until you have your goals and know what you are providing and why, you certainly can't know who will want to or need to participate.

Question 24   Section: Assessment

The correct answer is D
Fear of open spaces. This comes from the Greek word for open marketplace, agora. People with agoraphobia can end up

"trapped" in their house, unable to go to the store, or even go to the mailbox. It is a very serious and crippling phobia.

A is INCORRECT.

An abnormal and persistent fear of heights. Sufferers experience severe anxiety even though they realize as a rule that heights pose no real threat to them. You might think this could be dealt with by simply avoiding the top floor of buildings, however, Acrophobics report being unable to travel due to having to drive over bridges (which can be rather high) and to drive on mountain roads

Fear of heights is termed acrophobia. The word "acrophobia" is   derived from the Greek "acron" (height) and "phobos" (fear).

B is INCORRECT.

Ophidiophobia is the fear of snakes.   Given its unusual pronunciation it is no surprise we don't use it.

C IS INCORRECT

This is called Claustrophobia.

Question 25   Section: Clinical

Definition: A defense mechanism is a strategy used to cover up or change unconscious desires and wishes that may be inappropriate or difficult to express.

The correct answer is B
Most psychoanalysts believe this is the most primitive defense. Negative

[100]

and positive impulses are split off and un-integrated. The individual views other people as either innately good or innately evil, rather than a whole continuous being.

A is INCORRECT.

Examples of denial include:

- The refusal to accept external reality because it is too threatening;

- arguing against an anxiety-provoking stimulus by stating it doesn't exist

- resolution of emotional conflict and reduction of anxiety by refusing to perceive or consciously acknowledge the more unpleasant aspects of external reality.

C is INCORRECT.

Transformation of negative emotions or instincts into positive actions, behavior, or emotion.

Examples include:

A person is angry and goes outside to chop wood, thereby getting exercise and an expanded woodpile.

A person with a strong desire for control, becomes a business entrepreneur.

D is INCORRECT.

Projection is a primitive form of paranoia. Projection also reduces anxiety by allowing the expression of the undesirable impulses or desires without becoming consciously aware of them; attributing one's own unacknowledged unacceptable/unwanted thoughts and emotions to another; includes severe prejudice, severe jealousy, hypervigilance to external danger, and "injustice collecting". It is shifting one's unacceptable thoughts, feelings and impulses within oneself onto someone else, such that those same thoughts, feelings, beliefs and motivations are perceived as being possessed by the other.

Question 26   Section: Behavior

The correct answer is A
This is an individual service. A community organizer may help a community locate space to build a mental health clinic, but individual service provision is beyond its scope.

Community organization focuses on community group, empowerment through skills training involving organizational issues. It also deals with help neighborhoods organize services for their population and creating methods for neighborhoods to identify problems and focus solutions.

B is INCORRECT.
This is a function of community organizati

C is INCORRECT.
This is a function of community organizati

D is INCORRECT.
This is a function of community organizati

Question 27   Section: Clinical

The correct answer is D
The most important tool you have for building rapport is to develop an attitude with your client that their needs are important and they will be reflected, in the treatment plan and in the on-

going treatment. They need to understand they are the primary driver of therapy and their needs and desires will be respected.

A IS INCORRECT

The only goals that are best for the client are the goals they develop and chose. This will cause a "buy-in" effect, which will increase effectiveness. The agencies goals are not usually relevant to an individual client.

B IS INCORRECT

Confidentiality is NEVER COMPLETE. There are multiple exceptions where you will have to break confidentiality.

C IS INCORRECT

The client is already assured of your experience, because they are sitting in your office. Now, the trick is, "Can you meet their needs?"

Question 28   Section: Clinical

The correct answer is C
(Peace) A sense of peace is often reported by individuals in the fifth and final stage (Acceptance) but it is not one of the stages postulated by Dr. Kubler-Ross.

A is INCORRECT.

Is the second of the five stages. In this stage the individual recognizes that denial cannot continue. Because of anger, the person is very difficult to care for due to misplaced feelings of rage and envy. Any individual that symbolizes life or energy is subject to projected resentment and jealousy. Questions often heard by the patient during this stage are similar to:

"Why me? It's not fair!"

"How can this happen to me?"
"Who is to blame?"

B is INCORRECT.

Is the First of the five stages. It is often seen as a temporary ego defense for the individual. This feeling is generally replaced with heightened awareness of situations and individuals that will be left behind after death. Statements that might be heard by the patient during this stage are:

"I feel fine."
"This can't be happening, not to me."

D is INCORRECT.

The fifth and final stage. In this stage the individual begins to come to terms with their mortality or that of their loved one. Statements that might be heard by the patient during this stage are:

"It's going to be okay."
"I can't fight it, I may as well prepare for it."

The Full five stages are:

1. Denial –usually only a temporary defense for the individual. This feeling is generally replaced with heightened awareness of situations and individuals that will be left behind after death.

2. Anger – Once in this stage, the individual recognizes that denial cannot continue. Because of anger, the person is very difficult to care for due to misplaced feelings of rage and envy. Any individual that symbolizes life or energy is subject to projected resentment and jealousy.

[104]

3. Bargaining – involves the hope that the individual can somehow postpone or delay death. Usually, the negotiation for an extended life is made with a higher power in exchange for a reformed lifestyle. Psychologically, the individual is saying, "I understand I will die, but if I could just have more time..."

4. Depression – during this stage, the dying person begins to understand the certainty of death. Because of this, the individual may become silent, refuse visitors and spend much of the time crying and grieving. This process allows the dying person to disconnect oneself from things of love and affection. It is not recommended to attempt to cheer up an individual who is in this stage. It is an important time for grieving that must be processed.

5. Acceptance – The final stag, the individual begins to come to terms with their mortality or that of their loved one.

More Information can be obtained at:
http://www.ekrfoundation.org/about-grief

My favorite quote: "For those who seek to understand it, death is a highly creative force. The highest spiritual values of life can originate from the thought and study of death."

Question 29   Section: Assessment

The correct answer is B

Research has shown that long-term treatment groups are a very effective method for treating habitual sex offenders. The group allows the treatment to be supported by the other offenders and keeps the offenders from denying their role in their offenses.

A IS INCORRECT

[105]

Psychotropic medications have shown no success when used with sex offenders.

C IS INCORRECT
Individual therapy with sex offenders tends to be unsuccessful because they are, by the nature of their offenses, manipulative and devious. They tend to lie, minimize and shift blame. It is very easy to do this in an individual session.

D IS INCORRECT
There is no indication that family therapy is useful with sex offenders.

Question 30   Section: Clinical

The correct answer is C
Jung conceptualized libido as a free, creative, psychic—energy, that a person uses to energize personal development or individuation. Libido, may contain sexual energy, but is not constrained by sexual energy, as postulated by Freud.

A is INCORRECT.
Rogers was not concerned with libido. One of his 19 propositions, Optimal development, results in a specific process rather than static state. He describes this as the good life where the organism continually aims to fulfill its full potential. Rogers believed that a person raised in an environment consisting of "unconditional positive regard", which can be defined as accepting a person "without negative judgment of the individuals basic worth", will achieve Optimal Development.

B is INCORRECT.

Freud saw libido as psychic energy linked with both the sexual desire as well as all constructive human activity. A gross generalization of Freud's work could be summed up as his believe that "psychiatric illnesses were the result of misdirecting or suppressing the libido."

D is INCORRECT.
Beck is the father of Cognitive Behavior Theory. Our beliefs decide the course of our actions. Libido is not a part of his theory. Beck was convinced of positive results if patients could be persuaded to think constructively and forsake negative thinking.

His theory postulates "If beliefs do not change, there is no improvement. If beliefs change, symptoms change. Beliefs function as little operational units," which means that one's thoughts and beliefs (schema) affect one's behavior and subsequent actions. He believed that dysfunctional behavior is caused due to dysfunctional thinking, and that thinking is shaped by our beliefs.

Question 31   Section: Ethics

The correct answer is C
Always obtain informed consent. If you are not sure that you need to obtain informed consent before doing something, error on the side of caution and get informed consent.
If you believe that informed consent may cause the session to be distorted or the information to be altered, then you need to ask yourself... "why you I need this information?" You must determine your motives for the intrusion into your client's life. If you are at this point, a discussion with a peer social worker may

help you formulate your ideas regarding the intervention in question.

NASW Code of Ethics Section:
1.03 Informed Consent

A Social workers should provide services to clients only in the context of a professional relationship based, when appropriate, on valid informed consent. Social workers should use clear and understandable language to inform clients of the purpose of the services, risks related to the services, limits to services because of the requirements of a third-party payer, relevant costs, reasonable alternatives, clients' right to refuse or withdraw consent, and the time frame covered by the consent. Social workers should provide clients with an opportunity to ask questions.

A is INCORRECT.
A written Consent for treatment does not, in itself, equal informed consent. a written consent, you have no accurate way of knowing if the client understood the language (a critical area of the ethical code) and you also do NOT know if the client was given the opportunity to ask questions (another critical aspect).

B is INCORRECT.
The purpose of the observation is IRRELEVANT in terms of the informed consent. An informed consent gives the client the right to withdraw consent at any time, period. By not telling the client you have nullified their ability to decline participation… you have committed an ethical violation. As for recording, I would recommend getting a second, separate and specific release for any audio or video. If the video release is already signed then a complete review of the release before the session begins. A clear

question should be asked as to whether the client wants to withdraw their consent.

D is INCORRECT.
This does not meet the ethical criteria for informed consent.

Afterwards: Not all your clinical supervisors will be Social Workers and may not be experienced with the NASW code of Ethics. It is a good idea to keep a copy of the code readily available and to be able to reference the section immediately. If your supervisor orders you to do something unethical, they can be disciplined. If you follow the order, knowingly or unknowingly, you can be disciplined.

Question 32   Section: Assessment

The correct answer is D
Generally this disorder is short-term in duration unless it is the prodromal (beginning) phase of the development of schizophrenia.

Diagnostic criteria are:
A. Two (or more) of the following, each present for a significant portion of time during a 1-month period (or less if successfully treated):

   * delusions
   * hallucinations
   *disorganized speech (e.g., frequent derailment or
        incoherence)
   * grossly disorganized or catatonic behavior
   * negative symptoms, i.e., affective flattening, alogia, or
        avolition

Note: Only one Criterion A symptom is required if delusions are bizarre or hallucinations consist of a voice keeping up a running commentary on the person's behavior or thoughts, or two or more voices conversing with each other.

B. Schizoaffective Disorder and Mood Disorder With Psychotic Features have been ruled out because either:

(1) no Major Depressive, Manic, or Mixed Episodes have occurred concurrently with the active-phase symptoms; or
(2) if mood episodes have occurred during active-phase symptoms, their total duration has been brief relative to the duration of the active and residual periods.

C. The disturbance is not due to the direct physiological effects of a substance (e.g., a drug of abuse, a medication) or a general medical condition.

D. An episode of the disorder (including prodromal, active, and residual phases) lasts at least 1 month but less than 6 months. (When the diagnosis must be made without waiting for recovery, it should be qualified as "Provisional.")
Specify if:
   * Without Good Prognostic Features
   * With Good Prognostic Features: as evidenced by two (or more) of the following:
      − onset of prominent psychotic symptoms within 4 weeks of the first noticeable change in usual behavior or functioning
      − confusion or perplexity at the height of the psychotic episode good premorbid social and occupational functioning absence of blunted or flat affect

Associated features
  * Learning Problem
  * Hypoactivity
  * Psychosis
  * Euphoric Mood
  * Depressed Mood
  * Somatic or Sexual Dysfunction
  * Hyperactivity
  * Guilt or Obsession
  * Sexually Deviant Behavior
  * Odd/Eccentric or Suspicious Personality
  * Anxious or Fearful or Dependent Personality
  * Dramatic or Erratic or Antisocial Personality

A is INCORRECT.
The DSM-IV-TR indicated that "A. Two (or more) of the following, each present for a significant portion of time during a 1-month period (or less if successfully treated):" The duration of the symptoms are relatively brief.

B is INCORRECT. Substance abuse and dependency are often co-morbid disorders with Schizophreniform and schizophrenic disorders, there is no indication of a causal relationship.

C is INCORRECT.
By the time symptoms have existed for more than a year, a diagnosis of Schizophrenia is probably more appropriate if it meets all the additional diagnostic criteria.

Question 33   Section: Assessment

The correct answer is B

The feeling that casual incidents and external events have a particular and unusual meaning that is specific to the person. In this mindset, the incidents revolve around the person perceiving them. They are translated as having special significance to the individual. Indeed, they might appear very paranoid and bizarre, but they are not fully formed beliefs. Upon confrontation, the individual is able to distinguish these beliefs as unlikely or improbable.

A is INCORRECT.
Is an alteration in the perception or experience of the self so that one feels detached from, and as if one is an outside observer of, one's mental processes or body (e.g., feeling like one is in a dream).

C is INCORRECT.
A loss of, or alteration in, voluntary motor or sensory functioning suggesting a neurological or general medical condition. Psychological factors are judged to be associated with the development of the symptom, and the symptom is not fully explained by a neurological or general medical condition or the direct effects of a substance. The symptom is not intentionally produced or feigned and is not culturally sanctioned.

D is INCORRECT.
A delusion whose theme is that events, objects, or other persons in one's immediate environment have a particular and unusual significance. These delusions are usually of a negative or pejorative nature, but also may be grandiose in content.
- This would be a good answer if there were no indication of Caffeine overdose or other substance abuse. Delusions are false beliefs that ARE firmly held and FULLY organized into a true belief.

Question 34   Section: Clinical

The correct answer is A
Enmeshment is the inappropriate closeness of family members against a backdrop, of course, of developmental appropriateness.

As defined by Minuchin (1974), "family structure is the invisible set of functional demands that organizes the ways in which family members interact. A family is a system that operates through transactional patterns. Repeated transactions establish patterns of how, when, and with whom to relate, and these patterns underpin the system."

B is INCORRECT.
A relaxed attitude towards sexuality does not directly correlate with boundary issues and sexual abuse issues. In an incestuous family, it is possible to have a very strict attitude towards the inappropriateness of sex, and still have the incest occur. They can be co-occur, but are generally not causal.

C is INCORRECT.
Infants originally experience themselves as part of a symbiotic relationship with their mothers. Over the course of infant development, inevitable failures in perfect empathy and wish-fulfillment help children to recognize that their mother is a separate individual with her own thoughts and feelings.

However, in pathological development, emotionally deprived mothers may feel threatened by the infant's emergent sense of individuality and act in ways so as to promote and prolong this sense of parent-infant oneness. The consequences to the child can be severe, interfering with the ability to forge and assert a separate sense of identity. (Pine 1979).

D is INCORRECT.
Distorted patterns of communication may well be seen in an incestuous family, but it is not necessarily a causal link. Many non-incestuous family have distorted communication patterns

Question 35   Section: Clinical

The correct answer is C
Client's often have inconsistent views and values concerning a specific problem. This is a HUMAN problem we all fight with. Conflicts between what a client 'thinks' should be the solution and what the actual solution will be is the bread and butter of therapy. Just because we know we should do something does not mean we will act in the appropriate manner. (Think about cigarette smoking as an example)

A is INCORRECT.
You demonstrate an accurate understanding by reflective listening (telling the client what you think you heard them say) and by asking questions for clarification. This response back to the client is the primary component of active listening. Rather than passively saying...Uh huh...

B is INCORRECT.
This is the ultimate goal of many therapies and an end result you should always look to achieve. However, there are many ways to achieve it without confrontation.

D is INCORRECT.

[114]

This is definitely a part of therapy. Helping client's see alternatives and supporting them in their attempts to change their behavior is very powerful therapeutic intervention. But there are more ways to achieve this than through confrontation.

Question 36   Section: Behavior

The correct answer is D
Social Work always allows the client the right of self-determination. Just because you (the professional social worker) believes the client needs a certain services does not obligate the client to accept or utilize that service. The client is always in control.

A IS INCORRECT. *(This is a direct social work case management function!)*
The client's Biopsychosocial status and the state of the social system operating around the client are directly part of the definition of social work case management as promulgated by NASW.
        Reference:
http://www.naswdc.org/practice/standards/sw_case_mgmt.asp
The primary goal of case management is to optimize client functioning by providing quality services in the most efficient and effective manner to individuals with multiple complex needs. Like all methods of social work practice, case management rests on a foundation of professional training, values, knowledge, theory, and skills used in the service of attaining goals that are established in conjunction with the client and the client's family, when appropriate.

B IS INCORRECT
(This is a direct social work case management function!)

All social work services are provided at the micro and macro level. This is what makes social work different (and a more powerful intervention than other clinical services). *<in my humble opinion>*

The five (5) primary goals of social work case management are:

1. enhancing developmental, problem- solving, and coping capacities of clients
2. creating and promoting the effective and humane operation of systems that provide resources and services to people
3. linking people with systems that provide them with resources, services, and opportunities
4. improving the scope and capacity of the delivery system
5. contributing to the development and improvement of social policy.

C IS INCORRECT. *(This is a direct social work case management function!)*
Without the development and maintenance of a therapeutic relationship, the ability of the social worker to determine and respond to the multiple levels of need of the client in their environment becomes impaired. Client's will often have needs which they may consider trivial or embarrassing and will not allow these needs to be known to the social work case manager until a bond of trust and empathy is created.

Question 37   Section: Behavior

The correct answer is B
Secondary prevention, also called "screening," refers to measures that detect disease before it is symptomatic. The goal of secondary prevention is to identify and detect disease in its

earliest stages, before noticeable symptoms develop, when it is most likely to be treated successfully. With early detection and diagnosis, it may be possible to cure a disease, slow its progression, prevent or minimize complications, and limit disability.

Reference: http://www.libraryindex.com/pages/722/Prevention-Disease-SECONDARY-PREVENTION.html

A is INCORRECT.

Primary prevention is the inhibition of the development of disease before it occurs.

Primary prevention measures fall into two categories.

> The first category includes actions to protect against disease and disability, such as getting immunizations, ensuring the supply of safe drinking water, applying dental sealants to prevent tooth decay, and guarding against accidents.

> General action to promote health is the other category of primary prevention measures. Health promotion includes the basic activities of a healthy lifestyle: good nutrition and hygiene, adequate exercise and rest, and avoidance of environmental and health risks.
> *Reference:*

http://www.libraryindex.com/pages/721/Prevention-Disease-PRIMARY-PREVENTION.html

C is INCORRECT.

Tertiary prevention efforts focus on people already affected by disease and attempt to reduce resultant disability and restore functionality.

Tertiary prevention programs aim to improve the quality of life for people with various diseases by limiting complications and disabilities, reducing the severity and progression of disease, and providing rehabilitation (therapy to restore functionality and self-sufficiency). Unlike primary and secondary prevention, tertiary prevention involves actual treatment for the disease and is conducted primarily by health care practitioners, rather than public health agencies.

Reference: http://www.libraryindex.com/pages/ 723/Prevention-Disease-TERTIARY-PREVENTION.html

D is INCORRECT.
Crisis intervention is a particular type of intervention geared towards a specific circumstance, which can overwhelm the client. Crisis intervention, may be provided at the Primary, Secondary or even Tertiary levels of intervention.   Crisis intervention is not limited in scope.

Question 38   Section: Behavior

The correct answer is B
This theory was postulated by Douglas McGregor.
Theory Y managers believe that employees will learn to seek out and accept responsibility and to exercise self-control and self-direction in accomplishing objectives to which they are committed. They also believe that the satisfaction of doing a good job is a strong motivation.

It consists of the following tenets:
    1. Work can be as natural as play and rest.
    2. People will be self-directed to meet their work objectives if they are committed to them.

[118]

3. People will be committed to their objectives if rewards are in place that addresses higher needs such as self-fulfillment.

4. Under these conditions, people will seek responsibility.

5. Most people can handle responsibility because creativity and ingenuity are common in the population.

http://en.wikipedia.org/wiki/Theory_X_and_theory_Y

A is INCORRECT.

This might occur in a "Theory Y", but it would not be specifically dictated as part of the "Y" model.

C is INCORRECT.

This is a standard behavioral rewards system designed to foster initiative and performance using money as a token system. It also assumes that money is the primary motivator for the worker in question.

D is INCORRECT.

This concept comes from Max Weber's conception of the perfect bureaucracy. It does not specifically deal with a management style.

Question 39   Section: Clinical

The correct answer is D

(MOAI's then Tricyclics then SSRI's)

MOAI's were discovered accidently in 1951 Irving Selikoff and Edward Robitzek at the Sea View Hospital on Staten Island while testing two new anti-tuberculosis agents from Hoffman-LaRoche called ISONIAZID and IPRONIAZID. They noticed a dramatic improvement in their condition. Only patients with a poor prognosis were initially treated; nevertheless, their condition improved dramatically. Selikoff and Robitzek noted "a subtle general stimulation . . . the patients exhibited renewed vigor…"

In 1952, Cincinnati psychiatrist Max Lurie and Harry Salzer tried it on their patients and reported that ISONIAZOD improved depression in two thirds of their patients and coined the term antidepressant to describe its action.

Reference: Healy, D (2001). "The Antidepressant Drama". in Weissman MM. The treatment of depression: bridging the 21st century. American Psychiatric Pub. pp. 10–11. ISBN 978-0-88048-397-1.
http://books.google.co.uk/books?id=LAmBVollG5kC&printsec=fro ntcover#PPA7,M1.

A is INCORRECT.
(Tricyclics then MAOI's then SSRI's)
Roland Kuhn made the discovery that a tricyclic ("three ringed") compound had a significant antidepressant effect This discovery was made in 1957 in a Swiss psychiatric hospital. Kuhn first called it a "thymoleptic" (literally, "taking hold of the emotions," rather than a neuroleptic, "taking hold of the nerves") and reported his findings 1955-56. The first tricyclic antidepressant, imipramine, was soon developed and followed by numerous variants.
Reference: Kuhn, R (November 1958). "The Treatment of Depressive States with G 22355 (Imipramine Hydrochloride)". American Journal of Psychiatry (American Psychiatric Association) 115 (5): 459–464.

B is INCORRECT.
(MAOI's then SSRI's then Tricyclics)

SSRI's were the third class of antidepressants to be discovered and the primary SSRI was Fluoxetine Hydrochloride (Prozac).

C is INCORRECT.
(SSRI's then MAOI's then Tricyclics)
SSRI's came last.
Selective serotonin reuptake inhibitors (SSRIs) were first introduced in the late 1980s and available in America in 1988 as produced by Eli Lilly, INC.
Selective serotonin reuptake inhibitors or serotonin-specific reuptake inhibitor (SSRIs) are a class of compounds typically used as antidepressants in the treatment of depression, anxiety disorders, and some personality disorders. They are believed to increase the extracellular level of the neurotransmitter serotonin by inhibiting its reuptake into the presynaptic cell thus increasing the level of serotonin available to bind to the postsynaptic receptor. (Don't you wish you had taken Anatomy and Physiology 1)
They have also been used in the treatment of depressive disorders, anxiety disorders and obsessive-compulsive disorder (OCD).
Reference: Preskorn SH, Ross R, Stanga CY (2004). "Selective Serotonin Reuptake Inhibitors". in Sheldon H. Preskorn, Hohn P. Feighner, Christina Y. Stanga and Ruth Ross. Antidepressants: Past, Present and Future. Berlin: Springer. pp. 241–62. ISBN 978-3-540-43054-4.

Question 40   Section: Clinical

The correct answer is B
(Citalopram (Celexa), Escitalopram (Lexapro), Fluoxetine (Prozac), Fluvoxamine (Luvox),Paroxetine (Paxil), Sertraline (Zoloft))

All of these are SSRI's.

A is INCORRECT.
(Procarbazine (Matulane), Safrazine (Safra), Phenelzine (Nardil, Nardelzine), Pheniprazine (Catron), Iproniazid (Iprozid))

All of these drugs are MAOI's. A lot of MAOI's have the suffix – Zine. (Be careful because they do not all follow this pattern. When in doubt, look it up.)

C is INCORRECT.
(Amitriptyline (Elavil), Clomipramine (Anafranil), Desipramine (Norpramin), Doxepin (Sinequan), Imipramine (Tofranil), Nortriptyline (Pamelor))

All of these are Tricyclics

D is INCORRECT.
(Citalopram (Celexa), Fluoxetine (Prozac), Nortriptyline (Pamelor), Phenelzine (Nardil, Nardelzine), Amitriptyline (Elavil))

These are a mixture: SSRI – SSRI – TRICYCLIC – MAOI – TRICYCLIC

Question 41   Section: Clinical

The correct answer is C
This is a situation where one member of a structural unit needs to leave (or be pushed out) of the structural unit. Individual therapy and crisis intervention during the separation are the best possible therapy choices. Family therapy may be appropriate after the

separation and after a set period of time has passed, in order to explore the new role.

A is INCORRECT.

All families are a structural unit with various roles ascribed to each member. When one family member's role begins to change because of growing awareness in therapy, the entire system will begin to destabilize and cause other family members stress until it again reaches a state of equilibrium. Another way to look at it is that family therapy will cause everyone some distress. That is kind of its purpose as it helps the family re-shape themselves.

B is INCORRECT.

An eating disorder is almost always a family therapy issue. Structural Family Therapy (Salvador Minuchin) would argue that only by restructuring all the roles in the family, can you help the individual with an eating disorder.

D is INCORRECT.

Divorce is usually a nasty business and the children often get the nastiest end of the stick. If there ever was a time for family therapy, it would be now. The family should explore its new roles and the expectations, both stated and implied, which are going to change in the new structure.

Question 42   Section: Assessment

The correct answer is D
Discharge and termination are concepts that need to be addressed continually (and at the appropriate) times during therapy. Often the goals set during assessment can change and some goals will vanish naturally as therapy progresses and insight increases. By addressing termination issues continually

during therapy, you have the opportunity to review your goals, provide positive and negative feedback to the client naturally, assess the client's willingness to separate from therapy and ensure that a dependency bond does not occur which could jeopardize therapy and growth.

A is INCORRECT.
Most people would probably feel like you were pushing them out the door and trying to get rid of them. The possible outcomes of this action may include failure of the client to open-up and disclose issues, refusal to deeply engage in therapy and premature termination of therapy on the client's biased belief that you "don't feel their problems are important."

B is INCORRECT.
This would probably feel like the client was getting "blown off." Just as they start to get comfortable and begin deep disclosure you say, "Well, next week will be our last session." What they will hear is: "Your problems are not longer important so I am replacing your hourly slot with someone else."

C is INCORRECT.
Once again, it does not allow therapy to pace itself. The point of therapy is awareness and change. These require constant feedback and constant review. It is probable they will not remember the termination talk from the beginning of therapy and will feel the talk at the end comes "out of the blue."

Question 43   Section: Assessment

The correct answer is C
This answer shows her you are hearing her concerns and are able to meet her needs. It is an excellent way of showing

concern and understanding. It will most likely open a conversation that will allow the client to divulge their feeling and fears about their upcoming mood.

A IS INCORRECT

This statement is dismissive and talks down to the client. It lets the client know you are not very interested in their issues.

B IS INCORRECT

This statement has no therapeutic value and appears to be a challenge. It is unnecessarily argumentative.

D IS INCORRECT

This is your opinion stated as fact in an effect to allay a set of fears that you are not taking seriously. You will find that the client will also recognize your lack of concern.

Question 44   Section: Clinical

The correct answer is B

Remember that Carl Rogers entire theory is based on his 19 propositions. Of these propositions the 15th one states "Psychological maladjustment exists when the organism denies awareness of significant sensory and visceral experiences, which consequently are not symbolized and organized into the gestalt of the self structure. When this situation exists, there is a basic or potential psychological tension."

When a person denies the awareness of their situation there is an immediate conflict between their self (the whole of them) and their experience. In a psychodynamic perspective, using an ego defense mechanism which limits awareness of attempts to filter the interpretation of the experience would assist in creating, increasing or maintaining the "incongruence". and would be dysfunctional.

His 19 Propositions are:

1) All individuals (organisms) exist in a continually changing world of experience (phenomenal field) of which they are the center.

2) The organism reacts to the field as it is experienced and perceived. This perceptual field is "reality" for the individual.

3) The organism reacts as an organized whole to this phenomenal field.

4) A portion of the total perceptual field gradually becomes differentiated as the self.

5) As a result of interaction with the environment, and particularly as a result of evaluational interaction with others, the structure of the self is formed - an organized, fluid but consistent conceptual pattern of perceptions of characteristics and relationships of the "I" or the "me", together with values attached to these concepts.

6) The organism has one basic tendency and striving - to actualize, maintain and enhance the experiencing organism.

7) The best vantage point for understanding behavior is from the internal frame of reference of the individual.

8) Behavior is basically the goal-directed attempt of the organism to satisfy its needs as experienced, in the field as perceived.

9) Emotion accompanies, and in general facilitates, such goal directed behavior, the kind of emotion being related to the perceived significance of the behavior for the maintenance and enhancement of the organism.

10) Values experienced directly by the organism, and in some instances are values introjected or taken over from others, but perceived in distorted fashion, as if they had been experienced directly.

11) As experiences occur in the life of the individual, they are either, a) symbolized, perceived and organized into some relation to the self, b) ignored because there is no perceived relationship to the self structure, c) denied symbolization or given distorted symbolization because the experience is inconsistent with the structure of the self.

12) Most of the ways of behaving that are adopted by the organism are those that are consistent with the concept of self.

13) In some instances, behavior may be brought about by organic experiences and needs which have not been symbolized. Such behavior may be inconsistent with the structure of the self but in such instances the behavior is not "owned" by the individual.

14) Psychological adjustment exists when the concept of the self is such that all the sensory and visceral experiences of the organism are, or may be, assimilated on a symbolic level into a consistent relationship with the concept of self.

15) Psychological maladjustment exists when the organism denies awareness of significant sensory and visceral experiences, which consequently are not symbolized and organized into the gestalt of the self structure. When this situation exists, there is a basic or potential psychological tension.

16) Any experience which is inconsistent with the organization of the structure of the self may be perceived as a threat, and the more of these perceptions there are, the more rigidly the self structure is organized to maintain itself.

17) Under certain conditions, involving primarily complete absence of threat to the self structure, experiences which are consistent with it may be perceived and examined, and the structure of self revised to assimilate and include such experiences.

18) When the individual perceives and accepts into one consistent and integrated system all his sensory and visceral

experiences, then he is necessarily more understanding of others and is more accepting of others as separate individuals.

19) As the individual perceives and accepts into his self structure more of his organic experiences, he finds that he is replacing his present value system - based extensively on introjections which have been distortedly symbolized - with a continuing organismic valuing process.

> *HINT: If you want to become a Rogerian therapist, read these 19 propositions every single day for 4 years. This is a lot of material! Don't be intimidated by it.*

A is INCORRECT

Rogers never discussed EGO or BOUNDARIES. There are Psychodynamic Concepts. While he came to professional fruition during the psychodynamic years, he never adopted many of the issues of psychodynamic therapy of his day. This may be due to the influence of the post-Freudian psychotherapist, Otto Rank.

C is INCORRECT

According to Rogers, an organism could NEVER be unaware of their surrounding and environment. The crucial matter was how they interpreted and responded to in order to integrate the experiences.

D is INCORRECT

Rogers' theory did not directly address irresponsibility. If would probably have been a subject that he would have considered too judgmental and incongruent with actualization and integration.

Question 45   Section: Clinical

The correct answer is D
It is best to think of neurosis as DYSFUNCTION.

[128]

Neurosis is a class of functional mental disorders involving distress but neither delusions nor hallucinations, whereby behavior is not outside socially acceptable norms.

According to Dr. George Boeree, effects of neurosis can involve: ...anxiety, sadness or depression, anger, irritability, mental confusion, low sense of self-worth, etc., behavioral symptoms such as phobic avoidance, vigilance, impulsive and compulsive acts, lethargy, etc., cognitive problems such as unpleasant or disturbing thoughts, repetition of thoughts and obsession, habitual fantasizing, negativity and cynicism, etc.

Interpersonally, neurosis involves dependency, aggressiveness, perfectionism, schizoid isolation, socio-culturally inappropriate behaviors, etc.

A is INCORRECT

In Freudian terms, introjection is the aspect of the ego's system of relational mechanisms which handles checks and balances from a perspective external to what one normally considers.
One of the ways we develop is to introject or swallow the behaviors of our parent's whole and then slowly modify our responses.

Introjection can be a defense mechanism when you have an individual with weak EGO BOUNDARIES (which is to say the individual has rather soft and flexible rules about how they respond to certain situations) e.g. I believe stealing is wrong, but in order to fit in with my friends and not be called a 'chicken' I will engage in shoplifting. "Individuals with weak ego boundaries are more prone to use introjection as a defense mechanism.

B is INCORRECT

Introjection usually has the effect of decreasing awareness.

C is INCORRECT
is necessary for healthy growth
According to Fritz Perl's, "assimilation", as opposed to "introjection", was the prime means by which growth occurs in therapy.

In contrast to the psychoanalysts who believe the "patient" introjects the (presumably more healthy) interpretations of their analyst; Gestalt therapy states the client must "taste" his or her experience, and either accept or reject it, but not "swallow the experience whole" (Introjection).

This key point separates Gestalt Therapy from Psychoanalysis.

Gestalt Therapist avoid interpretation, and encouraging discovery instead. The therapist should not interpret but lead the client to discover the experiences for themselves.

EXTRA: *If you ever get the chance to read about Fritz Perls personal life, do not pass up the opportunity. I have had the pleasure of personally interviewing some psychoanalysts who attended Fritz Perls' trainings in the 60's. Fritz was a very 'colorful' fellow. This may have been in part to his tutorship under the Psychoanalyst Wilhelm Reich. Reich postulated his entire theory of Psychoanalysis on the function and condition of the sexual orgasm. It should be noted **(without negativity)** that there is a growing community of psychoanalysts who believe Wilhelm Reich suffered from an acute form of schizophrenia.*

Question 46   Section: Clinical
The correct answer is C

In psychoanalytic theory, reaction formation is a defensive process (defense mechanism) in which anxiety-producing or unacceptable emotions and impulses are mastered by exaggeration (hypertrophy) of the directly opposing tendency.

A man who is overly aroused by pornographic material and who utilizes reaction formation, may become very critical of all forms of pornography. He may devote a great deal of energy to fighting the availability of pornography and allow this "formation" to take over his life. He may end up sacrificing many of the positive things in his life, including family relationships, by traveling around the country to anti-pornography rallies. He continues his behavior and eventually it only brings temporary relief, because the deeply rooted arousal to an unacceptable behavior such as watching pornography is still present.

A is INCORRECT

When a client projects their own undesirable thoughts, motivations, desires, and/or feelings onto another person. The client is afraid to accept or acknowledge personal feelings so they attribute those feeling to another person. An alternative is to project idealized feeling onto another person and then respond to the projected feelings instead of the person.

> *HINT: If you have ever known someone who quickly "falls in love" with someone and several months later are splitting up because the person is not who I thought they were", only to quickly fall in love with another person and repeat the cycle, this person is probably using projection and responding to their own inner desires. They can maintain the false belief for a short period of time, but eventually the real person they projected onto comes through.*

B is INCORRECT

Transference is the process (in psychodynamic terms) of unconscious redirection of feelings from one person to another. It is common for people to transfer (put on other people) feelings from their parents to their partners or children. An example of this behavior would be the tendency to mistrust somebody who resembles an ex-spouse in manners, voice, or external appearance; or be overly compliant to someone who resembles a childhood friend.

> *HINT: If you have ever met someone that "Turns you off immediately" (assuming the social situation is appropriate), or felt an intense like or dislike for a person who you just met, it is possible you are "Transferring" issues from childhood or your past.*

D is INCORRECT

Transformation of negative emotions or instincts into positive actions, behavior, or emotion. In Freud's classic theory, erotic energy is allowed a limited amount of expression, due to constraints of human society. Sublimation is the process of transforming libido into "socially useful" achievements, mainly art

Question 47   Section: Clinical

The correct answer is A

This is clearly a frustrating experience for the client and given their age they probably do not have the experience to be able to process the experience, or even identify or name it. By naming it and allowing them to process similar feelings you should be able to encourage growth and understanding

B IS INCORRECT

This is a judgmental statement, which will undoubtedly put therapeutic distance between you and your client.

C IS INCORRECT

This statement is NON-THERAPUETIC. It is probably a statement, the client has heard many times in the past and is not useful.

D IS INCORRECT

While this may be a true statement and reflect reality, it is confrontational. If you do not have an exact reason to confront with a follow-up that will enable and encourage growth, you have missed an opportunity to foster change.

Question 48   Section: Clinical

The correct answer is A

excitation due to internal or external stimulation or stimulus

Excitation puts demands on the ego and it can feel overwhelming. These demands and conflicts cause an unpleasant inner state that acts to tell the EGO something is not right.

Freud identified three types of anxiety:

> **Neurotic anxiety** is the unconscious worry that we will lose control of the id's urges, resulting in punishment for inappropriate behavior.

> **Reality anxiety** is fear of real-world events. The cause of this anxiety, is usually easily identified. For example, a person might fear receiving a dog bite when they are near a menacing dog. The most common way of reducing this anxiety is to avoid the threatening object.

Moral anxiety involves a fear of violating our own moral principles.

B is INCORRECT

Anything that stimulates the EGO in Freudian psychoanalysis causes a reaction, usually physical and/or psychological. Construing or understanding an event is the outcome of psychoanalysis, not an ego motivator.

C is INCORRECT

"Splitting" is a term coined by Pierre Marie Félix Janet (May 30, 1859 - February 24, 1947) in his book L'Automatisme psychologique. Pierre Janet (Jan-eh) was a pioneering French psychologist, philosopher and psychotherapist in the field of dissociation and traumatic memory.

Splitting as a psychological phenomenon (defense mechanism) that can affect two separate area. The first of these is the splitting of the mind. This is used in understanding the concept of "disassociation". The second is the "splitting of mental concepts" (for example: Black and White thinking) which is often used to explain certain personality disorders. Splitting of mental concepts occurs naturally in the early years of development and must be integrated for healthy development.

D is INCORRECT

The concept of "unified self" belongs to Analytical Psychology as defined by Carl Gustav Jung. Jung believed that the anima (Jungian Archetype: feminine inner personality, as present in the unconscious of the male.) and animus (the masculine inner personality as present in women) act as guides to the unconscious unified self and that forming an awareness and a connection with the anima or animus is one of the most difficult and rewarding steps in psychological growth.

Question 49   Section: Assessment

The correct answer is C

In this particular situation, the child is receiving their reward in the form of the attention the teacher gives them. The more attention they get from the teacher, the more they feel reinforced. It does not matter that the attention is negative or punitive, just the simple fact of getting the teacher to stop what they are doing and focus on them is gratifying.

--- Positive reinforcement is the presentation of a consequence immediately following a response which increases the likelihood that the response happening again. In this case the response is the misbehavior and the reinforcer is the teacher's attention.

A is INCORRECT

Secondary reinforcers are ALWAYS conditioned reinforcers. They are secondary to the primary or the positive reinforcer but have become bonded to the response.

If you have ever been owned by a cat, and have opened a can of cat food, you will notice that the sound of the can opener releasing the air from the can, or the sound of the electric can opener will cause the cat to appear from almost anywhere, and then attempt to wrap itself around your ankles in an attempt to trip you, thus getting the food to the floor quicker. (Cats are devious!) This "can opening sound" is a secondary reinforcer.

B is INCORRECT

a negative reinforcer does its work by being removed from the scene in response to a behavior. Most children find being ignored to be very aversive. If you ignore a child's temper tantrum until they exhibit the behavior of stopping the tantrum, upon ending the process of ignoring them you have just provided negative reinforcement by removing the aversive stimuli (ignoring). If the tantrum behavior reduces in frequency and duration as a means of getting "attention" then the negative reinforcer if appropriate.

D is INCORRECT

A primary reinforcer is an UNPAIRED reinforcer. It exists because it is required for a species survival. Examples of primary reinforcers are food, air, water, sex and sleep.

Question 50   Section: Assessment

The Correct Answer is C

Regression is the Temporary reversion of the ego to an earlier stage of development rather than handling unacceptable impulses in a more adult way.

This would probably not be a serious step backwards in therapy, but should help the client identify the need for continued work in this area. During her mother's visit, you may want to have your client come in with her mother to help her come to grips with her feelings about "her mother's knowledge". You may find out mother did know and wants to apologize, but does not know how, or you may find out mother had no clue about the abuse. Either way, it Could yield some consciousness onto the problems reported by your client.

A is INCORRECT

Repression: is the defense where a person repels inner desires towards pleasurable instincts and situations in order to keep from acting on the impulse when the action would be associated with a very negative consequence. The user pushes the desire into the unconscious mind in order to remove it from awareness. As a therapist you can often see the effects of repression on your clients when you notice "unexplained naivety", "memory lapses", "seeming lack of awareness of certain situations in their life", or being "brushed off absent-mindedly when you ask about certain items during therapy."

The emotion (the client's emotion may be detectable to you, however, the client's cognition behind the emotion may be invisible or ethereal) will be noticeable to you, but the idea behind the emotion will be invisible, or ethereal.

> *Practice Note: When you are sitting in therapy and your client's response leads you to think; "What was that about?" or "What just happened?" you have probably rubbed up against the ego defense mechanism of REPRESSION.*

B is INCORRECT
Splitting: A primitive defense and one primarily found in childhood or in psychosis. It is in essence a "psychotic" defense mechanism because it allows the user to SPLIT a piece of their ego state or experience from themselves and remove it from reality.

D is INCORRECT
Introjection is the process of identifying with some idea or object so deeply that it becomes a part of that person.
In Freudian terms, folding something external into your internal world, where you can weigh and balance it against your internal values and desires. It is a "Safe" method of exploring change.

Question 51   Section: Assessment

The correct answer is D
All of these symptoms are associated with Fetal Alcohol Syndrome.

Poor growth while the baby is in the womb and after birth
Decreased muscle tone and poor coordination
Delayed development and problems in three or more major areas: thinking, speech, movement, or social skills
Heart defects such as ventricular septal defect (VSD) or atrial septal defect (ASD)
Problems with the face, including:
Narrow, small eyes with large epicanthal folds
Small head
Small upper jaw
Smooth groove in upper lip
Smooth and thin upper lip

A IS INCORRECT
Albino coloration has no correlation with FAS

B IS INCORRECT
Adolescents with FAS, have been known to be aggressive, but it is only one of many characteristics

C IS INCORRECT
There is no correlation between moral development and FAS

Question 52   Section: Assessment

The Correct Answer is A
An education technique for disciplining a child that involves removing the child from other children in order to extinguish

[138]

behavior. In the case of a child who is already withdrawn, it would most likely reinforce the ideas the child has about their separation and would possibly increase the level of withdrawal.

B is INCORRECT

Cognitive problem-solving skills training (CPSST) attempts to decrease a child's inappropriate or disruptive behaviors by teaching the child new skills for approaching situations that previously provoked negative behavior. Using both cognitive and behavioral techniques and focusing on the child more than on the parents or the family unit, CPSST helps the child gain the ability to self-manage thoughts and feelings and interact appropriately with others by developing new perspectives and solutions. The basis of the treatment is the underlying principle that children lacking constructive ways to address the environment have problematic behaviors; teaching these children ways to positively problem-solve and challenge dysfunctional thoughts improves functioning.

Reference:http://www.minddisorders.com/Br-Del/Cognitive-problem-solving-skills-training.html#ixzz10ASTSlRH

C is INCORRECT

Premack's Principle suggests that if a person wants to perform a given activity, the person will perform a less desirable activity to get at the more desirable activity. *Example: If you eat your brussel sprouts, you can have ice cream for dessert.*

D is INCORRECT

negative reinforcement does its work by being removed from the scene in response to a behavior. Most children find being ignored to be very aversive. If you ignore a child's temper tantrum until they exhibit the behavior of stopping the tantrum, upon ending the process of ignoring them you have just provided negative reinforcement by removing the aversive stimuli (ignoring). If the tantrum behavior reduces in frequency and duration as a means of getting "attention" then the negative reinforcer if appropriate.

Question 53   Section: Behavior

The correct answer is B
Coping skills are tools we all use. When you respond to a new situation you have used a coping skill. Some more obvious examples would be: "sitting up in your seat straight when the teacher addresses you in class." This set of skills in response to the teachers request is read by the teacher as a sign of respect , and the teacher feels valued and validated. If the teacher speaks and you continue to look away, this set of skills will be interpreted as being disrespectful, and may be followed by a punishment by the disrespected teacher as a means of displaying that they are in control.

Some ways to teach coping skills are:
Open communication within the family is vital to good relationships. During stressful times we frequently need people outside the family willing to listen when we need to vent our feelings. In some families, listening without judging is difficult because we want to help, but have strong feelings and opinions. Taking the extra effort to actively listen is important.

Communication Tips
        Be sensitive to nonverbal communication. Clenched fists, fidgeting, eye movements, and other body language can suggest very different meanings for what is said.

Avoid "you" statements. They can stifle communication. Sentences that begin with "you" can sound like accusations.

Share your feelings with "I" statements. "I" statements build trust in the relationship. They give you ownership for what is said. The model for this type of communication is:

1. Begin: "I feel"
2. Name situation: "when you"
3. Tell how you are affected: "because"
4. State what you would like to see in the future: "from now on please"

An example might be:

"I feel angry when I get home and find the dishes undone because it makes the place look so messy. In the future, would you please put the dishes in the dishwasher?"

Give feedback or clarify what is said. Ask questions such as "Do you mean...?" "I understood you to say..."
Reference:
http://www.extension.org/pages/Teaching_Children_Coping_Skills

A is INCORRECT

This is a broad emotional range which could be related to many topics and require many interventions.

C is INCORRECT

This is a broad emotional range which could be related to many topics and require many interventions.

D is INCORRECT

A cognitive behavioral technique developed by Richard Bootzin to be used in the treatment of insomnia. Stimulus control is designed to overcome the conditioning that occurs with repeated and unsuccessful attempts to sleep that result in negative associations being built up between the preparation for sleep and the sleep environment with the effort to fall asleep.

The stimulus control instructions are designed to re-associate bedtime with the rapid onset of sleep and to establish a regular sleep-wake schedule that is consistent with the circadian (24 hour) sleep/wake cycle. The instructions are:

1. Only go to bed when sleepy. Bear in mind being sleepy is not the same thing as being tired. It is important to be aware of this difference. Behavioral signs such as dropping eyelids, involuntary head nodding and yawning signal sleepiness. This rule helps prevent lying in bed engaging in negative sleep thoughts. Thoughts about how you don't feel like sleeping, how bad it will be tomorrow if you don't sleep tonight, going over everything you have to do in the morning and so on just create arousal and make it harder to fall asleep.

2. If after about 20 minutes you are unable to fall asleep or awaken and find it difficult to fall back asleep, leave the bed and go to another room and engage in a relaxing activity such as some light reading or using a relaxation technique until you do feel drowsy. Then return to bed and repeat as often as necessary until you do fall asleep. It is important to not watch the clock while doing this. It is your subjective estimate of time that is important. It is also important to not engage in stimulating activities such as watching late night horror movies on Fear Net.

3. Use the bed only for sleep and sexual activity. Do not engage in sleep-incompatible activity in bed such as eating snacks,

watching TV (especially the evening news with the reports of the several murders that happened in a nearby neighborhood earlier today), or working on your IRS tax audit. These activities obviously will result in arousal and make it difficult to fall asleep. Repeatedly engaging in these kinds of activities helps condition arousal to the bed environment when instead you want to condition a feeling of relaxation to being in bed.

4. Keep a regular morning rise time no matter how much sleep you got the night before. This will help regularize the circadian (24 hour) schedule and if you don't sleep well one night, the drive to sleep
will be higher the following night - if you don't dissipate it with low quality, light morning sleep by staying in bed later than planned.

5. Avoid napping. (There is more to napping that will be discussed in a future post but for now the stimulus control instruction is to avoid it.) This prevents reducing sleep drive earlier in the day that can make it harder to fall asleep at night. With the use of stimulus control many people can begin to overcome their insomnia. In the next post further techniques for managing insomnia will be reviewed.

Reference:
http://www.psychologytoday.com/blog/sleepless-in-america/200905/cognitive-behavioral-therapy-insomnia-part-2-stimulus-control

This is a form of Dialectic Behavioral Therapy (DBT) designed to learn and refine skills necessary for the change of behavioral, emotional, and thinking patterns associated with problems in interacting which causing misery and distress.

Specific DBT Goals

Decrease in the following behaviors: (1) Interpersonal chaos, (2) Labile (not steady) emotions and or moods, (3) Impulsiveness, (4) Confusion about self, (5) cognitive dysregulation, and (6) Relationship difficulties

Followed by an increase in the following behaviors: (1) Interpersonal effectiveness skills, (2) Emotions regulation skills, (3) Distress tolerance skills, (4) Core mindfulness skills

Reference:
http://www.dbtselfhelp.com/html/general_handout.html

Question 54   Section: Assessment

The correct answer is B
Premack's Principle suggests that if a person wants to perform a given activity, the person will perform a less desirable activity to get at the more desirable activity.

A is INCORRECT
In OPERANT CONDITIONING, punishment is the reduction of a behavior via application of an adverse stimulus ("positive punishment") or removal of a pleasant stimulus ("negative punishment").

Examples include: Extra chores or spanking are examples of positive punishment, while making an offending student lose recess or play privileges are examples of negative punishment.

Important: The definition requires that punishment is only determined after the fact by the reduction in behavior; if the offending behavior of the subject does not decrease then it is not considered punishment.

C) is INCORRECT
In classical conditioning, when the occurrences of a conditioned response decrease or disappear. In classical conditioning, this

happens when a conditioned stimulus is no longer paired with an unconditioned stimulus.

D is INCORRECT

an OPERANT CONDITIONING TERM, if positive reinforcement strengthens a response by adding a positive stimulus, then response cost has to weaken a behavior by subtracting a positive stimulus. After the response the positive reinforcer is removed which weakens the frequency of the response.

Question 55   Section: Clinical

The correct answer is D

One of the hallmarks of psychological distress is the overwhelming of an individual's coping strategies and tools. During a crisis, we tend to use "tools" and "skills" we have learned before. If these work, the crisis lessens. Often they do not work and the crisis deepens. It is easy to go through your entire "toolbox" and run out of options. At this crucial point, giving advice may be appropriate, however, you should limit your advice to as small an area as possible. For example, you might give someone advice to take several days off work and visit a supportive family member, but it would not be prudent to advise them to quit their job and move to Taos, New Mexico.

A is INCORRECT

Resistance is a part of therapy. Everyone is resistant to anything other than superficial change. Therapy gives a clearly defined and safe area to explore resistance and to learn to modify behavior and expectations.

B is INCORRECT

This is also a standard part of therapy. It is sometimes referred to as psychoeducation. It is appropriate to discuss all sorts of options, however, when asked, you should avoid given direct advice. A couple of good stock phrases that may be useful are, "Our situations are different, any advice I gave you would be appropriate for me but not for you!" and "I am not going to be effected by the consequences of your decisions, you are…you need to decide for yourself."

C is INCORRECT

This is probably one of the reasons she has come into therapy to begin with. You need to act as a reflective, pleasant, accepting "wall" for her to "bounce her ideas" off of. You will create a safe environment where she will be able to figure out her problem on her own.

Supplemental: As a therapist, I have always seen my job as being a type of "trail guide". I know several specific sections of the trail we walk through life and can guide a person along that section. We generally walk side by side and I can often point out obstacles along the trail that will cause them problems. But, sooner or later we will reach a portion of the trail where I will no longer be able to guide the client. Then I wish them well and assure them (as I truly believe) that they will find another "Trail Guide" up ahead who will be able to assist them.

They may need to stumble for a while before they find this guide, but we must trust that all people have the right and should be allowed the dignity of choosing their own trail.

You should also be able to accept the possibility that your client will "leave the trail into the wilderness" or "go down an unknown sidepath" or even "simply sit in the middle of the trail and cry, refusing to move or help themselves."

As social workers, we MUST allow the client to choose their own option. We can assist them, however, only they can live their own lives.

Question 56 Section: Clinical

B is CORRECT
Impulsive, excessive and uncontrollable use of foul or obscene language, including words related to feces (bowel waste). Coprolalia is a typical symptom of Tourette syndrome and can sometimes be a symptom of schizophrenia.

SUPPLEMENTAL: (Or more information than you wanted to know about Copro-related vocabulary)
> *"Coprolalia" is derived from the Greek words "kopros" (dung) and "lalein" (to babble). "Kopros" has also given us such English words as "coprolith," a hard lump of feces in the intestines, and "coprophobia" (an abnormal and persistent fear of feces).*

A is INCORRECT
An impulse control problem involving the compulsive stealing of items not needed for their monetary value. There is usually a feeling of tension before stealing, and a sense of pleasure at the time of the theft. These items are not usually stolen as an expression of anger or vengeance.

C is INCORRECT
Ornithophobia - is the fear of birds (I don't know what else could be said about this.)

[147]

D is INCORRECT
Pulling out your own hair habitually, to the point of seeing noticeable hair loss, and experiencing pleasure or tension relief from the behavior. This does not include hair loss as a result of medical conditions, and the disorder must result in clinical distress or impairment in life functioning.

Question 57   Section: Clinical

The correct answer is D
Freud's oral stage was from birth to about 24 months. Freud felt oral needs where an integral aspect of human development and were satisfied by nursing. If the individual did not get enough satisfaction to fulfill this stage, they would develop a fixation on oral behaviors, which would allow them to recreate this phase to achieve the necessary level of oral satisfaction. Smoking could act as a substitute for the nursing needs missed at this stage. A person who was fixated at this stage would be labeled as "oral-retentive"

A is INCORRECT
Anal is his stage from 24-48 months where the primary purpose is to learn to control the body's elimination of waste by learning to be toilet trained. A person who had a problem with learning to control their bowels would have had a problem with the anal phase. Failure to learn proper elimination could lead a person to be labeled "anal-retentive" or "anal-expressive"

B is INCORRECT
The Phallic stage is the discovery of the genitals and would generally occur after age 3-4. The primary mission of this stage is to integrate a sense of pleasure.

IMPORTANT: When reading Freud, you must understand that he lived in a different century and the meanings associated with the words he used have changed linguistically over time. He will often use the term "sex" or "sexual". In his day, these were commonly interpreted as "pleasure". When you read Freudian psychoanalysis you should substitute the word "pleasure" for "sex" and the word "pleasurable" for "Sexual". He will make a lot more sense.

C is INCORRECT
Latency is his final stage which begins at age 10-12 and continues until death.

BY THE WAY: The American Culture seems to have an odd view of sex. We routinely use it and its promise to sell merchandise, however we do not talk about it openly. This conflict has caused many young social workers to avoid learning about Freud. If you are going to work with people you will need to deal with your reluctance to talk about all sorts of "taboo" subjects. If you are, for example, uncomfortable discussing "adolescent masturbation" with your colleagues when presenting a case, there may be issues which go unaddressed and can cause damage to the client later. If will take time and a supportive atmosphere to overcome your culturally embedded views of sex. It cannot be done overnight, but if you are to do clinical work, it cannot be ignored.

Question 58   Section: Clinical

The correct answer is C
Reflection is usually obtained in a calm and serene state. It is the antithesis of a crisis situation.

Crisis Overview:
Crisis always has a precipitating event. Then it occurs in a series of phases. The phases usually include (1) Baseline/In Control – (2) Escalation [Increased tension] – (3) Crisis – (4) Calming Down (De-escalation) – (5) Recovery [Re-integration]

A is INCORRECT
This is the initial phase of the increasing energy. This is when the fight/crisis/anxiety/aggression begins to build. Often this is the best stage to plan an intervention or to train the client to respond to. The emotional energy of the situation has not overwhelmed the parties.

B is INCORRECT
This is the final stage where de-escalation occurs and the system either, returns to its baseline normal or to a slightly less "energetic" situation. This is the "let down after the storm".

D is INCORRECT
This event sets off the crisis cycle. It will be different for everyone. Sometimes the event will be clear to all parties involved and other times it will be "the straw that broke the camel's back."

SUPPLEMENTAL:

Baseline/In Control- Person is calm and displaying their normal everyday behavior.
Trigger- Person experiences a stressor which may be physical, environmental or social (e.g. a loud noise, crowd, hunger, demand, etc.)

Escalation- Person continues to show increased signs of agitation. Behaviors may intensify (e.g.; pacing, swearing, attempting to hit, verbally threatening, etc.)

Crisis- Person is out of control and loses ability to process information. Person may be physically aggressive (e.g., hitting, kicking, biting, etc), engage in self-injurious behavior(e.g., biting hand, head banging, etc.), verbally assaultive (e.g., swearing, name calling, racially offensive remarks), running away, etc.

Calming Down- Person begins to regain control, and behavior becomes less intense.

Recovery- Person has regained control but remains fragile.

Crash- Person may drop below normal activity level and need quiet time (e.g. sleep, relax).

Baseline/In Control – Escalation – Crisis - Calming Down (De-escalation) – Recovery

Question 59   Section: Clinical

The correct answer is C
The ego state is an internal set of feelings and responses to thoughts, feelings, ideas and external events. This is not part of the Ecological Model.

A is INCORRECT
The normal expectations of the culture in which a person lives, both internal and external are excellent predictors of external stressor and needs for a client. You should always be aware of cultural norm that affect your client, regardless of how remote or distant they may seem.

B is INCORRECT
Stress caused by environmental factors and financial, employment, or academic concerns can have a very profound

impact on the emotional and psychological condition of your client. Eliminating, moderating or teaching coping skills to minimize stress are essential to helping your client become healthy.

D is INCORRECT
Where you live has a direct impact on your well-being. If you live in an isolated area without public transportation and you have no vehicle, you will experience stress due to isolation. Many other neighborhood and habitat (state of the physical plant of your house) will impact your level of stress and therefore your well-being.

SUPPLEMENTAL
Ecological Approaches are not really theories as such but eclectic combinations of ideas from various disciplines that focus on the unity of individuals and groups with their environments.

These approached are generally considered a refinement of General Systems Theory. This approach is popular in social work because it on the intra-psychic life of individuals but also the environmental and social conditions.

Also, people need to be understood in their natural environments and settings and personality needs to be understood as the product of the historical development of the transactions between the person and the environment over time.

Question 60   Section: Behavior

The correct answer is A
Always begin an intervention by setting goals and planning actions. If you don't know where you are going it is hard to get there. Many people fail to take time to set proper goals and end up "wandering in the desert."

B is INCORRECT

Until you know where you are going and then what you need to get there, it is impossible to know what resources you will need.

C is INCORRECT

You can not apply for thing you do not know you need.

D is INCORRECT

Once you know what is needed, you can decide what parameters would allow you to successfully chose your markers of achievement.

Question 61   Section: Behavior

The correct answer is D

Remember, a schema is a cognitive framework or concept that helps us organize and interpret our information. A depressogenic schema is a cognitive framework that bolsters depression.

Aaron Beck argued that depression was the result of three core schemas.

These internal concepts are:

    1) The self is defective or inadequate;

    2) All experiences are defeats or failures; *and*

    3) The future is hopeless.

Beck also put forth the idea that depressed people (who are using depressive/faulty schemas) also use faulty information processing. This faulty information processing includes selective attention or only paying attention to the details that maintain their view of the world, to maintain their negative core schemas in spite of evidence to the contrary.

Beck believed that once the core schemas are modified, the symptoms will go away and will not return.

A is INCORRECT
Actually, the opposite is true. Depressogenic schemas distort reality and lead to faulty reality testing.

B is INCORRECT
These schemas only affect the client when they are active. If, they are not activated by stress, anxiety or overwhelming emotional considerations, they will remain dormant. Once they have been replaced with more positive schemas they will disappear.

C is INCORRECT
Once activated they may persist for some time, however, they can be modified and again become dormant.

Supplemental:
Another form of Cognitive Behavioral Therapy for treating depressogenic schemas is called Behavioral Activation (BA).
BA emphasizes idiographic interventions, encouraging each patient to perform those behaviors that will improve the patient's mood and achieve the patient's goals. If a depressed patient stays in bed in the morning in order to avoid the pain of getting up, going to work, and facing failure, guess what intervention the BA therapist makes. That's right, "What are the consequences of staying in bed?" Of course the patient reports feeling worse, and the BA therapist suggests that she try out a new behavior, such as getting up and going to work, to see if that makes her feel better. The BA therapist will also point out that staying in bed may cause her to lose her job and feel even more like a failure.
Reference: http://www.nj-act.org/article13.html

Question 62   Section: Behavior

The correct answer is D
The task-centered model is a short-term, problem-solving approach to social work practice. It is a major approach in clinical social work. The model consists of three phases.

Initial phase
The initial phase normally takes from one to two interviews although some cases may require more. It ends with setting up initial tasks.

Middle Phase
The middle phase starts with the next session. Changes in the problems and the outcome of the tasks are reviewed at the beginning of the interview. If tasks have been accomplished, new tasks are developed. If tasks have not been attained, an effort is made to identify obstacles to task accomplishment. Some obstacles may be resolved in the session, others may require tasks in their own right. Still others might prove insurmountable, in which case a different task strategy may be adopted.

Termination Phase
Although only one session (the final one) is devoted to termination, the process of terminating is actually begun in the initial phase when the duration of treatment is set. Reminders of number of sessions left as well as discussion of modifications of the original limits keep termination alive throughout the course of service. The final session is designed to emphasize what clients have learned and accomplished.

A is INCORRECT

Originally put forth in 1980, this is the first model to introduce an ecological perspective into social work practice. It states the social work profession is distinct from other service professions. This theory stresses the "what" (theories and concepts) and the "how" (practice methods) to help people with their life stressors and, simultaneously, to influence communities, organizations, and policymakers to be more responsive to them.

B is INCORRECT

The functional model of social work practice was based on the personality theory of Otto Rank. A member of Freud's inner circle in Vienna, a psychologist and psychoanalyst, first Secretary of the Vienna Psychoanalytic Society, member of Freud's Committee, or "Ring" of 7 and his closest associate

C is INCORRECT

Erik Erikson's psychosocial crisis life cycle model - the eight stages of human development. Erikson's model of psychosocial development is a very significant, highly regarded and meaningful concept. Life is a serious of lessons and challenges, which help us to grow. Erikson's wonderful theory helps to tell us why.

Question 63   Section: Behavior

The correct answer is C

Always assess and gather information. You need to have an understanding of the issues and concerns in the client's life. What environmental impacts they are coping with and what support resources they have at their disposal.

A is INCORRECT

If you do not know the causative factors to the anxiety, you will miss an opportunity to help. There are situations where intense anxiety and panic are appropriate and functional

B is INCORRECT
This should be done only after an assessment, and with the understanding that some physical effect may be causing, sustaining or exacerbating the situation.

D is INCORRECT
If you do not know causal and/or environmental factors, which support or feed the dysfunctional behavior, it is impossible to create therapeutic goals.

Question 64   Section: Behavior

The correct answer is D
During the review, you should only provide the general information. Specifics about sexual abuse incidents are, not generally needed for a reviewer to determine if the therapeutic needs of the client have been met. If this is not enough information for the reviewer then you should contact the client and review the specific requests of the reviewer with them, and determine what information the reviewer should have.

The primary concern is to protect the safety of the client. Sexual abuse details can be very humiliating. The rights of the client, should always be balanced against the demands of the insurance carrier.
If the request for more sessions, is refused because the information is not provided then you have the right to engage in an appeals process.

EXTRA ANALYSIS: It is possible the reviewer is just being nosy or voyeuristic. It is also possible that they are reading from a manual, which specifically states they need to ask these questions (the manual may not have been written by social workers). You do not need to ascertain the motives of the reviewer in order to meet the needs of your client.

If the sessions, are denied because of your refusal to answer detailed questions, you can assist the client with lodging a grievance of their own against the HMO.

A is INCORRECT

This will probably not be very helpful, because Releases of Information (ROI's) tend to be written in an overly broad manner. The issue at the heart of this question is whether the details requested are too intimate or whether they are inappropriately requested.

B is INCORRECT

Only choose this answer if you want to drive your supervisor crazy (this of course assumes your supervisor is currently sane! Not always a good assumption!). Chances are the contract is not easily available, very lengthy and written in "legalese". Reviewing a contract is best done by an agency's lawyer.

C is INCORRECT

Never provide any information without thinking about the ramifications first. You are a social worker, not a mindless automaton. One of the first duties of a social worker is to protect their client, and sometimes this means standing up to the agency's demands as well as that of outsiders.

Question 65   **Section: Behavior**

The correct answer is B

This may seem counter-intuitive since the client is in your office talking about the abuse, so why deny? The denial shown by the client is usually centered around denial of the effects the abuse has on their current day-to-day functioning, or denial on the overall impact of the abuse on their current situation. Sexual abuse had a tremendously large impact on most areas of adult functioning. However, over the years, the client has successfully found numerous ways to blunt or mitigate the impact of the abuse. They are unlikely to see its total effect. Part of the therapeutic process is to bring that effect out into "the light of day" so it can be recognized by the client, dealt with and then put to rest.

A is INCORRECT

This will only occur after the initial abuse is acknowledged. They may suppress certain events and certain ideas, but not the entire abuse history. Suppression is more of a temporary defense mechanisms which allows the user to control the speed of the flow of the information, not access to the information. Access to the information is controlled more readily by the defense mechanism – repression.

C is INCORRECT

You will see this defense mechanism when you are working with certain clients. It is not very useful at holding back the sheer chaos and pain associated with the boundary violations of child sexual abuse. Also: This is a defense mechanism you are more likely to see in the ABUSER, not the VCITIM.

D is INCORRECT

This ego defense mechanism is the reverse of suppression. It is probably not going to be seen, by the therapist, in child abuse survivors before admission of the abuse. It would tend to rear it head as a response in therapy like: "I think all abusers should be jailed!"

Question 66   **Section: Behavior**

The correct answer is A
Client's almost always show some resistance at different times during therapy. Confronting their issues is always difficult and the process of therapy can be rather painful. This is increased by the possibility, in this case, they are court ordered and do not want to be there anyway. Exploring their feelings and validating them when you can will help develop a therapeutic bond between you and the client which could lead to some great therapeutic success.

Validating a response: (An Example)
> Client: "I am only here because the court says I have to see you before they will give my kids back."
>
> Social Worker: "Being forced to do anything never feels good. I am sorry we have to meet under these circumstances, however, the fact you have agreed to come here means you must care for your children a lot. Let's see what we can do to help you get done what the court is demanding?"

B is INCORRECT
Direct confrontation rarely works the way you want it to. It often works in TV Dramas, mainly because it is written in the script, but seldom works in real life. Therapeutic confrontation needs to be subtle, well thought out in advance, and there has to be a clear

[160]

plan in place (in the social workers mind) as to alternative responses if the confrontation goes badly.

C is INCORRECT

A behavioral contract will only be effective if the client has acknowledged the behaviors and seems them as counter-productive. The resistance may be very productive for the client in trying to get their point across that they feel forced or coerced.

D is INCORRECT

Once again, this re-ordering can only take place after the client owns or accepts the behavior. This requires insight and acceptance to be a viable strategy.

Question 67   Section: Assessment

C is CORRECT

Unless clearly stated by your company, a consultant has no authority to alter the work place issues or to order employees around. Your direct supervisor is always your supervisor. Consultants are usually detached from the administration of an agency because it helps them focus on the solutions they need to find.

        --- You should always be polite to a consultant. Remember your company paid a lot of money for their presence and is looking to benefit by their report. A good way to hand any conflict would be to say… "Let me clear that with my supervisor and I will get back with you."

A is INCORRECT

Almost never. Consultants have no direct line authority.

B is INCORRECT

Nope. Unless presented in the initial meeting, assume the consultant is employed just like you.

D is INCORRECT

Again, unless stated directly by your agency or supervisor they have no authority over you.

Question 68   Section: Ethics

B is CORRECT

NEVER BARTER WITH A CLIENT FOR SERVICES!
The NASW Code of Ethics SECTION 1.13 … PARAGRAPH 2 … States:
"Social workers should avoid accepting goods or services from clients as payment for professional services. Bartering arrangements, particularly involving services, create the potential for conflicts of interest, exploitation, and inappropriate boundaries in social workers' relationships with clients. Social workers should explore and may participate in bartering only in very limited circumstances when it can be demonstrated that such arrangements are an accepted practice among professionals in the local community, considered to be essential for the provision of services, negotiated without coercion, and entered into at the client's initiative and with the client's informed consent. Social workers who accept goods or services from clients as payment for professional services assume the full burden of demonstrating that this arrangement will not be detrimental to the client or the professional relationship" (Section 1.13, para. 2).

A is INCORRECT

It is not a conflict of interest to accept this service in lieu of CASH payment...It is a violation of the NO BARTER section of the ethical code.

C is INCORRECT

You have just committed an ethical violation which could result in being investigated by the State Licensing Agency and possible SANCTIONS, LIMITING OF, OR LOSS OF your license.

DO NOT PASS GO...Do Not collect $200.

D is INCORRECT

You have just committed an ethical violation which could result in being investigated by the State Licensing Agency and possible SANCTIONS, LIMITING OF, OR LOSS OF your license.

Wait until you see your next year's MALPRACTICE INSURANCE PREMIUMS...

Question 69   Section: Behavior

The correct answer is A

Task Centered treatment is rather behavioral in it conception. Cognitive Behavioral Therapy (CBT) would be considered a type of task centered treatment. It revolves around helping a client review the specific behaviors or tasks they use to navigate their life and then helping them attempt to change the responses.

B is INCORRECT

This is a standard CBT intervention. Get the client to describe how they see other people's behavior or how they view the world. Then working with them to see it from another angle.

C is INCORRECT

[163]

Once a behavior or perception is identified, it is often useful to role-play the change to help the client perform the task in the future. This is a case when "practice makes perfect."

D is INCORRECT
Behavioral approaches tend to be rather directive. They are not "insight" oriented. If insight occurs, it is secondary to the process.

Question 70   Section: Diversity

The correct answer is B
It is best to think of interventions as occurring on three different levels. The first level is often called by two names; the "meta" or the "macro" level (the grand scale of things; affecting everything in a client's life), the second level has no name. It is the individual level and affects only the client. The third level affects the smallest area of the client/environment, the "micro" level.
The functional model usually involves intervention on the on the "micro" level. The intervention is geared towards functional behaviors, evaluating the functional behaviors of the client, and teaching new skills (in the form of behaviors) to deal with problems.

A is INCORRECT
This answer emphasizes the "meta" or "macro" level. Remember, the functional model is not a macro level model.

C is INCORRECT
This is also a "macro" level intervention and does not fit with the functional model.

D is INCORRECT

This is a "micro" level intervention, however, it is more insight oriented and less functional. Just because you know the diagnosis, does not mean you can plan a functional intervention. Some diagnoses do not lend themselves to functional intervention. This "micro" level intervention does give the social worker information which they can use to analyze the information in a "Macro" level manner.

Question 71   Section: Clinical

The correct answer is B
Alprazolam is used to treat anxiety disorders and panic attacks. Alprazolam is in a class of medications called benzodiazepines. It works by decreasing abnormal excitement in the brain.
Alprazolam comes as a tablet and a concentrated solution (liquid) to take by mouth. It usually is taken two to four times a day. You will probably start you on a low dose of Alprazolam and gradually increase your dose, not more than once every 3 or 4 days.
Alprazolam can be habit-forming.
Do not stop taking Alprazolam without talking to your doctor. Suddenly stopping to take Alprazolam may worsen your condition and cause withdrawal symptoms (anxiousness, sleeplessness, irritability, and seizures). Withdrawal symptoms may be worse if you take more than 4 mg of Alprazolam every day. Your doctor will decrease your dose gradually.
Ref: http://www.ncbi.nlm.nih.gov/pubmedhealth/PMH0000807

A is INCORRECT
An analgesic (also known as a painkiller) is any member of the group of drugs used to relieve pain (achieve analgesia). Aspirin, Ibuprofen, Motrin, Vicodin, etc are all analgesics..

C is INCORRECT

The most popular metabolic interferant is ANABUSE, used to treat alcoholism by making the user violently ill if they take the drug and drink.

D is INCORRECT
Common stimulants are Ritalin, Adderall, Vyvance, Straterra, etc and are all used to treat ADHD and ADD.

Question 72   Section: Assessment

The correct answer is F
Clonidine is an anti-hypertensive (high blood pressure) medication. It can be used to help juveniles calm down and get to sleep at night. If a juvenile is having problems falling asleep or sleeping through the night, the disrupted sleep patterns can lead to anger, aggression and violent behaviors the following day. In group home settings, it can assist a juvenile in obtaining better sleep and is non-narcotic. This is the best answer because it is an anti-hypertensive medication and when used to help juveniles get good sleep. It can (secondarily) reduce anger and aggression as well as helping them sleep through the night.

A is INCORRECT
The most common medication to treat this issue are a class of medications called benzodiazepines. They work by decreasing abnormal excitement in the brain.

B is INCORRECT
Technically this is an "off-label" usage of this medication. However, it is NOT your BEST ANSWER.

C is INCORRECT

[166]

This is another 'Off-label" usage for Clonidine. However, it is NOT your BEST ANSWER.

D is INCORRECT
This is the only "On-Label" use for this medication. However, it is NOT your BEST ANSWER.

E is INCORRECT
Answers A & B

Definitions:
Off-label use = When a medication is prescribed for a condition that is not approved by the FDA. Once a medication has been approved for use by the FDA for a specific condition, Physicians can prescribe it for that condition and for any other condition they see fit.

On-Label Use = Prescribed for exactly what the FDA approved the medication for use with.

Po AM = shorthand medical chart script for "per oral in the Morning" or take by mouth in the morning.

Po HS = shorthand medical chart script for "per oral at Hour of Sleep" or take by mouth at bedtime.

Clonidine:
Clonidine is used alone or in combination with other medications to treat high blood pressure. Clonidine is in a class of medications called centrally acting alpha-agonist hypotensive agents. It works by decreasing your heart rate and relaxing the blood vessels so that blood can flow more easily through the body.

Reference:
http://www.ncbi.nlm.nih.gov/pubmedhealth/PMH0000623

Question 73   **Section: Clinical**

The correct is C
Phenytoin is an anti-convulsant used in the treatment of seizure disorders and does not mix well with alcohol and many other drugs. Use of simple over the counter (OTC) medications can also have a serious affect on how much the body can absorb (Maalox, Mylanta, Tums can adversely affect how it operates in the body.)
All of the behaviors are classic symptoms of a Dilantin (Phenytoin) overdose and should be reported to the EMT's as such.

The following are classic signs of a Dilantin overdose:
uncontrollable eye movements
loss of coordination
slow or slurred speech
uncontrollable shaking of a part of the body
nausea
vomiting
difficulty understanding reality
coma (loss of consciousness for a period of time)

For more information on Phenytoin go to:
http://www.ncbi.nlm.nih.gov/pubmedhealth/PMH0000549

The number to POISON CONTROL is

1-800-222-1222

[168]

(YOU SHOULD HAVE THIS NUMBER MEMORIZED!!!!)

A is INCORRECT
Fluoxentine is the generic name for Prozac.

B is INCORRECT
Catapres is the generic name for Clonidine

D is INCORRECT
Ibuprofen is the generic name for MOTRIN.

Question 74   Section: Diversity

The correct answer is C
One of the most important tenets of Adlerian theory is the concept that the individual will create a "fiction" or story about themselves during their childhood and this "fiction" will guide their perceptions and choices throughout life. Another major belief in Adlerian Psychology is ..."the ability to work with others for a common good was the hallmark of sound mental health."
ref: http://www.nndb.com/people/256/000097962/

He also created the concept of 'Birth Order in the Formation of Personality', and the impacts of neglect and pampering on personal development.

Adler's notion of the "self-perfecting drive", the belief that all humans try to become better and perfect their behavior if they have sound mental health. In the above question, the addict or criminal would have created a "fiction" where they were a failure and they were unable to perfect their behavior, so they would "wallow" in a belief that they could not change their behavior and therefore would have no motivation to change. This would account for their continued irresponsible behavior.

A is INCORRECT
Personal responsibility is not a primary concept in Adlerian Psychology. Someone could create a "fiction" where they were personally responsible, but it would not been seen as a psychopathic issue, simply a mis-created fiction..

B is INCORRECT
Adler would have felt social interest was a product that everyone had in the same quantity, but their view of how it pertained to them would be determined by Birth Order.

D is INCORRECT
Adler would probably not have differentiated between experience and self-concept outside of birth order. (This answer is sure to cause me trouble with Adlerian Therapists)

Question 75   Section: Clinical

A is CORRECT
Transactional analysis

B is INCORRECT
Gestalt Therapy is concerned with transference and counter-transference issues and does not acknowledge the "pre-dispositioning" of a life script.

C is INCORRECT
Adlerian Psychotherapy

D is INCORRECT

Reality therapy

Question 76   **Section: Clinical**

The correct answer is D
Conditions of worth refer to conditions after which affection is given. It is a term used by Carl Rogers to describe social influences on the self-concept; for example, a child might not include anger in her self-concept because her parents' scolding has established a condition of worth such that anger is inappropriate.

A is INCORRECT
Conflict perspective refers to an analytical perspective on social organization which holds that conflict is a fundamental aspect of social life itself and can never be fully resolved. It is a theoretical approach, that holds that crime is the natural consequence of economic and other social inequities. Conflict theorists highlight the stresses that arise among and within social groups as they compete with one another for resources and for survival. The social forces that result are viewed as major determinants of group and individual behavior, including crime.

B is INCORRECT
Factor analysis refers to statistical technique used to reduce large amounts of data (e.g. answers to personality questionnaires given to large numbers of people) into groups of items or factors that correlate highly with each other but not with other items.

C is INCORRECT
Oedipus complex refers to the Freud's theory where the boy wants to kill his father and sleep with his mother because of sexual attraction to mother. This complex was named after the

mythical Greek King, Oedipus who unwittingly killed his father and married his mother.

Question 77   **Section: Clinical**

The correct answer is B
Margaret Schönberger Mahler (May 10, 1897 – October 2, 1985) worked as a psychoanalyst with young disturbed children. She was especially interested in mother-infant duality and carefully documented the impact of early separations of children from their mothers.

Her phase theory follows:

Normal Symbiotic Phase - Lasts until about 5 months of age. The child is now aware of his/her mother but there is not a sense of individuality. The infant and the mother are one, and there is a barrier between them and the rest of the world.

Separation-Individuation Phase - The arrival of this phase marks the end of the Normal Symbiotic Phase. Separation refers to the development of limits, the differentiation between the infant and the mother, whereas individuation refers to the development of the infant's ego, sense of identity, and cognitive abilities. Mahler explains how a child with the age of a few months breaks out of an "autistic shell" into the world with human connections. This process, labeled separation-individuation, is divided into sub-phases, each with its own onset, outcomes and risks. The following sub-phases proceed in this order but overlap considerably.

Hatching – first months. The infant ceases to be ignorant of the differentiation between him/her and the mother. "Rupture of the shell".

(1) Increased alertness and interest for the outside world.
(2) Using the mother as a point of orientation.

Practicing – 9-about 16 months.
Brought about by the infant's ability to crawl and then walk freely, the infant begins to explore actively and becomes more distant from the mother. The child experiences himself still as one with his mother.

Rapprochement –15-24 months.
In this sub-phase, the infant once again becomes close to the mother. The child realizes that his physical mobility demonstrates psychic separateness from his mother. The toddler may become tentative, wanting his mother to be in sight so that, through eye contact and action, he can explore his world. The risk is that the mother will misread this need and respond with impatience or unavailability. This can lead to an anxious fear of abandonment in the toddler. A basic 'mood predisposition' may be established at this point. Rapprochement is divided into a few sub phases:

+ Beginning - Motivated by a desire to share discoveries   with the mother.
+ Crisis - Between staying with the mother, being emotionally close and being more independent and exploring.
+ Solution - Individual solutions are enabled by the development of language and the superego. Disruptions in the fundamental process of separation-individuation can result in a disturbance

in the ability to maintain a reliable sense of individual identity in adulthood.

A is INCORRECT
Erikson developed the psychosocial developmental model to postulate different stages in a child's development.

C is INCORRECT
Murray Bowen felt that severe problems within the family unit stem from a multigenerational transmission process whereby levels of differentiation among family members can become progressively lower from one generation to the next. He developed an extended family systems therapy with the goal to increase individual family members level of differentiation.
Bowen summarized his theory using eight interlocking concepts
- Differentiation of Self (the most important concept)
- Nuclear Family Emotional System
- Triangles
- Family Projection Process
- Multigenerational Transmission Process
- Emotional Cutoff
- Sibling Position
- Societal Emotional Process

D is INCORRECT
Sigmund Freud had many theories.

Question 78   Section: Assessment

The correct answer is C
You have just confronted them on their paradoxical ideations and forced them to reassess their views. It is controlled, because you

[174]

set it up with the question about the other brothers first, and then issued the confrontation.

> NOTE: Not all therapeutic confrontations need to be controlled; they can just be "shot from the hip" as long as you are comfortable with the client's possible responses.

A is INCORRECT

Unconditional positive regard is a Rogerian technique and is very supportive. If you had replied with something like, "That seems like you are very angry at your brother and I accept you feeling that way." You may have been using unconditional regard.

B is INCORRECT

Paradoxical intent is where you "throw back" the opposite instruction to the client that you think should happen. It often 'derails' the client's current thought process and allows them to refocus away from their current ideations. An example may be, "You seem to really love your brother!" When they stop and try to figure out why you "misinterpreted the situation so badly", you then have the ability to re-present to them the two dichotomous views they presented to you.

D is INCORRECT

I just made this term up on the fly. But it sounds pretty cool…huh? The real question is whether you could wear it over a Freudian slip?

Question 79   Section: Assessment

The correct answer is C

Whenever you ask a person to explain how someone else would describe them, you are really asking them to describe how they feel about themselves.

Documentation tip: While documenting this type of intervention, I would use the following configuration:
"While assessing self-concept, the client related (Person/their (mom, dad, sister, etc…) would describe them as (description).

Then: "Client's self-perception appeared normal/intact."

OR: "Client's self-perception appeared distorted-unusual-odd/(Etc) due to …."

A is INCORRECT
Reality testing is an individual's objective evaluation of the external world and the ability to differentiate adequately between it and the internal world. Reality testing in a 7 year old is rather difficult because they still show signs of 'magical thinking'**.

** Swiss psychologist Jean Piaget used the term "operation" to refer to an act of logic, such as could be translated into a mathematical equation. He thought of preschool-age children as "preoperational" because they do not yet use logic. Instead, they understand the world through magical and egocentric thinking.

B is INCORRECT
This could be assessed by asking questions like, "How do you feel when you are left with a babysitter? (assuming the babysitter is not abusing) and "Do you miss your mommy and daddy when you are at school?"

D is INCORRECT

I wish I knew of a way to measure the level of conscious awareness of a 7 year old. Having ushered 4 of my 5 children through the 7 year-old stage, and looking at number 5 going through it in 3 years, I must admit to total and complete failure. (long sigh…)

It should also be noted that measuring the level of conscious awareness of the average adolescent is equally frustrating.

Question 80 Section: Diversity

The correct answer is C

Absolutely essential to therapy is a clear grounding and a self-awareness. You need to know your triggers, both good and bad, what interests and what bores you. What makes you happy, sad, angry, mad, disgusted or sick. When you know how you respond, then therapy becomes easier and more productive for your client. A personal example: When I first started out, I would not work with female victims of domestic violence. The 'victimhood' of the abused made no sense to me. Why not just walk away? After having children and understanding their visceral impact on your life, and understanding, on a level far deeper than consciousness, that they come first, I was able to come to grips with the issues of conflict faced by a domestic violence survivor. Until this self-awareness occurred, I also would have been a terrible counselor for them and may well have done more harm than good.

A is INCORRECT

The ugly truth is that you do not have to identify with your client, or even like them for that matter. In reality, they can make you feel uneasy and you can still provide constructive therapy for them. I would hope that no therapist has ever identified with a child sexual predator or an abusive spouse.

B is INCORRECT
All therapy requires transference. It would not be therapy without transference, however, it generally happens naturally.

D is INCORRECT
Most client's do not communicate well or openly. Part of the need for therapy and part of the goal of therapy is to help a client develop their communication skills, both with other people and with themselves.

Question 81   Section: Clinical

The correct answer is B
A false belief based on INCORRECT inference about external reality that is firmly sustained despite what almost everybody else believes and despite what constitutes incontrovertible and obvious proof or evidence to the contrary. The belief is not one ordinarily accepted by other members of the person's culture or subculture.

A is INCORRECT
Delirium is sudden severe confusion and rapid changes in brain function that occur with physical or mental illness.

Alternative Names:
Acute confusional state;
Acute brain syndrome

Causes

[178]

Delirium is most often caused by physical or mental illness and is usually temporary and reversible. Many disorders cause delirium, including conditions that deprive the brain of oxygen or other substances.

Causes of DELIRIUM include:

☐ Drug abuse
☐Infections such as urinary tract infections or pneumonia (in people who already have brain damage from stroke or dementia)
☐ Poisons
☐ Fluid/electrolyte or acid/base disturbances

Patients with more severe brain injuries are more likely to get delirium from another illness.

Symptoms of Delirium involve a quick change between mental states (for example, from lethargy to agitation and back to lethargy).

They include:
☐ Changes in alertness (usually more alert in the morning, less alert at night)
☐ Changes in feeling (sensation) and perception
☐ Changes in level of consciousness or awareness
☐ Changes in movement (for example, may be inactive or slow moving)
☐ Changes in sleep patterns, drowsiness
☐ Confusion (disorientation) about time or place
☐ Decrease in short-term memory and recall
☐ Unable to remember events since delirium began (anterograde amnesia)
☐ Unable to remember past events (retrograde amnesia)

- ☐ Disrupted or wandering attention
- ☐ Inability to think or behave with purpose
- ☐ Problems concentrating
- ☐ Disorganized thinking
- ☐ Speech that doesn't make sense (incoherent)
- ☐ Inability to stop speech patterns or behaviors
- ☐ Emotional or personality changes
- ☐ Anger
- ☐ Anxiety
- ☐ Apathy
- ☐ Depression
- ☐ Euphoria
- ☐ Irritability
- ☐ Movements triggered by changes in the nervous system psychomotor restlessness)

C is INCORRECT

Dissociation is a partial or complete disruption of the normal integration of a person's conscious or psychological functioning.

It is not necessarily pathological: In general, dissociation is a defense mechanism that everyone uses every day. In its most common form, mild dissociation includes day dreaming, "zoning out," or doing things on "autopilot." For example, when you find yourself staring out the window thinking about what you are going to do after your class, driving a car and not recalling the details of how you got from one point to the next, or getting so caught up in a movie you don't hear someone whispering behind you - these are all examples of normal dissociation. Dissociation is a form of self-hypnosis. Everyone experiences dissociation.

D is INCORRECT

Dysphoria refers only to a condition of mood and may be experienced in response to ordinary life events, such as illness or grief. Additionally, it is a feature of many psychiatric disorders, including anxiety disorders and mood disorders. Dysphoria is usually experienced during depressive episodes, but in people with bipolar disorder, it may also be experienced during manic or hypomanic episodes. Dysphoria in the context of a mood disorder indicates a heightened risk of suicide.

Question 82   Section: Clinical

The correct answer is D
Paradoxical directive: a technique in which the therapist directs family members to continue their symptomatic behavior. Change occurs through defying the directive.

A is INCORRECT
Reframing: relabeling a family's description of behavior by putting it into a new and more positive context.

B is INCORRECT
Coaching: the role of the therapist in assisting clients in the process of differentiating the self.

C is INCORRECT
Disengagement: a family organizational pattern characterized by psychological isolation that results from rigid boundaries.

Question 83   Section: Assessment

The correct answer is D
Tell Mr. Smith that you will be able to talk to him after you have contacted your client's parents, as he is a juvenile, and received

their permission to discuss their son's issues with the guidance counselor.

You should not release information regarding the client until you have the consent of the parents, because he is a juvenile. You probably should also let your client know before you talk with Mr. Smith, because, you do not know the details of their relationship, and your client may feel 'betrayed' if you give information to Mr. Smith prior to discussing it with him.

A is INCORRECT

There are many reasons not to talk to Mr. Smith, but his status as a clinician is not one of them. However, when you get permission to talk to him, you should keep your language simple and plain. Avoid the use of jargon and 'clinical-speak'.

B is INCORRECT

When you do get permission, you should confine your discussion to topics that deal with the specific issue at school. If you are working on an issue that is not part of the peer issue at school, it should not be divulged to the guidance counselor.

Teaching moment: For the new clinician it is often exciting to get to discuss your ideas with another person. In this role, you are the expert and that feeling of authority is powerful stuff. It would be easy to overstep your bounds and discuss more than you should as a way of "showing off" (which, by the way is a perfectly human and normal response). Be careful. Before you give specific information ask yourself, "Do they need to know this?" If they don't need to know, you don't need to tell them!"

C is INCORRECT

Should provide Mr. Smith with any necessary information because you are both working with the youth and both want what is best for him.

OOOPS! Two problems. Release without consent is a problem and there is no way for you to know that you both have the same interest in the outcome. Mr. Smith may or may not feel the same way you do about the youth.

You are assuming he does....assuming is problematic...

Question 84   Section: Clinical

The correct answer is C
Discuss the client's feeling and acknowledge their ideas. Offer to continue therapy if they choose, and if they don't, offer to help them locate another therapist to meet their needs.

Remember the client always has the right of self-determination. They can terminate at any time. You must honor and acknowledge this right. During therapy, nothing for you (the therapist) should be taken personally. You are the professional. Doing therapy will give you some bumps, bruises, cuts and scars. Welcome to the club. It is not personal. If you are to be an effective agent of change, you will need this objectivity.

A is INCORRECT
Your decision to continue therapy without allowing the client the right to decide to terminate or choose another therapist is probably rooted in some form of arrogance. You must let the client decide. They may want out because you are a very poor therapist...or they may want out because you are an excellent

[183]

therapist and are challenging them to look at things they would rather avoid. Either way, they get to choose.

B is INCORRECT
Yikes!!! ...this is real arrogance. It is also controlling and manipulative and if you feel this, you have probably lost your objectivity and need to refer.

D is INCORRECT
Discuss the situation with your supervisor and ask them for advice.
This is half of the way there. Whenever in doubt, discuss with a supervisor or a peer who will not readily agree with you. But you still have to give a client a choice.

Question 85   Section: Ethics

The correct answer is D
Now we get a chance to split hairs....Technically the contents of the file belong to the client, and the actual physical make-up of the client file, the paper, belongs to the agency. Nothing belongs to you. The clients 'belong' to the agency and you are acting as the agent of the agency. Many people will tell you that you have no right to keep a copy of the file after it is closed because it is not 'your' client. All files belong under lock and key. They should never be left laying around.

Professional Note: When you leave a position, it is not only a good idea to complete all the paperwork and documentation you are responsible for in the file, it is a professional obligation. Leave your files in excellent working order. Just because you are going, does not mean someone else is going to sort out the file for you. Failure to do this may complicate the life of the client or actually cause them harm. I have seen client's whose file have been closed after a social worker left, because there were no notes in them for several months and the supervisor just assumed they were non-compliant. Then the client show up asking why they have received no services for six months. (This will make people say very bad things about you!)

A is INCORRECT

This is probably a violation of your company policies and may also be a violation of HIPPA standards. Remember, the files are not yours.

B is INCORRECT

This is an extremely bad idea. There may be information in the file from other agencies. Some of that information may subject the releaser (you) to civil penalties or criminal charges upon re-release. Generally, if you receive a psychosocial or psychological report from another agency, it is NOT RE-RELEASE-ABLE (what a horrible word).

C is INCORRECT

Only chose this option if you have made a decision that you no longer wish to practice (for the rest of your life) and are turning in your license. After doing this, you should probably practice the following phrase for your new job, "Would you like fries with that..."

Question 86   Section: Ethics

The correct answer is A

Social workers treat each person in a caring and respectful fashion, mindful of individual differences and cultural and ethnic diversity. Social workers promote clients' socially responsible self-determination. Social workers seek to enhance clients' capacity and opportunity to change and to address their own needs. Social workers are cognizant of their dual responsibility to clients and to the broader society. They seek to resolve conflicts between clients' interests and the broader society's interests in a socially responsible manner consistent with the values, ethical principles, and ethical standards of the profession.

B is INCORRECT

Ethical Principle: Social workers recognize the central importance of human relationships.

Social workers understand that relationships between and among people are an important vehicle for change. Social workers engage people as partners in the helping process. They seek to resolve conflicts between clients' interests and the broader society's interests in a socially responsible manner consistent with the values, ethical principles, and ethical standards of the profession.

C is INCORRECT

Ethical Principle: Social workers behave in a trustworthy manner. Social workers are continually aware of the profession's mission, values, ethical principles, and ethical standards and practice in a manner consistent with them. Social workers act honestly and responsibly and promote ethical practices on the part of the organizations with which they are affiliated.

D is INCORRECT

Value: Competence
Ethical Principle: Social workers practice within their areas of competence and develop and enhance their professional expertise.

Social workers continually strive to increase their professional knowledge and skills and to apply them in practice. Social workers should aspire to contribute to the knowledge base of the profession.

Question 87   **Section: Ethics**

The correct answer is A

Social workers are encouraged to volunteer some portion of their professional skills with no expectation of significant financial return (pro bono service).

> *Ethical Principle: Social workers' primary goal is to help people in need and to address social problems.*

B is INCORRECT

… social work's core values of service, social justice, dignity and worth of the person, importance of human relationships, integrity…

> *Ethical Principle: Social workers challenge social injustice.*

C is INCORRECT

Social workers promote clients' socially responsible self-determination.

> *Ethical Principle: Social workers respect the inherent dignity and worth of the person.*
>
> *Social workers engage people as partners in the helping process.*
>
> *Ethical Principle: Social workers recognize the central importance of human relationships.*

D is INCORRECT

Social workers engage people as partners in the helping process.

Ethical Principle: Social workers recognize the central importance of human relationships.

Question 88 **Section: Ethics**

The correct answer is B
Social workers continually strive to increase their professional knowledge and skills and to apply them in practice. Social workers should aspire to contribute to the knowledge base of the profession.

A is INCORRECT
Social workers are continually aware of the profession's mission, values, ethical principles, and ethical standards and practice in a manner consistent with them. Social workers act honestly and responsibly and promote ethical practices on the part of the organizations with which they are affiliated.

C is INCORRECT
Social workers elevate service to others above self-interest. Social workers draw on their knowledge, values, and skills to help people in need and to address social problems. Social workers are encouraged to volunteer some portion of their professional skills with no expectation of significant financial return (pro bono service).

D is INCORRECT
Social workers pursue social change, particularly with and on behalf of vulnerable and oppressed individuals and groups of people. Social workers' social change efforts are focused primarily on issues of poverty, unemployment, discrimination, and other forms of social injustice. These activities seek to promote sensitivity to and knowledge about oppression and cultural and

[188]

ethnic diversity. Social workers strive to ensure access to needed information, services, and resources; equality of opportunity; and meaningful participation in decision making for all people.

Question 89　　　　Section: Ethics

The correct answer is A
1.03 Informed Consent
Social workers should provide services to clients only in the context of a professional relationship based, when appropriate, on valid informed consent. Social workers should use clear and understandable language to inform clients of the purpose of the services, risks related to the services, limits to services because of the requirements of a third-party payer, relevant costs, reasonable alternatives, clients' right to refuse or withdraw consent, and the time frame covered by the consent. Social workers should provide clients with an opportunity to ask questions.

B is INCORRECT
1.04 Competence
Social workers should provide services and represent themselves as competent only within the boundaries of their education, training, license, certification, consultation received, supervised experience, or other relevant professional experience.

C is INCORRECT
1.05 Cultural Competence and Social Diversity
Social workers should have a knowledge base of their clients' cultures and be able to demonstrate competence in the provision of services that are sensitive to clients' cultures and to differences among people and cultural groups.

D is INCORRECT

1.06 Conflicts of Interest

Social workers should be alert to and avoid conflicts of interest that interfere with the exercise of professional discretion and impartial judgment. Social workers should inform clients when a real or potential conflict of interest arises and take reasonable steps to resolve the issue in a manner that makes the clients' interests primary and protects clients' interests to the greatest extent possible. In some cases, protecting clients' interests may require termination of the professional relationship with proper referral of the client.

Question 90 **Section: Ethics**

The correct answer is D

1.13 Payment for Services

C Social workers should not solicit a private fee or other remuneration for providing services to clients who are entitled to such available services through the social workers' employer or agency.

A is INCORRECT

2.01 Respect

a) Social workers should treat colleagues with respect and should represent accurately and fairly the qualifications, views, and obligations of colleagues.

b) Social workers should avoid unwarranted negative criticism of colleagues in communications with clients or with other professionals. Unwarranted negative criticism may include demeaning comments that refer to colleagues' level of competence or to individuals' attributes such as race, ethnicity, national origin, color, sex, sexual orientation, gender identity or expression, age, marital status, political belief, religion, immigration status, and mental or physical disability.

c) Social workers should cooperate with social work colleagues and with colleagues of other professions when such cooperation serves the well-being of clients.

B is INCORRECT

1.15 Interruption of Services

Social workers should make reasonable efforts to ensure continuity of services in the event that services are interrupted by factors such as unavailability, relocation, illness, disability, or death.

C is INCORRECT

2.02 Confidentiality

Social workers should respect confidential information shared by colleagues in the course of their professional relationships and transactions. Social workers should ensure that such colleagues understand social workers' obligation to respect confidentiality and any exceptions related to it.

Question 91   Section: Ethics

The correct answer is D

All of the above.

The NASW Code of Ethics prescribes all of these actions.

A is INCORRECT *(When chosen alone)*

Social workers should advocate for living conditions conducive to the fulfillment of basic human needs

6.01 Social Welfare

Social workers should promote the general welfare of society, from local to global levels, and the development of people, their communities, and their environments. Social workers should advocate for living conditions conducive to the fulfillment of basic human needs and should promote social, economic, political, and cultural values and institutions that are compatible with the realization of social justice.

B is INCORRECT *(When chosen alone)*
should provide appropriate professional services in public emergencies

6.03 Public Emergencies
Social workers should provide appropriate professional services in public emergencies to the greatest extent possible.

C is INCORRECT *(When chosen alone)*
Social workers should act to expand choice and opportunity for all people

6.04 Social and Political Action
B Social workers should act to expand choice and opportunity for all people, with special regard for vulnerable, disadvantaged, oppressed, and exploited people and groups.

Question 92   Section: Diversity

B is CORRECT
The Poor Relief Act 1662 was enacted by the "Cavalier Parliament of England". It was also known as the Settlement Act or the Settlement and Removal Act.

[192]

Its purpose was to establish the parish to which a person belonged "their settlement" and make that parish financially responsible for him should he become in need of Poor Relief. This is the first time that documentation of one's domicile became enshrined in law. The documents were called "settlement certificates".

PS: We use this system today. When someone applies for any type of public assistance they need to prove their residency (usually by showing an electric bill in their name) to "prove" they qualify for money from the local government agency.

A IS INCORRECT

The Liberal welfare reforms (1906–1914) were acts of social legislation passed by the British Liberal Party after the 1906 General Election. It has been argued that this legislation shows the emergence of the modern welfare state in the UK. They shifted their outlook from a laissez-faire system to a more collectivist approach.

C is INCORRECT

Poverty was felt to be the result of character weakness, not as a social problem. The 1834 Poor Law Amendment, also known as the "The Workhouse Amendment", believed that those in dire need would accept the workhouse.

The "working Class" of 19th-century society was poor by modern standards. Most people were likely to be in poverty at some point in their lives due to sickness, old age or unemployment. The zeitgeist of the day purported that the fear of having to rely on their children, friends or credit for support, when times were tough was right and proper because it encouraged the poor to work.

D is INCORRECT

The Act for the Relief of the Poor 1601 or , the "Elizabethan Poor Law", created a created a national poor law system for England and Wales.

The "Old Poor Law" aka "the Act for the Relief of the Poor 1597" was not one law but a collection of laws passed between the 16th and 18th centuries.

The "Elizabethan Poor Law", made individual parishes responsible for Poor Law legislation.

Important Point:

Why should we, as Clinical Social Workers care about these old Laws? Clinical Social Work is the "New Psychology" for the PEOPLE. The venue of a social worker does not end at insurance reimbursement, or ability to pay in cash. We serve all clients equally. The old British Laws are the underpinning of our current bureaucratic social care safety net. They have shaped how we think about the poor. As a clinician, it is vitally important to understand where you came from and why you think the way you do

Question 93   Section: Clinical

The correct answer is C
These four diagnoses make up the Cluster B
(dramatic, emotional or erratic disorders)
Borderline personality disorder (DSM-IV code 301.83)
Histrionic personality disorder (DSM-IV code 301.50)
Narcissistic personality disorder (DSM-IV code 301.81)
Antisocial personality disorder (DSM-IV code 301.7)

A is INCORRECT
Avoidant Personality Disorder (DSM-IV code 301.82)
    - This belongs to the Cluster C (anxious or fearful disorders)

[194]

Paranoid Personality Disorder (DSM-IV code 301.0)
- This belongs to the Cluster A (odd or eccentric disorders)
Histrionic Personality Disorder (DSM-IV code 301.50)
- This belongs to the Cluster A (odd or eccentric disorders)
Schizotypal personality disorder (DSM-IV code 301.22)
- Major characteristics: odd behavior or thinking.
- This can look a lot like SCHIZOPHRENIA

B is INCORRECT

Paranoid Personality Disorder (DSM-IV code 301.0)
- This belongs to the Cluster A (odd or eccentric disorders)
Dependent personality disorder (DSM-IV code 301.6)
-This belongs to the Cluster C (anxious or fearful disorders)
Schizoid personality disorder (DSM-IV code 301.20)
- Major characteristics:
1) lack of interest in social relationships,
2) seeing no point in sharing time with others,
3) anhedonia.
Schizotypal personality disorder (DSM-IV code 301.22)
Major characteristics: odd behavior or thinking.
This can look a lot like SCHIZOPHRENIA

D is INCORRECT

Avoidant personality disorder (DSM-IV code 301.82)
-This belongs to the Cluster C (anxious or fearful disorders)
Dependent personality disorder (DSM-IV code 301.6)
-This belongs to the Cluster C (anxious or fearful disorders)
Obsessive-compulsive personality disorder (DSM-IV code 301.4)
-This belongs to the Cluster C (anxious or fearful disorders)
-DO NOT CONFUSE this with Obsessive-Compulsive
Disorder
Paranoid personality disorder (DSM-IV code 301.0)
- This belongs to the Cluster A (odd or eccentric disorders)

Helpful TIP:

If you memorize two of the clusters, anything that is not in them is in the third cluster. Cluster A and Cluster B are the easiest to memorize. Think of it like this:

Cluster A (odd or eccentric disorders)

Paranoid PD	Being PARANOID is ODD.
Schizoid PD	Schizoid (Prefix for Schizophrenia)
Schizotypal PD	Schizotypal (Prefix for Schizophrenia)

Cluster B (dramatic, emotional or erratic disorders)

Antisocial PD	People with this diagnosis often end up in prison. That is dramatic!
Borderline PD	Para-suicidal gestures are both dramatic and emotional
Histrionic PD	Hysteria is very emotional (and dramatic)
Narcissistic PD	Narcissistic people are often very dramatic in pointing out why their needs are more important than any other persons

REMEMBER: Narcissistic Personality Disorder gets its name from the tale told by the Roman poet, OVID.

"Narcissus became thirsty and went to drink from a stream. As he saw his reflection, he fell in love with it, not knowing that it was him. As he bent down to kiss it, it seemed to "run away" and he was heartbroken. He grew thirstier but he wouldn't touch the water for fear of damaging his reflection, so he eventually died of thirst and staring at his own reflection. The narcissus flower is closely identified with the boy and was said to spring from the ground around the pool where Narcissus died. "

*** He DID NOT fall in love with himself – He fell in love with the IMAGE of himself. This is a very important distinction!*

Question 94   Section: Ethics

The correct answer is D
People frequently chat about their problems with co-workers and acquaintances. If they begin to talk, you should listen attentively and try to determine the purpose of their approach. They may tell you some things, which would allow you to assist them with a referral later on if that is what is needed. Sometime the most powerful communication tool we have as therapists and as people is just listening and honoring or respecting that person's issues, problems or pain. We do not always need to "solve" issues.

A is INCORRECT
This would be seen as a passive-aggressive attempt at interacting with someone and would be unfair and below your level as a therapist. That is not to say you can never "act" in a passive-aggressive manner in therapy, but you should be entirely conscious of your actions at the time they occur and have a good reason for using this technique.

B is INCORRECT
This would be very snobbish and elitist. If you respond this way, take a look at whether you are feeling undervalued in your own life. This may help you restore some balance.

C is INCORRECT
Until you listen, you will not be able to understand if there are any referral needs and even what they may be.

Question 95   Section: Diversity

The correct answer is C
A semi-restrictive grant of money by a central or federal government to a local or state government with strings attached. For instance, "Here is a large chunk of money and you can only spend it on children's medical services and food for your citizens." Medicaid and Food Stamp funding are categories of spending restrictions.

A is INCORRECT
The least restrictive grant of money is the block grant. It is a chunk of money given by the federal government to a state or local government with very few to no restrictions. Kind of like, "Here...take this large chunk of money and try to spend it wisely!"

B is INCORRECT
Grants-in-Aid are very specific grants of money for very specific functions. When the Federal government gives "Federal Transportation Funds" to a state in order to repair and maintain their roads, this is a grant-in-aid "of repairing your roads."

D is INCORRECT
In-Kind assistance has a value but does not involve money. This is when you give an item or materials to someone in order to assist them. The local food bank gives bags of groceries to people as a form of in-kind assistance. Also, when the Federal Emergency Management Agency (FEMA) gave trailers to people displaced after Hurricane Katrina, this is a form of "IN-KIND" assistance. Now only if the trailers had not been soaked in FORMALDEHYDE (A known cancer causing agent)...but...this is one of the drawbacks with this type of aid.

[198]

Question 96   Section: Legal

The correct answer is A
The Gault decision gave up the Juvenile Justice System, which we labor under today.

In re Gault, 387 U.S. 1 (1967), was a landmark U.S. Supreme Court decision which established that under the Fourteenth Amendment to the United States Constitution, juveniles accused of crimes in a delinquency proceeding must be afforded many of the same due process rights as adults such as the right to timely notification of charges, the right to confront witnesses, the right against self-incrimination, and the right to counsel. The court's opinion was written by Justice Abe Fortas, a noted proponent of children's rights.

On the morning of June 8 1964, the sheriff of Gila County, Arizona, took fifteen-year-old Gerald Gault into custody — without notifying Gault's parents — after a neighbor, one Mrs. Ora Cook, complained of receiving an inappropriate and offensive telephone call. After returning home from work that evening to find her son missing, Gault's mother eventually located him at the county Children's Detention Home but was not permitted to take him home.
According to Gault, it was his friend Ronald Lewis who made the call from the Gault family's trailer in Globe. Gault claims that Lewis had asked to use his telephone while the former was getting ready for work. Then — not yet knowing to whom Lewis was speaking — Gault relates, "I heard him, ahem, using some pretty vulgar language … so I — all I did was walk out, took the phone off him, hung it up, and told him — I says, 'Hey, there's the door. Get out.'"

[199]

In an 8-1 decision the United States Supreme Court ruled that Gault's commitment to the State Industrial School was a clear violation of the 14th Amendment, since he had been denied the right to an attorney, had not been formally notified of the charges against him, had not been informed of his right against self-incrimination, and had no opportunity to confront his accusers. Justice Potter Stewart was the sole dissenter. He argued that the purpose of juvenile court was correction, not punishment, and the constitutional procedural safeguards for criminal trials should not apply to such juvenile trials.

B is INCORRECT
Kelly v. Goldberg is a case involving the deprivation of a welfare recipient's benefits without due process of law. Goldberg v. Kelly, 397 U.S. 254 (1970), is a case in which the United States Supreme Court ruled that the Due Process Clause of the Fourteenth Amendment to the United States Constitution requires an evidentiary hearing before a recipient of certain government benefits (welfare) can be deprived of such benefits. The individual losing benefits is not entitled to a trial, but is entitled to an oral hearing before an impartial decision-maker, the right to confront and cross-examine witnesses, and the right to a written opinion setting out the evidence relied upon and the legal basis for the decision.
The case was decided 5-3.

C is INCORRECT
Ginsberg v. New York. This case gave us the 18-year-old age limit on the sale of pornography and relegated playboy (and the other magazines) into the "must have spotlight" of most teenage boys.
Ginsberg v. New York was a 1968 Supreme Court of the United States decision. The Warren Court ruled that material that is not

[200]

obscene may nonetheless be harmful for children, and its marketing may be regulated.

Under New York Law it was illegal to willfully sell to a minor under 17 any picture which depicts nudity, is harmful to minors and any magazine which taken as a whole is harmful to minors. Ginsberg and his wife operated Sam's Stationery and Luncheonette in Bellmore, Long Island. In it they sold magazines including those deemed to be "girlie". He was prosecuted from two informants in whom he personally sold two 16-year-old boys the "girlie" magazines. He was tried in Nassau County District Court and found guilty. The court had found that the pictures were harmful to minors under the law.

The Conviction was upheld by the Appellate Term of the Supreme Court of New York and was denied an appeal to the New York Court of Appeals.

D is INCORRECT
District of Columbia v. Heller
This decision allows people to carry guns in Washington DC. It pushed the latest interpretation of the second amendment to the new understanding that being allowed to own a pistol, rifle or assault weapon is an inalienable right. No matter where you live. District of Columbia v. Heller, 554 U.S. 570 (2008), was a landmark case in which the Supreme Court of the United States held that the Second Amendment to the United States Constitution protects an individual's right to possess a firearm for private use within the home in federal enclaves. The decision did not address the question of whether the Second Amendment extends beyond federal enclaves to the states,[1] which was addressed later by McDonald v. Chicago. It was the first Supreme Court case in United States history to decide whether the Second

Amendment protects an individual right to keep and bear arms for self defense.

Why should I know this?

A good question. Since you were not born yesterday, we can assume that where you are today is a culmination of your past. Things have happened which have shaped your world. Things have happened which have shaped the world for our clients as well.

Why do we have a separate system for Juvenile Offenders? Because in 1964, an Arizona Judge sentences a 14-year-old boy to reform school for 6 years for making a prank phone call. If he had been an adult, his maximum sentence would have been 2 months in jail and a $50 fine. His parents fought and won. They did not win on the craziness of the sentence but instead on the fact he did not receive "due process." There were no clear set of rules the court had to follow.

Why can't the State just tell an AFDC recipient, "Sorry, we are not going to give you any more help...Good Luck!" Because they tried it and the Supreme court said NO!

---The next time your client asks you, "Can they just take my benefits away?" you can say, "No! Not after Goldberg v. Kelly (1970)."

Why can't a 14-year-old boy walk into a store and buy a "Hustler" magazine? Why do certain magazines in stores have to be kept behind the counter and wrapped in plastic?

Because, in the mid-60's, Mr. Ginsberg sold some "girlie" magazines to two 16-year-old boys.

Why do local governments no longer have the power to enact "No SALE gun regulation in certain municipalities? Welcome to "District of Columbia v. Heller". A brave new world!

Question 97   Section: Clinical

The correct Answer is C
The HMO or managed care model is designed around the concept of brief, focused therapies to SOLVE a particular issue. Chronically ill patients do not have a SOLVABLE problem. They have problems, which must be DEALT WITH daily, and have no clear solutions. This makes them a poor fit for the HMO model and there, traditionally, HMOs have had a non -productive track record when it comes to patient care for chronic illness. A shorter way of saying it is, "If you have a chronic illness, HMOs STINK."

A is INCORRECT
HMO's do provide mental health services; they are provided in a variety of formats but are expressly tied to the concept of "Medically Necessary". Because of the payment schedules imposed by HMO's, most therapy provided is behaviorally based and time-limited.

B is INCORRECT
Regardless of your opinions on HMOs, this general statement is not applicable to HMOs.

D is INCORRECT
Payments for services are simply what they are. Personally, I have never had a positive experience with payment from ANY insurance company. I should also add, PAYMENT for services have always seemed inadequate for my tastes.

Question 98   Section: Clinical

The correct answer is A

People who are treated for Alcohol abuse are at a 10 times greater risk for suicide than the general population. Dealing with this type of client requires skills and training in understanding the suicidal patterns of alcoholics. If you want to work with substance abusers, you need to seek specialized training and education.

Reference: Wilcox, H. C., Conner, K. R., & Caine, E. D. (2004). Association of alcohol and drug use disorders and completed suicide: an empirical review of cohort studies. Drug and Alcohol Dependence, 76, S11–S19.

B is INCORRECT
Injectable substance abusers have a risk 14 times as great the general population. Wilcox, Conner, & Caine, 2004)

C is INCORRECT

Individuals who have detoxed (dried out) have the same risk as those who are still abusing. To stop using is considered to be DRY and to achieve a state where you NO LONGER DESIRE to use is to be CLEAN. These are not precise definitions. Once a person is DRY, they have to deal with all the problems caused by their addiction.

D is INCORRECT

Individuals just entering care are at an elevated risk for suicidal ideations and attempts according to Kessler, Borges, & Walters 1999)
Reference: Kessler, R. C., Borges, G., & Walters, E. E. (1999). Prevalence of and risk factors for lifetime suicide attempts in the National Comorbidity Survey. Archives of General Psychiatry, 56, 617–626.

Question 99   **Section:**   **Clinical**

The correct answer is D

According to Ross, Et al, 2005, some of the reasons substance abusers have a higher risk of suicide after entering treatment are 1) entering treatment at a point when their substance abuse is out of control, 2) entering treatment when a number of co occurring life crises may be occurring, 3) entering treatment at peaks in depressive symptoms, and also entering treatment with Co-occurring mental health issues.

A is INCORRECT
It is only one of many reasons for the increased suicide risk

B is INCORRECT
It is only one of many reasons for the increased suicide risk

C is INCORRECT
It is only one of many reasons for the increased suicide risk

E is INCORRECT
This is only a partial answer.

Ross, J., Teesson, M., Darke, S., Lynskey, M., Ali, R., Ritter, A. et al. (2005). The characteristics of heroin users entering treatment: findings from the Australian treatment outcome study (ATOS). Drug and Alcohol Review, 24, 411-418.

Question 100   **Section: Clinical**

[205]

The correct answer is B

According to Freud, if you have developed in any remotely health way, you are primarily an EGO with a small ID attached and supervised or maintained by the SUPEREGO. The ID is the child-you, the EGO is the adult-you, and the SUPEREGO is the parent/controller-you. Most of the time your interactions with a client are "adult-you" to "adult-them". If, during an interaction, you see the "child-them" (ID) slip out you need to be asking yourself, Why? What about our interaction may have caused or released this? Also, if during an interact you notice the "child-you" slipping out you also need to review 'What Happened?' in order to understand the interaction. This holds true to the 'slipping-out' of the SUPEREGO as well.

For Example: During therapy your client responds to a situation "like a child would". You need to ask yourself, What situation caused them to become "child-like" in their response? This "child-like" response is probably associated with fear, concern, anxiety, anger, etc and is linked to one of the primary defense mechanisms. Knowing how they will respond is very helpful in understanding and possibly predicting trouble areas in their life,

A is INCORRECT

This is not a Freudian Personality Structure

C is INCORRECT

The SUPEREGO is the adult or parent. It tries to control and place rules on you. If is very rule-bound. You can often see it exhibit itself in parents with young children and their constant NO! statements

D is INCORRECT

The ID is the CHILD. All wants, needs and desires. You often see examples of ID behavior in young children with ME-ME-ME or MINE-MINE!

Question 100+   **Section: Clinical**

The correct answer is C
Conscious and unconscious motivations fall under the realm of psychoanalytic theory. He will be concerned about what a client has done as well as why it was done. Motives, reaction and defense mechanisms are all part of this training set.

A is INCORRECT
a behavioral orientation would be interested in WHAT was happening, specifically what behaviors were manifest. They would then work with modification techniques in order to alter the behavioral patterns of a person and cause them to respond differently.

B is INCORRECT
a structuralist is primarily interested in the structure of the family and intimate, as well as congenial relationships, with others in the persons social milieu. They are interested in, WITH WHO and HOW the client interacts

D is INCORRECT
A person who practices Bowenian theory would be very interested in the Micro and Macro systems in a client's life, how they interact and at what particular level are all of these systems integrated with each other.

Question 100++   **Section: Clinical**

The correct answer is C
The focus of reality therapy is to increase the client's responsibility and help them learn different methods of coping. Reality therapy uses four basic questions to address the issues of a client.

1. What do you want to accomplish/to do? (Main Goal)
2. What have you done today/ What can you do to get....? (Examine current behavior)
3. What prevented you from reaching your goal or accomplishing task? (Obstacles)
4. What are you going to do about what blocked you from your goal? (Solution focused now and in the future)
                    Reference: http://www.realitytherapy.org.uk/

A is INCORRECT.
Increasing a client's social interest may be functional but would not be a specific goal of Reality Therapy. It could be an outcome of a Reality Therapy Goal.

B is INCORRECT.
One goal of therapy is always awareness. Awareness of self, others, environment, internal feelings, drives, motivations, resources, ideas, spirituality and on...and on...

To a Reality Therapist, awareness will come as a by-product of using and applying the four major questions and the analysis of the results of applying them. As you accept responsibility for your behavior, your awareness of the motivation and drives behind your behavior become greater.

D is INCORRECT.
A therapist always hopes the interactions will increase a client's self-esteem. Self-esteem is a very broad and poorly defined

concept, which often makes it difficult to define and conceptualize in therapy. You will often know self-esteem has improved by your client's behavior without ever knowing what triggered it of how it got better.

> Clinical Pearl: Personally, I have found that giving a client permission to feel certain things during the beginning of therapy can help reshape and bolster their self-esteem. Example: a client is angry at a family member for perceived attacks, which seem ambiguous. The client perseverates on the feelings of anger because they do not feel it is right for them to be angry. Once you define the difference between anger (a feeling) and aggression (a behavior), you can give the client your permission to be angry about the perceived treatment but deny them the right to behave with aggression toward the family member.

When people feel they have a "right" to their feelings, they can generally stop focusing on their "right" and begin to focus on the problem and solutions.

Answers to Questions 1-100++

1. D	35. C	69. A
2. C	36. D	70. B
3. B	37. B	71. B
4. A	38. B	72. F
5. B	39. D	73. C
6. C	40. B	74. C
7. C	41. C	75. A
8. C	42. D	76. D
9. B	43. C	77. B
10. D	44. B	78. C
11. B	45. D	79. C
12. A	46. C	80. C
13. C	47. A	81. B
14. B	48. A	82. D
15. B	49. C	83. D
16. C	50. C	84. C
17. D	51. D	85. D
18. D	52. A	86. A
19. C	53. B	87. A
20. C	54. B	88. B
21. A	55. D	89. A
22. D	56. B	90. D
23. C	57. D	91. D
24. D	58. C	92. B
25. B	59. C	93. C
26. A	60. A	94. D
27. D	61. D	95. C
28. C	62. D	96. A
29. B	63. C	97. C
30. C	64. D	98. A
31. C	65. B	99. D
32. D	66. A	100. B
33. B	67. C	100+. C
34. A	68. B	100++. C

Volume II

Another 100 Questions Every Social Worker Should Know: ASWB-LCSW Exam Preparation Guide

Volume II

Harvey Norris, MSW, LCSW

TURTLE PRESS

Library of Congress Cataloging in Publication Data

Norris, Harvey S.

ACKNOWLEDGEMENTS

This book is dedicated to my friend,
James V. Cook, ESQ
If the practice of law had not grabbed him, he would
have made a great social worker.

He sees the good in everyone, even those who appear
to be his adversaries. He has taught me about human
nature and how to fight better.

...and how not to carry a grudge...

Thank you for every breakfast...and every chance to do
good...

CONTENTS

differences between cultures

122	who has been assigned to see a Guatemalan immigrant	Cultural
123	they are seeing you because their son is GAY	Cultural
124	a case involving an Asian-American youth	Cultural
125	You are asked to assess a man from New Guinea	Cultural
126	you realize her guilt is related to spending so much on tuition and	Clinical
127	on a 36 year old Arab-American	Clinical
128	on a 22 year old female whose parents are very concerned	Clinical
129	He is convinced that most people dislike him	Clinical
130	Juan and Isobel come to their first couple's session	Clinical
131	rather consistent with attending sessions	Clinical
132	You have developed an eco-diagram	Clinical
133	Tommy's parents say he just sits around	Clinical
134	You have taken a job as a prison social worker	Clinical
135	a 35 year old male who has served two brief prison terms	Clinical
136	You have completed your MSW	Ethical
137	You are hospital social worker in charge of discharge planning	Ethical
138	sessions to a 23 -year-old female client, who is indigent and has a nine month old baby boy	Ethical
139	insurance has authorized two sessions for assessment	Ethical
140	You are a hospice social worker	Clinical
141	You would be able to estimate his FSIQ	Clinical

142	therefore is more sensitive, more creative and more emotional	Clinical
143	she recently went to the doctor and he gave her an EEG	Clinical
144	You are seeing Sylvia for anxiety and depression	Clinical
145	they exhibit a belief of a "hands-off" attitude	Clinical
146	She appears delusional and disorganized	Human Diversity
147	The stage of the school age child is the	Clinical
148	You are working with an inter-generational family	Clinical
149	a 47 year old white female who is characteristically very shy	Clinical
150	One of the most powerful ethical cases	Ethics
151	she has been diagnosed with Borderline Personality Disorder	Clinical
152	he wishes he could understand the ONTOGENESIS	Clinical
153	His history is unremarkable before his current symptoms	Clinical
154	she is unable to afford the fees for therapy	Ethics
155	of sexual abuse by her stepfather	Clinical
156	diagnosed with a dysthymic disorder	Clinical
157	explain the difference between post-traumatic stress disorder	Clinical
158	He initially presented with moderate to severe depression	Clinical
159	You are supervising an intake worker at a	Clinical
160	One of your ethical commitments that is implicit in the NASW Code	Ethics
161	Your level of concern about their potential to commit suicide should	Clinical
162	who is diagnosed with a Bipolar Disorder	Clinical

163 a 43 year old female with a long history of chronic alcoholism	Clinical
164 referral reports problems with reality testing	Clinical
165 seeing a 23 year old female client who appears rather manipulative	Clinical
166 Each time the child begins to express emotions	Clinical
167 white male with an alcoholic wife who	Clinical
168 clients who suffer from drug or alcohol addiction	Clinical
169 Substance Abuse programs that use cognitive behavioral	Clinical
170 Of the four common groups of medications taken	Clinical
171 an intake for a court ordered client.	Psychothx
172 You are working with a client in a hospital	Ethics
173 when you can break confidentiality and disclose confidential	Ethics
174 You run into the client and learn they are a gardener and	Ethics
175 you decide the family is not appropriate for family therapy	Psychothx
176 Incest and family dynamics have several	Clinical
177 she spends entire days in her pajamas	Psychothx
178 Children reared in family environments	Psychothx
179 diagnosed with an anxiety disorder and an alcohol use disorder	Clinical
180 You have decided to administer the "Draw-a-Person" test	Diagnosis
181 states she is frustrated, overwhelmed and feels like she is drowning	Psychothx
182 There are many different theories for intervention	Psychothx
183 Of the four following childhood behaviors	Behavior

184 A repetitive and persistent pattern of behavior	Behavior
185 mother has just brought her eight year old boy	Diagnosis
186 You are completing the first session with a women	Psychothx
187 views a patient with unexpressed guilt as	Psychothx
188 The client's mother was killed in a single car accident	Psychothx
189 A cognitive bias is a pattern	Psychothx
190 have started an admission on a 38 year-old female client	Psychothx
191 lists a series of diagnoses which can only be used with children under the age of 18	Diagnosis
192 for personality disorders and mental Retardation	Diagnosis
193 Psychoanalytic theory postulates	Diagnosis
194 All other countries use the International	Diagnosis
195 working with a client who has a full scale IQ	Diagnosis
196 with a child who has been diagnosed with a conduct disorder	Diagnosis
197 who is described as "latency aged".	Diagnosis
198 issues including anger, aggression, and impulse control	Ethics
199 As an emergency room social worker	Diagnosis
200 You begin to explain confidentiality for	Assessment

Question 101   Section: Psychotherapy

A 19-year-old girl, upon returning from her first year away at college sits her parents down and tells them she is a lesbian. She tells them she has known of her orientation since she was 16 but has been afraid to tell them until now. The family normally has good relations and treats each other well. Her mother and father are angry, embarrassed and confused. Both parents feel disappointed in their daughters' orientation, embarrassed by her revelation and unsure of how to deal with her situation. Although the family typically gets along well, they are angry, confused, and embarrassed. Her father feels alienated from his daughter, and neither parent feels able to express their feelings about their daughter's sexuality nor their disappointment in her. Mother indicates that her husband has confided in her that he feels he is to blame because he was strict with her dating during high-school. How could you best help this family?

A) offer the girl and her family access to a re-orientation program in order to alter her sexual orientation.
B) Provide the girl with individual therapy to deal with her feelings about her orientation.
C) Provide crisis counseling to the family and refer the mother and father to a support group for parents of gay and lesbian children.
D) Educate the parents about the homosexuality and address their prejudices in a direct, blunt manner.

Answer on Page: 74

Question 102   Section: Psychotherapy

You have been referred a case of a seven year old boy. He has been tested and is in the low-average range of intellectual functioning. His motor skills are delayed and while he is able to walk between objects he often refuses to stand and pulls himself across the floor. The referral is due to risk of self harm because he persistently eats sand, bugs, houseplants, paint, dog food and has recently been caught eating cat feces from the cat litter box. He started this behavior four months ago and it has been continuous since. His primary diagnosis would MOST likely :

A) mental retardation
B) encopresis.
C) Asperger's
D) Pica

Answer on Page: 76

Question 103   Section: Psychotherapy

Jayne's parents divorced 18 months ago, after 2 years of almost constant daily bickering, when she was 14 years old. She lives with her mother and has started staying out all night, has come home drunk several times and has been caught smoking pot with her friends at least twice. Both mom and dad are upset about the behavior. Since she lives with mom, dad feels left out and unable to help his daughter. They come in to see you together and it is clear they are still grieving over the loss of their marriage, and they feel guilty because they blame the constant arguing that occurred before their divorce as the starting point for their daughter's rebellion. Both are concerned their daughter will continue to get in trouble and may end up in the legal system.
You have been seeing the daughter at school for a behavioral referral from a teacher. What would be your best option going forward?

A) Attempt to get Jayne involved in different after-school activities with the opportunity to meet and get involved with a different peer group.
B) Continue individual therapy with Jayne and provide and referrals to support groups and provide linking services
to   them for the parents dealing with the after-effects of divorce and co-parenting issues.
C) Continue individual therapy and tell the parents this is a stage that Jayne will mature out of.
D) Refer Jayne to a church youth group so she can develop a new set of friends.

Answer on Page: 78

Question 104   Section: ETHICS

You are a new female social worker at a mental health center. You have scheduled a client for tomorrow at 8 PM when you realize that none of your co-workers or your supervisor is going to be in the building. You have never met with this client and it will be your initial screening and interview. Your best course of action is to:

A) talk to your co-workers and ask if they can stay late that night so you are not alone.
B) Call the client and reschedule for a time when there are other people in the office.
C) Don't worry about the situation and see the client alone as scheduled.
D) Call your significant other and ask them if they can stay in the office waiting room while you see your client.

Answer on Page: 80

Question 105 **Section: ETHICS**

You have an appointment with Margaret scheduled for the evening. You receive a call from her husband around 3 in the afternoon, stating he wanted to confirm the time of his wife's appointment for her. You just attended training on HIPAA awareness. You should…

A) Tell the husband you cannot answer the question and then call Margaret and verify she asked her husband to confirm the appointment.
B) Ask the husband why he is calling instead of Margaret.
C) Let the husband know the time of the appointment so he can make sure Margaret is on time.
D) Refuse to acknowledge that Margaret is your client and refuse to discuss any appointment times with the husband.

Answer on Page: 81

Question 106 **Section: CLINICAL**

Psychosis is defined as a person who is out of touch with reality. There are five basic types of symptoms that define psychosis. If a person exhibits one or more of these symptoms you can say they are suffering from psychosis and then if you gather enough information you can arrive at a more exact diagnosis, e.g. Schizophrenia, Schizophreniform… Which of the following is NOT a symptom of PSYCHOSIS?

A) Delusions
B) Negative Symptoms
C) Alopecia
D) Disorganized Speech

Answer on Page: 82

Question 107   **Section: CLINICAL**

Negative Symptoms are one of the major symptoms of psychosis. A person with negative symptoms will often present with a FLAT or BLUNTED affect. They are called negative symptoms because...

A) they are characterized by a reduction in amount and fluency of speech.
B) They give the impression something has been taken away from the client.
C) they reduce the apparent TEXTURAL RICHNESS of a patient's personality.
D) All of the above

Answer on Page: 82

Question 108   **Section: CLINICAL**

Once during the beginning of my career, as I sold my time to an inpatient psychiatric facility for $4.97 per hour, I walked into the dayroom to find a male client, approximately 55 years of age sitting on a couch and pushing on his face from different angles. As I watched, he pushed harder and harder from different directions and seemed perplexed. I approached him and asked him how he was doing. He replied, "OK, I guess." And continued to touch his face. I then asked him what he was doing and he replied that he was making sure his face was all right? I commented that his face appeared fine and he said, "Now it does, but during the night THEY come and rearrange all the bones in my face while I sleep and I have to make sure they get them back in the right places!" Trying not to react strongly, I said, "That must be kind of painful!" He replied, "Not really, unless I wake up while they are doing it!" This client was experiencing a

A) Disorganized thought
B) A False Belief
C) Hallucination
D) Bizarre Delusion

Answer on Page: 83

Question 109   Section: CLINICAL

When dealing with psychosis, in order to diagnose correctly, you must look at longitudinal factors and associated disorder features. Which of the following is NOT a factor used to assist with diagnosis:

A) Duration of symptoms
B) Precipitating Factors of illness
C) Premorbid Personality
D) Previous employment history.

Answer on Page: 84

Question 110   Section: CLINICAL

In order to properly diagnose schizophrenia, it is important that the patient's occupational and social functioning be materially impaired. For example a person with this diagnosis would not be likely to marry or be in an intimate relationship (Material Social Impairment) and would not likely be able to hold a job (Material Occupational Impairment). Once you have determined that a person has PSYCHOSIS, you must then exclude other issues. PSYCHOSIS alone is not enough to diagnose schizophrenia. Which of the following would NOT be an exclusionary factor?

A) Substance Abuse Disorders
B) Mood Disorders
C) Family Illness
D) General Medical Condition

Answer on Page: 85

Question 111   Section: CLINICAL

In the diagnosis of schizophrenia, there are other features which need to be considered in order to properly complete the differential diagnosis. Which of the following features need to be considered...

A) Family History of Illness
B) Age of onset of illness
C) Response to Medications
D) All of the above

Answer on Page: 86

Question 112   Section: CLINICAL

John has withdrawn from his social circles and has begun to display rather peculiar habits when his friends come over to visit. All of his friends notice small behavior changes which include odd statements, reference to things that "cannot be" and comments regarding his belief's that his dog may be listening into his telephone conversations. He is not known to use any drugs and has had no medical history. Because John is mild mannered and pleasant, his friend have felt his behavior is odd but not a major concern. When Cecelia went to visit him yesterday, he had not bathed in several days. His bird feeder was removed from the backyard and was sitting on the table. When she asked about it he smiled pleasantly and said in a calm tone of voice, "The birds have been gathering around the bird feeder in order to spy on me and watch what I do during the day. So, I took down the birdfeeder so they can't come around anymore." He mentioned that he was happy because his brother started to call him again and they had a great conversation on the telephone that lasted for about an hour this morning. Cecelia knows that John had only one brother and he died in a car crash several years ago. Cecelia reported this to her friends and is very concerned. She calls a social worker she knows from work and they recommend John be evaluated for a psychotic disorder. Her social worker friend tells her that it is possible John is suffering from Schizophrenia. Cecelia goes online and learns the following about the onset of schizophrenia:

A) It affects about 5% of the population and once treated with medications the person should have no further problems.

B) It affects about 5% of the populations and most people continue to have symptoms throughout their lives.

C) It affects about 1% of the population and treatment is often provided using neuroleptic medications which can cause Tardive Dyskinesia and may have to be taken on a lifelong basis.

D) It affects about 1% of the population and can cause some incapacity of social and work functioning, but the functioning incapacity is seldom profound.

Answer on Page: 86

Question 113   Section: CLINICAL

You are dealing with Michael, a 19-year-old male with a diagnosis of Schizophrenia. Among all the symptoms he presents with, you notice the most prominent are the material impairment of his ability to socialize with other people and his inability to study his texts for his college courses. He is very distractible and at times can become disoriented as to his place and time, although this usually fades after 20-25 minutes. This constellation of behaviors is grouped under the psychotic symptom label of:

A) Absence of Insight
B) Cognitive dysfunction
C) Dysphoria
D) None of the above

Answer on Page: 87

Question 114 Section: CLINICAL

You are reviewing a chart for a client you are about to start seeing and you read the following diagnostic classification:

Axis I 295.60 Schizophrenia, Residual Type, Episodic With Interepisode Residual Symptoms.

What behavior would you expect to see in this individual?

A) A client who is primarily mute, with catalepsy (when some moves a client's body part, like raising their hand above their head – it will stay in the same position for several minutes)
B) A patient who would present with no impulse control problems, fully oriented and without suicidal ideations, and would be able to describe her most scary experiences with the same emotional tone as she would use for describing her dishes.

C) A patient who will present as appropriate but can deteriorate rapidly, talk gibberish, neglect their appearance and neglect their hygiene.
D) a patient who presents with a reduced or attenuated psychotic   symptoms such as odd speech or peculiarities of behavior that exist but are rather slight in presentation.

Answer on Page: 88

Question 115   Section: CLINICAL

In clinical parlance, the word mood is used to describe "a sustained emotion that colors the way we look at life". We used to use the term AFFECTIVE DISORDER instead of MOOD DISORDER, so be careful when reading older reports or talking to clinicians who received their initial training in the seventies and eighties, as they may use AFFECTIVE to mean MOOD. Which of the following facts are true about mood disorders?

A) Their prevalence is about 20% among adult females and 10%   among adult males
B) They occur regardless of social class and race
C) They are more common among single adults
D) All of the above

Answer on Page: 89

Question 116   Section: CLINICAL

A BIPOLAR DISORDER is a shorthand way of describing any cyclic mood disorder that includes at least one MANIC Episode. A MANIC Episode consists of a classic triad of symptoms (1) heightened self-esteem, (2) increased motor activity, and (3) pressured speech. Symptoms must be obvious and outrageous. You receive a patient with a diagnosis of 296.0

Bipolar Disorder, Single Manic Episode. Which of the following items can you infer from this diagnosis?

A) The patient has had AT LEAST one manic episode and one major depressive episode in the past.
B) The patient has had just one manic episode and no major depressive episodes.
C) All the client's episodes have been Hypomanic
D) The client may have been misdiagnosed as an alcoholic.

Answer on Page: 89

Question 117   Section: CLINICAL

What is the difference between Bipolar Disorder I and Bipolar Disorder II?

A) Bipolar Disorder I has no depressive episodes
B) Bipolar Disorder II has no depressive episodes
C) Both have very similar symptoms, but type II does not have any "High" phases which lead to hospitalization
D) Both have very similar symptoms, but type I does not have any "High" phases which lead to hospitalization

Answer on Page: 90

Question 118   Section: CLINICAL

A client is referred to you by his family. After an intensive interview with several members of the family you are able to document the following data; 1) For the past 5 days your client has exhibited a mood that is vastly more expansive and elevated than his usual mood. 2) This mood has been sustained for the past 5 days with no reduction, 3) During the past 5 days, they have shown a reduced need for sleep, racing thoughts and grandiosity. 4) There are no signs of psychosis 5) every family member has observed the same behavior. The current episode does not require hospitalization. Your BEST diagnosis would be:

A) Hypomanic Episode
B) Mixed Episode
C) Manic Episode
D) Depressive Episode

Answer on Page: 91

Question 119   Section: CLINICAL

You have just reviewed a case brought to you by a younger and less experienced social worker. It is clear that you are dealing with a Mood Disorder. The current diagnosis is Bipolar I Disorder. It is also clear that the diagnosis is incomplete because the most current episode needs to have a specifier attached. You ask several questions of the social worker and you get the following answers. The patient is extremely sensitive to feelings of rejection, they often feel as if there body is "leaden" (so heavy they cannot do anything) and they tend to overeat and are obese. You tell the social worker they need to add WHICH of the following specifiers:

A) With Atypical Features
B) With Melancholic Features
C) With Catatonic Features
D) With Postpartum Onset

Answer on Page: 92

Question 120   Section: CLINICAL

Which of the following disorders can present the clinical social worker with symptoms of Depression and Mania that can look like a Mood Disorder?

A) Vascular Dementia
B) Personality Disorders
C) Bereavement
D) All of the above

Answer on Page: 92

Question 121   Section: CULTURAL

You practice as a culturally competent social worker, which means you honor and respect the differences between cultures. You are assigned a new client that is a member of an ethnic, racial or social group unfamiliar to you. Your best course of action would be to...

A) Ask the client to help educate you on their culture and
      ethnicity
B) actively seek out information and knowledge on the new
      culture.
C) continue therapy without additional training
D) refer the client to someone who is of their own ethnic
      or cultural group.

Answer on Page: 93

Question 122   Section: CULTURAL

You are a culturally competent social worker who has been assigned to see a Guatemalan immigrant. The immigrant has received a notice from the U.S. Immigration and Customs Enforcement Agency (I.C.E.) requiring him to come in for an interview within the next two weeks. Like most Guatemalan's who have fled the country, he is fearful of all authorities. During your second session he tells you that he is afraid he will be deported if he goes to the appointment because he made a false statement on his immigration paperwork. He is concerned that if he is deported, he will be separated from his girlfriend and their 2 year old son, and they will be forced to fend for themselves. Your primary task to solve this issue is...

A) Convince the client to go the I.C.E. Office and confess the truth.
B) Call I.C.E. yourself and inform them about his status because lying on an immigration application is a crime.
C) Continue to provide services as you have no obligation to report the behavior to I.C.E.
D) Discuss the client's concern and discuss the need for him to get a lawyer and assist him in a referral to a lawyer.

Answer on Page: 95

Question 123   Section: CULTURAL

You are assigned a family and during the assessment, mom and dad tell you that they are seeing you because their son is GAY and they want him changed. The son sits quietly during the exchange and does not respond to any questions other than to shrug and sigh. Mom and dad tell you they want you to refer them to an agency that can provide Reparative or Conversion psychotherapy in order to retrain their son to become a heterosexual. You should respond with...

A) a referral to an agency that practices reparation psychotherapy.

B) Explain to the parents that there is no shame in being homosexual

C) Let the parents know that NASW, APA and the American Psychiatric Association consider this type of therapy to be UNETHICAL and you will not be able to make a referral.

D) Set up a time to speak with the son alone to see how he feels about Reparation Psychotherapy.

Answer on Page: 96

Question 124   Section: CULTURAL

You have received a case involving an Asian-American youth who is a first-generation immigrant. His parents were born in the far-east and he was born in Texas. As you begin to assess his support system and draw up a treatment plan, you know one of the problems you will face with this client, due to a familiar psychological characteristic, of some Asian cultural groups is ....

A) difficulties in understanding some of the eligibility requirements for psychotherapy

B) an overly exaggerated feeling of shame and possible loss of face due to being "unable" to handle his problems.

C) extreme resistance from his family of origin because they feel "outsiders" should not be involved in their life.

D) None of the above

Answer on Page: 97

Question 125   Section: CULTURAL

You are asked to assess a man from New Guinea regarding a recent behavior he displayed at his work place. He works on the loading docks of a shipping company. The episode was seen by an EAP counselor at the shipping company and they wrote a description of it which included a period of brooding; followed by a violent outburst where he was extremely aggressive towards several dock workers who were taunting him. Immediately after the episode, he began talking about his feelings. He stated he was being persecuted by his fellow workers and then appeared exhausted and quickly returned to his pre-aggressive state. Several minutes later, when questioned about his behavior he appeared to be displaying a significant amount of amnesia. You pinpoint the behavior as...

A)   Amok
B)   Psychotic Disorder
C)   dhat
D)   Hwa-byung

Answer on Page: 98

Question 126   Section: CLINICAL

Bobbi is a 23 year old female who has recently graduated from college and has been unemployed for about 8 months. She is seeking ways to cope with her feelings of depression and guilt. After several sessions, you realize her guilt is related to spending so much on tuition and not having gotten employment. She reports she has very few friends, belongs to no organizations or social clubs and often talks about her most enjoyable times as when she is sitting around home daydreaming. You realize her primary ego defense to cope with this stressor is...

A) Rationalization
B) projection
C) autistic fantasy

D) devaluation

Answer on Page: 99

Question 127   Section: CLINICAL

You begin an assessment on a 36 year old Arab-American, named Saheed. He is self-referred because he feels he is "not-good enough". After extensive questioning, you find it difficult to identify any particular event or person in his life who is negative. When he discusses his family members or his relationships at work, he talks glowingly about people. His entire outlook on life is one of overt optimism. You begin to wonder what brought him to therapy when you realize that his primary ego-defense mechanism is…

A) intellectualization
B) idealization
C) humor
D) isolation

Answer on Page: 100

Question 128   Section: CLINICAL

You have just received a referral on a 22 year old female whose parents are very concerned that she "is unable to stand on her own two feet." They state that she cannot make decisions by herself. After your initial assessment, she is unable to state any specific problems but does tell you that she has several close friends and they always help her when she has problems. When you ask about the type of help they offer, she replies, "They listen and give advice." While you are unable to locate any pathology, you realize she is adept at using the defense mechanism known as....

A) Acting Out
B) Affiliation
C) Altruism
D) Anticipation

Answer on Page: 102

Question 129   Section: CLINICAL

Marcus comes into your clinic with the following self-reported issues. He is convinced that most people dislike him and are upset with him. He states that no matter how hard he tries to start a conversation, he just drives people away. He states that when someone begins to become irritated by him in a conversation he tends to get upset with them, which pushes them away faster.   He stated that one of his only friends has often told him that he causes people to dislike himself because of how he behaves towards them, but he is unable to see this side of himself. His friend also tells him he should "repress" his anxiety.   You realize he is using the ego-defense mechanism of…

A) Passive Aggression
B) Projective Identification
C) Reaction formation
D) Repression

Answer on Page: 103

Question 130   Section: CLINICAL

Juan and Isobel come to their first couple's session and begin to talk about their issues. Juan is very active in his church and spends a great deal of time traveling to other churches talking about his views on abortion. He is adamantly opposed to Roe V. Wade. He spends so much time spreading his "ministry" that he is hardly ever home and Isobel is tired of being left alone. This has been going on for almost 3 years. Further questioning reveals that about 5 years ago their only daughter went to college and did not come home the first summer. Over winter break of her second year, she revealed to her parents that she had gotten pregnant and had terminated the pregnancy because she did not want to drop out of school. She felt devastated by this and eventually left school to join the Peace Corp. Juan states that he has "come to terms with his daughter's betrayal" and no longer even thinks about it. In fact, he said it has been more than a year since it even crossed his mind. You realize that Juan is using the ego defense mechanism called....

A) Self-observation
B) Self-assertion
C) Sublimation
D) Suppression

Answer on Page: 104

Question 131   Section: CLINICAL

You are working with Mary, a 32 year old divorced mother of three and she has been rather consistent with attending sessions. She often shows up early and never has to be prompted to begin her session. Usually, she brings complaints and problems with her. She complains about her neighbors, her children's teachers, her ex-husband, her new boyfriend and just about everyone involved in her life. When you discuss ways of coping with individual issues she tends to spurn them and when you try to teach or role-play social skills, she seems dismissive. You have assigned several sets of homework and she has not done any of them. When asked about her refusal to do homework, she states, "It won't work anyway, so why waste the time." Your first impression is a person with a personality disorder, however, you also realize Mary is using a specific ego defense mechanism which could mask a personality disorder or cause you to pursue a personality disorder diagnosis when it is not warranted. You know the ego defense mechanism is ...

A) Denial
B) Displacement
C) Dissociation
D) Help-rejecting

Answer on Page: 105

Question 132   Section: CLINICAL

You have seen Silvio two times as a referral from the court system. Silvio has been charged with several misdemeanor crimes which do not include battery or violence. You have developed an eco-diagram of his functioning and have noticed he has a very poor relationship with his father, who is not in the home. Silvio does not feel his father is supportive of anything he does. You ask Silvio if he would try a homework task of calling his father and talking to him for two minutes to "just make contact." Silvio's response is quick and harsh, "I know my father hates me, and so there is no point in trying to have a relationship with him!" Because you have worked with adolescents you realize this statement comes directly from a STANDARD THINKING ERROR called...

A) Entitlement
B) Emotional Reasoning
C) Fortune-telling

D) Externalization

Answer on Page:106

Question 133   Section: CLINICAL

You complete an assessment on Tommy, a 14 year-old boy who was brought in by his parents. Tommy's parents say he just sits around and refuses to do anything. When they want to go to a movie, he does not feel like it. When they want to go shopping he would rather stay home. He has no friends and does not appear to be interested in making any.

When you question Tommy about his behavior he seems slightly depressed. When you ask a direct question about his refusal to participate in family life, he responds by saying "it would not be any fun and besides they don't really want me to come anyway." Several more questions return similar answers. Tommy's parents think he may be having a 'nervous breakdown." You have seen similar behavior in adolescents in the past and you believe he actually perceives the world through the lens of a thinking error known as…

A) Image
B) Catastrophizing
C) Jumping to conclusions
D) Mind-Reading

Answer on Page:107

Question 134   Section: CLINICAL

You have taken a job as a prison social worker and one of your first clients of the day is a man serving a life sentence without the possibility of parole. He has served 8 years up to the point where you meet him. When you ask him why he requested an appointment with mental health he begins a long tirade about how everyone is against him. He tells you the dorm sergeant hates him and his fellow dorm members are always causing him problems. You have read his "prison jacket" and realize he has been sentenced for 1st Degree Murder. When you ask about the crime he was sentenced on he tells you it was not his fault. Upon further questioning he decides to tell you his story. He went out one night to rob a local drug dealer because he needed cash. He took his brother's pistol. As he was robbing the dealer, the dealer pulled out a gun and shot him, wounded, but not incapacitated he fired back and killed the drug dealer. He was convinced that since the drug dealer shot him first, he was only acting in self-defense. He then stated that his lawyer "screwed him" because his lawyer refused to use self-defense as a legal defense for his actions. You realize the primary issue facing this inmate/client is his internalization of a specific criminal thinking pattern. You recognize this criminal thinking pattern to be...

A) The "good person" stance
B) the "victim" stance
C) the "lack of time" stance
D) the "unique person" stance

Answer on Page: 108

Question 135   Section: CLINICAL

You have just completed your 4th session with Matthew, a 35 year old male who has served two brief prison terms. The first incarceration was for two years and the second for three. He has been out of prison for 7 years. He identifies himself as a devout church-goer who never misses a service and enjoys being part of his church community. During your sessions he peppers his language with bible quotes and admonitions. He came to therapy for complaints about stress and anxiety in his life. At this beginning of this session he admitted that his stress was caused by a letter he received from the State Police Agency declaring him a "person of interest" in a current investigation involving insurance fraud. He stated that while he is an insurance agent he is also very religious. He does not understand why he is being "targeted" in this investigation. Upon questioning, he admits his prior two incarcerations involve fraud and larceny. He also shows no remorse for his prior actions and seems more upset about getting arrested and losing his job than disappointing his church friends. You realize you may be dealing with a client who has a past diagnosis of anti-social personality disorder and he is deeply involved in the thinking error known as …

A) fragmented personality
B) justifying
C) fronting
D) grandiosity

Answer on Page: 110

Question 136   Section: ETHICAL

You are a 32 -year-old social worker. You have completed your MSW and are 10 weeks shy of completing your two years of licensure supervision. You have passed the ASWB exam and are simply waiting to finish your last 10 hours of supervision with your clinical supervisor, and then file the paperwork to become fully licensed.

Your agency refers you a case involving a man and woman, who are currently divorced, and are in a dispute over the custody and arrangements for their two children. Your initial meeting is with the husband. During your initial assessment, he lets you know that he feels his ex-wife will be very irate at the fact that they have not been assigned a licensed clinician. He states that his wife is an LCSW. He states she has been licensed for the past 10 years and was adamant in her referral process that she and her ex-husband receive services from a licensed clinical social worker.

It becomes clear to you during your assessment with the ex-husband, that the custody and arrangements for the children, are going to be a very contested issue. You have a number of concerns about the case. You have concerns about the possibility of a clinical intern providing services to a licensed clinical social worker. You decide to call your LCSW clinical supervisor and get feedback on your concerns. After detailing the situation with your supervisor, your supervisor recommends that you do the following actions:

A) continue seeing the divorced couple in therapy.
B) continue seeing the ex-husband in therapy and ask your office to schedule a different commission for the ex-wife.
C) contact the ex-wife and discuss the situation with her and ask if she would be willing to accept you as a clinician.
D) contact your office and explain to them that the case needs to be referred to a licensed provider.

Answer on Page: 111

Question 137   Section: ETHICAL

You are hospital social worker in charge of discharge planning for people in need of inpatient and outpatient rehab. Many of the clients you're responsible for have had traumatic brain injury due to motor vehicle accidents. You have a very firm working knowledge of the different services that Medicaid and Medicare will pay for. You also have good working relationships with most of the rehab centers within a 250 mile radius of your hospital. As part of your job responsibility you often have to interface with the State Department of Health coordinator for brain and spinal cord injury. You have completed your licensure requirements, and are three weeks from being able to file an application to become an LCSW. The state coordinator for the brain and spinal cord injury program is an MSW, approximately your age, who has never signed up as a clinical intern and is not currently seeking licensure. You are meeting with the mother of a 35 -year-old female patient who was severely injured in a motor vehicle accident. You have been trying to find rehab for the client for the past 30 days. The client has been discharged from the hospital 22 days prior however mother refuses to bring her home and no rehab has been willing to except her until today. During your consultation with the mother, the spinal cord injury project coordinator is involved. Multiple times during the conference, the MSW interrupts you and gives the mother inaccurate information regarding the benefits available to her daughter. Several times during the conference, the MSW tells mother that she should demand the hospital pay for certain things, and provide her with certain services before she agrees to take her daughter home.

Your ethical obligation is to respond by:

A) you should ignore the MSW and continue to provide accurate information to mother.
B) you should interrupt the MSW and point out the incorrect information and then continue to try to provide correct information to mother.
C) you should gracefully terminate the conference and reschedule with mother at a time when the social worker is not present.
D) Because you are almost an LCSW you should call down the social worker, point out her errors, and ask her to excuse yourself from the conference.

Answer on Page: 113

Question 138 Section: ETHICAL

You are a clinical social work intern one year post-graduation. You've been providing pro bono counseling services at a local drop-in agency that is a nonprofit. Most of your clients are extremely low income and often have interactions with the department of children family services. You have provided six sessions to a 23 -year-old female client, who is indigent and has a nine month old baby boy. She has a prior mental health history and has been in voluntarily hospitalized three times since age 17. While you have no direct paperwork on her hospitalizations you believe the general diagnosis is psychotic disorder, NOS. You have learned that during her last hospitalization, the nine -month-old child was picked up by the birth father, and is currently living with the birth father and his grandmother. You have no reason to suspect there's any problem with the child living with the birth father and his mother. While you are away from the drop in center you receive a phone call from the secretary saying that "Judy" called you and left a telephone number asking you to call about your client. The secretary told you that the caller identified themselves as someone from the Department of Children and Family Services. You have no verification of any information on Judy, your client has never mentioned this name, and the best of your knowledge the client is not involved Department of Children Family Services. You call your clinical supervisor to staff the case and determine what should be done. Your clinical supervisor recognizes the name of the caller and the phone number from the caller. Your clinical supervisor informed you that the caller is a DCF attorney. Your clinical supervisor then advises you to take the following actions:

A) return the call to Judy and provide her with all information she requires.

B) return the call to Judy and tell her you are unable to give her information without a signed release from your client.

C) asked the secretary to call the call her back and instruct her that all information requests need to come in writing.

D) throw the number away and don't worry about it.

Answer on Page: 115

Question 139   Section: ETHICAL

You have begun seeing a 16 year old female who has health insurance. The insurance has authorized two sessions for assessment but require a diagnosis and treatment plan for further sessions. The parents inform you that they feel their daughter needs services and they do not have the money to pay without the insurance support. Your first session is with the family and your second session is with the girl alone. You have identified the following features: 1) the behavioral or emotional symptoms developed in response to an identifiable event(s) and began within three months of the event (which occurred at school). 2) The behaviors are clinically significant due to responses after exposure to the event that were in excess of what would be expected by someone else, and 3) they cause significant impairment to her schooling because her grades and attendance at school is suffering.

After considering all the facts you have gathered, you decide that she meets the criteria for an Adjustment Disorder with Mixed Emotional Features. Upon reviewing the insurance treatment plan forms, you realize the insurance will not pay for any diagnosis of Adjustment Disorder. You realize that with a little "fudging" of your criteria you could apply a diagnosis of Post-Traumatic Stress Disorder, for which the insurance company would pay. You feel you can help the client and would like to work with them, and you realize the parents are not able to pay you privately. You also do not feel you have the time to provide the services in a pro bono fashion. Your best course of action would be to:

A) Give the diagnosis of Adjustment Disorder and refer the parents to a free clinic where their daughter can see another counselor without the insurance impediment.
B) Give the diagnosis of PTSD and continue to provide services to the girl and receive insurance money for it.
C) Discuss the situation with the parents and ask them if they would be comfortable with you giving the PTSD diagnosis for insurance reimbursement.
D) Provide the services Pro Bono.

Answer on Page: 117

Question 140   Section: ETHICAL

You are a hospice social worker, employed by a for-profit hospice. You have a number of clients on your caseload. You have been asked to get a client to sign some paperwork for the office. When reading the paperwork, you realize it is financial in scope. It is paperwork that binds the client to pay for the services provided by the hospice regardless of whether or not the Medicaid, or Medicare will cover the cost. You remember a staff meeting approximately one month ago, where all staff were told that certain clients did not have the Medicaid information entered correctly and therefore Medicaid did not pay for the services. You present the client with the paperwork and explain the purpose of the paperwork. The client states they do not want to sign the paperwork. They stated that upon acceptance to hospice, they were told their Medicaid or Medicare would pay the bill completely. Your best action at this point is:

A) explain to the client that the paperwork must be signed in order for the billing department to have a complete file.

B) tell the client to write the word refused across the signature space and you will turn the paperwork back into the office.

C) tell the client if they do not sign the paperwork you will have to discontinue seeing them and their case may be closed.

D) refuse to present the paperwork to the client and return it to the office unsigned.

Answer on Page: 118

Question 141   Section: CLINICAL

You have been asked to do a family assessment. One member of the family, Michael, is diagnosed with mental retardation. After your assessment you find that Michael can carry out work and self-care tasks with moderate supervision from his family members. You would be able to estimate his FSIQ (Full Scale IQ) as being between:

A) 20-40
B) 50-70
C) 35-55
D) Below 20

Answer on Page: 120

Question 142   Section: CLINICAL

You are working with Jodi and during your second session she states that she is a left handed individual and therefore is more sensitive, more creative and more emotional than many other people who are right handed. You ask her how she knows this and she says, "I just heard it and it fits me." You are aware that she may be correct according to a theory created by Nobel-prize-winners Roger Sperry and Robert Ornstein. This theory is known as...

A) Brain Schism Theory
B) Brain Lateralization Theory
C) Inherent Lobe Theory
D) Corpus Collosum Effect

Answer on Page: 121

Question 143   Section: CLINICAL

You have been seeing Marsha for 3 sessions. Marsha has a rather limited knowledge about medical practices. She stated she recently went to the doctor and he gave her an EEG. She is convinced there is something seriously wrong with her and does not want to go back to the doctor. You understand that an EEG is used to...

A) to provide a graph of the alpha waves of the brain
B) maps the biological conditions inherent in goal-directed behavior.
C) classify mental retardation caused by the presence of an extra chromosome.
D) measure autonomic nervous system functions

Answer on Page: 123

Question 144   Section: CLINICAL

You are seeing Sylvia for anxiety and depression. You have seen her every other week for about 4 months. She is extremely addicted to nicotine, and often has to take a break during your 50 minute session to sneak outside for several puffs on a cigarette. She reports smoking 4 packs a day and is considered a "Chain-smoker". She has just told you she had a positive pregnancy test and is excited about having a baby. She asks if her smoking will have any harmful effects on developing baby. You let her know that the nicotine from the cigarettes could have the following effect on her child...

A) lower than normal birth weight
B) mental retardation
C) flaccid muscle tone
D) Tay Sachs Syndrome

Answer on Page: 123

Question 145   Section: CLINICAL

Michael and Amy have begun seeing you because of problems they report with their two pre-teen age children. When asked to describe how they respond to different parenting situations, it is clear they exhibit a belief in a "hands-off" attitude and letting the children set their own rules. They state this type of attitude will help their children become more internally driven, focused and more self-initiating. They are exhibiting which major style of parenting?

A) Authoritarian
B) Authoritative
C) Uninvolved
D) Permissive

Answer on Page: 125

Question 146   Section: HUMAN DIVERSITY

A 22-year-old homeless woman appears at your community mental health agency. She appears delusional and disorganized. However she states she has eaten daily and knows how to get help. She refuses hospitalization but agrees to maintain phone contact with you.   What is your best response to this situation?

A) Respect her self-determination and ask her what kind of help   she would like.
B) Accompany her to a walk-in psychiatric outpatient emergency   facility.
C) Tell her family to proceed with an involuntary commitment.
D) Determine if other sheltered environments or supports are available to her.

Answer on Page: 127

Question 147   Section: CLINICAL

Eric Erikson's psychosocial stages of development theory postulate that each stage presents a conflict which the individual must resolve before advancing to the next stage. The stage of the school age child is the fourth stage in his theory and deals with...

A) Industry vs. inferiority
B) Intimacy vs. isolation
C) Integrity vs. despair
D) Identity vs. role confusion

Answer on Page: 127

Question 148   Section: CLINICAL

You are working with an intergenerational family, mom, dad, paternal grandma, maternal aunt and three children. Your treatment plan is to help them create and structure boundaries in order to have a greater sense of control and appropriate behavior. This tactic would be most likely to cause...

A) More family enmeshment
B) Less family enmeshment
C) no change in enmeshment
D) no change in differentiation level

Answer on Page: 130

Question 149   Section: CLINICAL

Pris is a 47 year old white female who is characteristically very shy and withdrawn. She will participate when asked, but will not seek out company. She has decided to enter group treatment and will participate in an "assertiveness training" group. Over the first couple sessions, she experienced lots of self-doubt and uncertainty as to whether this was the "right choice" for her. Her counselor urges her to stay in group because he realizes the mental health process occurring here will subside rather quickly and she will feel better. The mental health process is known as...

A) dissociation
B) acculturation
C) cognitive dissonance
D) individuation

Answer on Page: 131

Question 150   Section: ETHICS

One of the most powerful ethical cases in social work and mental health is the Tarasoff case. The decisions in this case have changed the landscape of how we practice in certain areas. Which of the following areas does the Tarasoff decision NOT AFFECT...

A) Malpractice liability
B) Privileged communication
C) Assessment procedures
D) Confidentiality

Answer on Page: 132

Question 151   Section: CLINICAL

You begin working with a new female client, Dawn, Age 21. Upon reading her history, you learn she has been diagnosed with Borderline Personality Disorder. Which of the following symptoms would the clinician have had to see in order to arrive at this diagnosis?

A) a sustained pattern of excessive emotionality and attention seeking behavior which could be traced back to adolescence.
B) abrupt mood shifts with a poorly developed self-image, and a history of intense and unstable relationships
C) an individual who expects others to perceive them as special or gifted and exhibiting a grandiose and inflated sense of their own worth.
D) an excessive need to be taken care of that leads to submissive and clinging behavior and fears of separation

Answer on Page: 133

Question 152   Section: CLINICAL

You have a social work colleague who is discussing a case with you. He describes several behaviors and the internal as well as social motivation, which drives the client to commit these behaviors. He says he wishes he could understand the ONTOGENESIS of the client. What does he want to know?

A) the various conditions which stimulate an emotional state and/or arousal
B) the overall course of development of an individual
C) the aspects of the behavior which can be used to classify the disorder.
D) the perceptions of the client and their interactions with friends and family.

Answer on Page: 135

Question 153   Section: CLINICAL
You have completed an assessment and initial interview with Jon, a 22-year old male who began having problems 4 months ago. His history is unremarkable before his current symptoms. He presents with an organized delusional system which has an overarching theme of persecution. Your best initial diagnosis would be...

A) Schizoid Personality Disorder
B) Schizophreniform Disorder
C) Paranoid Schizophrenia
D) Schizophrenia, undifferentiated

Answer on Page: 153

Question 154   Section: ETHICS

You are working in a private practice and complete an intake session with the female client, 35 years old. At the end of the assessment she tells you that she is unable to afford the fees for therapy. Her problems appear rather serious, and she appears to be in need of help rather quickly. She also tells you that she is very much interested in receiving help. Your most ethical response, as a social worker is to…

A) tell her that you are sorry that she cannot afford your fee and that she will have to look for services elsewhere.
B) tell her that you believe this is an important set of services for her, given your assessment, and that she should think about approaching her family members in order to borrow money to pay your fees.
C) ask her if she has really explored all the resources around her, and whether or not there was a friend, family member, or a bank that could provide her with the money she needs to pay for your services.
D) tell her you will see what kind of an arrangement you can work out with her, and determine whether or not you can enter into a satisfactory contract with her. Explain to her that if you cannot enter into a contract with her, you will be happy to refer her, and follow up on the linkage, to an agency or another social worker who is able to help her.

Answer on Page: 137

Question 155   Section: CLINICAL

You are a school social worker approached by Maggie, a 17 - year-old female. After several minutes of discussion she confides in you that both she and her 11 -year-old sister has been the ongoing victims of sexual abuse by her stepfather.

She relates to you that her stepfather is an alcoholic, and has been unemployed for the past three years. She states she wishes she had told her mother about the abuse, but she was afraid of what her stepfather would do if she told her mother. She stated the reason she has come forward now is because her stepfather promised not to abuse her 11-year-old sister if she kept "the secret." When she discovered her 11 -year-old sister was being abused, she decided that she could no longer keep "the secret." If this problem were left unreported, which of the following a long-term outcomes might be expected of both the 17 -year-old and in the 11 -year-old abuse victim.

A) you would expect both girls to develop sexual dysfunction in their primary relationships.
B) you would expect both girls to develop long-term patterns of alcohol abuse and alcoholism as a coping mechanism.
C) you would expect both of them to get involved in unhealthy and destructive relationships with the possibility of suicidal thoughts, behaviors, or self cutting behavior.
D) You would expect the girls to choose primary partners in their adult relationships, which would replicate the abuse on their children.

Answer on Page: 138

Question 156   Section: CLINICAL

You have begun seeing a 26 year old female, diagnosed with a dysthymic disorder. Of the following symptoms, which one will most likely be prevalent?

A) Vivid olfactory hallucinations that have begun in the last three   months and have occurred daily.
B) Long-term chronic depression which lasts for most days for approximately 2 years.

C) Drug dependency and drug abuse centered specifically on methamphetamine and stimulants.
D) an inability to maintain a job for any length of time due to intrusive thoughts and flashbacks.

Answer on Page: 139

Question 157   Section: CLINICAL

During a monthly staff meeting your supervisor asks every social work clinician to explain the difference between post-traumatic stress disorder and acute stress disorder as described in the DSM-IV TR. Your best response is

A) The duration of the intrusive thoughts and flashbacks occur for more than one month and can be debilitating.
B) the length of time between the trauma and the onset of the symptoms experienced by the client.
C) The level of somatization which can be observed in the responses to stressors or situations.
D) the degree of trauma, including the nature of the trauma and any pathology that results from it.

Answer on Page: 140

Question 158   Section: CLINICAL

You have been seeing Paul, a 33 year old married male, weekly for 3 months. He initially presented with moderate to severe depression. During your first 3 sessions you convinced him to seek a psychiatric evaluation for possible medication, and he was placed on Luvox, an SSRI (Selective Serotonin Reuptake Inhibitor).   Within 4 weeks of his taking the medications you saw his symptoms of irritability, hopelessness and lack of energy virtually disappear.   He also related an increase in his overall energy level. Over the last two weeks you have noticed the re-occurrence of his irritability and hopelessness. After several avoided questions, he admits he stopped taking the medication about 2 weeks ago. He states he had problems with it but will not discuss specific issues with you. You should be aware that one of the potential side effects of an SSRI with male clients is...

A) SSRIs can cause symptoms similar to neuroleptic malignant syndrome.
B) SSRIs are almost never covered by health insurance because they are considered experimental in nature.
C) While SSRIs reduce symptoms of depression, they make it all but impossible to feel happiness.
D) SSRIs can cause a loss of sex drive in males and can cause sexual dysfunction, in the form of "lack of erection" and problems "with ejaculation".

Answer on Page: 141

Question 159   Section: Ethical

You are supervising an intake worker at a local mental health clinic. She calls you at 11:15 AM to tell you that a father has just brought his 17 year old daughter into the intake area and she is actively suicidal. You inform the intake worker that she needs to take the client to the psychiatric emergency unit immediately for evaluation and report back afterwards. The intake worker takes the client to the emergency center but they are unable to see her and state it will be about 4 hours before they can evaluate her. The worker is unable to stay away from intake that long and makes an appointment for evaluation the following morning. She sends the client home with her father instructing them to come back in the morning and for the father to keep an eye on his daughter. She does not call you back and inform you of her actions. You do not follow up with her and confirm her actions. During the night, the daughter manages to kill herself. The father sues the agency for malpractice. Which statement best described the liability of the professionals involved?

A) The supervisor bears primary responsibility
B) The intake worker bears primary responsibility
C) The Agency bears primary responsibility
D) The Agency, the intake worker and the professional all bear equal responsibility.

Answer on Page: 141

Question 160   Section: Ethical

In becoming a professional social worker, one marries the NASW Code of Ethics. One of your ethical commitments that is implicit in the NASW Code of Ethics is ...

A) Your obligation to the client trumps your obligation to your employer.
B) Your representation of your client trumps your obligation over society as a whole.
C) Your representation of your client is subordinate to your obligation over other aggrieved individuals.
D) mobilization of clients is secondary to social work advocacy.

Answer on Page: 142

Question 161   Section: Clinical

You have been seeing a patient with depression for several weeks. The patient has not made any direct statements about suicide. They are beginning to show some signs of recovery from their depressive symptoms. Your level of concern about their potential to commit suicide should…

A) Increase
B) Decrease
C) Remain the same
D) Decrease if the client is medicated with an SSRI

Answer on Page: 143

Question 162   Section: Clinical

You are working with a male patient, age 48, who is diagnosed with a Bipolar Disorder. While no direct statements are made, the client shows various signs that would suggest they are contemplating suicide. Your best intervention is to...

A) complete a family genogram and an eco-map in order to determine familial history and support systems.
B) Complete collateral interviews with spouse and possible adult children to determine the extent of the effect of the bipolar disorder.
C) Avoid discussing suicide because people who are not actively contemplating it will be more likely to think about it if you, as the therapist, discuss it.
D) Address your concerns honestly and frankly. Begin a dialogue regarding suicide and your concerns and feelings aboutthe "signs" they are showing.

Answer on Page: 144

Question 163   Section: Clinical-Diagnostic

You have been asked to evaluate a 43 year old female with a long history of chronic alcoholism. You get some history from the family member who brought her to the appointment. She has been battling alcoholism since age 16 and has had long periods of time when she was homeless and her whereabouts were unknown. She presents with short-term memory loss. She compensates for this loss by confabulating (a natural process where she invents memories in order to fill in the blanks caused by the memory loss) and also displays anosognosia (a marked lack of insight or awareness of her current condition). She appears apathetic, confused and often disoriented. The most likely diagnosis is...

A) Korsakoff's syndrome
B) Tardive dyskinesia
C) psychogenic amnesia
D) Alzheimer's disease

Answer on Page: 145

Question 164   Section: Clinical

You have received a referral to work with a male client with schizophrenia. The referral reports problems with reality testing and medication compliance. Which or the following strategies should you NOT worry about when dealing with this client.

A) maintaining present levels of functioning
B) resolving internal psychological conflicts.
C) reorienting patients to present reality.
D) modifying adaptive behavior

Answer on Page: 147

Question 165   Section: Clinical

You are seeing a 23 year old female client who appears rather manipulative. She lives at home with her mother and father and does not work or attend school. She makes the following statement during your second session, "If you really cared about me like my mother cares, you would not charge me for treatment." The client has just performed a ....

A) Displacement reaction
B) counter-transference reaction
C) transference reaction.
D) sublimation experience.

Answer on Page: 148

Question 166   Section: Clinical

You are working with a mother and father who have an 8 year old male child. During the first family session you notice the child does not seem very expressive. Each time the child begins to express emotions the parents jump in and squash it. Twice while describing an incident at school the child becomes emotional and then parents tell him "get control of yourself" and "boys don't whine." With this type of parenting you would expect to see which of the following symptoms currently?

A) high anxiety levels.
B) eating disorders.
C) psychomotor problems.
D) acting-out behavior and somatization

Answer on Page: 149

Question 167   Section: Clinical

You have received a referral for Mr. Candor, a mid-forties married white male with an alcoholic wife who has just been hospitalized after an 11 day drinking binge where she had at least one blackout. In order to cope with his wife's problem drinking, he has read several popular books on the subject and consulted with his medical doctor who is NOT a substance abuse specialist. He also has acquired a book on abnormal psychology and reads it avidly. He admits when his wife is sober, he reads portions of the book that deal with personality disorders and eccentricity out loud to her. He is concerned that his wife is trying to get him to "rescue her" and is being "dependent." Your initial steps in therapy would involve...

A) Support his approach as a clear way to understand his wife
B) explore his feelings about his wife and her possible
   "dependency on him"
C) Assume his behavior is a defense mechanism which will
   pass as soon as he accepts his wife's illness
D) work with him to understand his approach is overly
   intellectual and probably will bear little fruit.

Answer on Page: 150

Question 168   Section: Clinical

As a generalization regarding clients who suffer from drug or alcohol addiction, which of the following statements regarding POOR TREATMENT PROGNOSIS is the MOST accurate?

A) When they suffer from a concurrent anxiety disorder
B) When they are homeless or unemployed
C) When they are over 50 years old
D) When they are also diagnosed with a Borderline Personality Disorder

Answer on Page: 151

Question 169   **Section: Clinical**

Substance Abuse programs that use cognitive behavioral treatment programs have as their major goal…

A) reducing the need for illegal drugs.
B) changing the cognitive and behavioral processes that lead to drug use
C) altering the drug-abusers' emotional need for mood altering drugs
D) offering alternative and less dangerous medications in place of illegal substances

Answer on Page: 152

Question 170   **Section: Clinical**

Of the four common groups of medications taken by the population generally seen in a mental health center, the Selective Serotonin Reuptake Inhibitors (SSRI), The Tricyclic Antidepressants (TCA.s), The monoamine oxidase inhibitors (MAOI's) and the Atypical Antipsychotics . Which of these drugs have the greatest chance of being lethal in a drug overdose?

A) SSRI's
B) MAOI's
C) TCA's
D) Atypicals

Answer on Page: 153

Question 171　　　　　　**Section: Psychotherapy**

You have just accepted an intake for a court ordered client. When you work with court-ordered clients, often the most difficult issue you will address during the early phases of treatment will be:

A) Your feelings about the crime that brought the client into your office
B) Your client's attempts at manipulation
C) The lack of help available to your client in his community
D) The anger your client feels towards being ordered into treatment.

Answer on Page: 154

Question 172　　　　　　**Section: Ethics**

You are working with a client in a hospital setting. They indicate that want to run down to the cafeteria and get themselves a cup of coffee and asks you if they can get you a cup of coffee as well. The BEST thing to do is to...

A) Decline the coffee but thank the client for their thoughtfulness.
B) Accept the offer because it is "just a cup of coffee" and it is a token gesture of respect.
C) Decline the offer but offer to walk down to the cafeteria with the client and get your own cup of coffee.
D) Accept their invitation but offer to pay for your coffee.

Answer on Page: 155

Question 173　　　　　　**Section: Ethics**

You have been seeing a client and started the relationship with a standard informed consent document. There are very few times in the relationship when you can break confidentiality and disclose confidential information about the client without obtaining the informed consent of the client. The BEST answer is...

A) the client's lawyer
B) the client's spouse
C) a law enforcement authority
D) your spouse

Answer on Page: 156

Question 174   **Section: Ethics**

You were seeing a client up until 6 months ago and therapy was successfully terminated. You run into the client and learn they are a gardener and you need gardening work done at your house. You decide to hire them as a gardener. Which of the following BEST describes the situation?

A) You may hire the ex-client as long as you have a clearly written contract explaining duties and expectations.
B) You may hire the client as long as you do not feel the relationship is exploitive.
C) The relationship will be considered a dual relationship but may be acceptable as long as personal issues are not discussed.
D) The relation is considered a dual relationship and is therefore not acceptable under the social worker code of ethics.

Answer on Page: 157

Question 175   **Section: Psychotherapy**

You have received a referral from intake for a family referred for family therapy. After reviewing the file, you focus on one specific "constellation of facts" discovered during the intake. Because of this specific "constellation" of information you decide the family is not appropriate for family therapy and you refer them back for individual sessions. Which is the BEST answer to justify your decision that family therapy would be ineffective with these clients?

A) interpersonal boundaries are routinely violated.
B) family dynamics indicate that members are deceitful and deliberately destructive.
C) the family has an overt pattern of secret-keeping.
D) two of the family members have no desire of intent to cooperate with therapy.

Answer on Page:158

Question 176   **Section: Psychotherapy**

Incest and family dynamics have several commonalities. You are evaluating a family who has been referred for possible incest issues. After the evaluation, you have identified several interaction styles and familial roles which cause you concern. Which of the following family characteristics, would be the BEST indicator incest occurring:

A) serious enmeshment in family relationships with highly stylized roles.
B) attitudes of permissiveness regarding sexuality.
C) permeable boundaries and extreme chaos.
D) Relationships that are high in conflict.

Answer on Page: 160

Question 177   **Section: Psychotherapy**

You have been asked to evaluate a 50 year old female who has spent the last twenty years as a top performer in an advertising firm. Her income was in the six-figures range and she ran an entire department of junior executives. Five month ago, she was released from her contract when the advertising agency was bought out by an international firm. She was told she was no longer in touch with the current market. Multiple networking contacts have left her with no leads. She relates that during the last three months her drinking, which she never considered a problem, has become an issue. She states she spends entire days in her pajamas and sometimes will not leave the house for three or four days in a row. She states she has begun to drink heavily. She stated that in the past two months she has begun hearing voices which tell her she is worthless and stupid. She stated she has never heard these before but she has discovered that drinking more makes the voices go away. The BEST diagnosis for the client is ...

A) 311 Depressive Disorder NOS
B) 296.22 Major Depressive Disorder, Single Episode
C) 296.24 Major Depressive Disorder with Psychotic Features
D) 291.8 Alcohol Induced Mood Disorder

Answer on Page: 161

Question 178   **Section: Psychotherapy**

Children reared in family environments in which parents or other family members abuse or are dependent on alcohol or other substances are likely to be at higher risk for

A) serious physical mobility problems.

B) schizophrenia and bipolar disorders

C) social anxiety and panic attacks

D) neglect, physical or sexual abuse and behavioral problems.

Answer on Page: 164

Question 179   Section: Psychotherapy

You are seeing John, a 20 year old client diagnosed with an anxiety disorder and an alcohol use disorder. Because the anxiety is a mental health issue and the alcohol use is a substance abuse issue, this client is said to have a...

A) Primary Axis II Diagnosis

B) Dual Diagnosis

C) Multi-axial Diagnosis

D) non-axial Diagnosis

Answer on Page: 165

Question 180   Section: Diagnosis and Assessment.

You have been asked to assess a five-year-old child. You have decided to administer the "Draw-a-Person" test in order to help understand a specific dimension of the child's functioning. The BEST reason to administer the test is to determine...

A) Child's gross and fine motor functioning

B) Basic Personality structures

C) Abnormal or pathological thought structures

D) Level of cognitive development/self-image.

Answer on Page: 165

Question 181   Section: Psychotherapy

You are a supervisor at a crisis counseling center. One of your social workers approaches you and reports the following symptoms. She states she is frustrated, overwhelmed and feels like she is drowning in the endless stream of complaints she has to field from her clients. She feels she has almost no energy and cannot cope with the different clients on her caseload. You recognize the social worker is suffering classic symptoms of...

A) Counter-transference
B) Depression
C) Projection
D) Stress/Compassion fatigue

Answer on Page: 167

Question 182   Section: Psychotherapy

There are many different theories for intervention with a variety of clients. Each different theory focuses on listening to a different aspect of a client's life story. If a therapist listens attentively to understand the issues involved in their client's life currently and does not focus on how the issues of gender and race play into the client's story, It is MOST likely the therapist is using a/an _____ approach.

A) Rogerian person-centered
B) The cognitive behavioral
C) psychodynamic
D) multicultural

Answer on Page: 168

Question 183   **Section: Behavior**

You have been engaged in a supervision session with a less experienced social worker. He asks the following question. Of the four following childhood behaviors, which is more common among boys than girls, you know the BEST answer is…

A) Acting out sexually
B) Aggression
C) Running away
D) Wetting the bed (Enuresis)

Answer on Page: 170

Question 184   **Section: Behavior**

You have been assigned a client who has been diagnosed with a conduct disorder 312.XX. You know this disorder is characterized by the following behavioral set:
A repetitive and persistent pattern of behavior in which the basic rights of others or major age-appropriate societal norms or rules are violated. The disturbance in behavior causes clinically significant impairment in social, academic, or occupational functioning:
Of the following specific behaviors, the client must display three of more within the past 12 months and at least one in the past 6 months. (1) often bullies, threatens, or intimidates others (2) often initiates physical fights (3) has used a weapon that can cause serious physical harm to others (e.g., a bat, brick, broken bottle, knife, gun) (4) has been physically cruel to people (5) has been physically cruel to animals (6) has stolen while confronting a victim (e.g., mugging, purse snatching, extortion, armed robbery) (7) has forced someone into sexual activity (8) has deliberately engaged in fire setting with the intention of

causing serious damage (9) has deliberately destroyed others' property (other than by fire setting) (10) has broken into someone else's house, building, or car (11) often lies to obtain goods or favors or to avoid obligations (i.e., "cons" others) (12) has stolen items of nontrivial value without confronting a victim (e.g., shoplifting, but without breaking and entering; forgery) (13) often stays out at night despite parental prohibitions, beginning before age 13 years (14) has run away from home overnight at least twice while living in parental or parental surrogate home (or once without returning for a lengthy period) (15) is often truant from school, beginning before age 13 years.

According to Sigmund Freud and psychoanalytic theory, the client MOST LIKELY lacks which of the following structures...

A) Ego functioning
B) Structured family system
C) Superego functioning
D) An Authoritative Figure

Answer on Page: 170

.

Question 185   **Section: Diagnosis**

You have just received a referral for assessment. The mother has just brought her eight year old boy into your office. She is stating that two days ago she found her eight -year-old son in a walk-in closet with a neighborhood child. The door to the walking closet was closed and both children were naked. She has no other information she can give you. She is extremely worried. Your BEST response would be to...

A) Assess the child for oppositional defiant disorder
B) Assess the child for a conduct disorder.
C) Assess the child for attention deficit hyperactivity disorder.

D) Assess the child for possible sexual abuse victimization.

Answer on Page: 171

Question 186 Section: Psychotherapy

You are completing the first session with a women recently separated from her significant other after 7 years of co-habitation which she was hoping would culminate in marriage. She has been separated for 6 weeks and she has met "the man of her dreams." She can't stop thinking about him or talking about him to her friends. You realize she is using a common ego defense mechanism. The ego defense mechanism BEST describing her situation is ...

A) Distortion
B) Projection
C) Displacement
D) Intellectualization

Answer on Page: 172

Question 187 Section: Psychotherapy

With the publication of his work, Gestalt Therapy Verbatim, Fritz Perls, MD became the most visible and leading proponent of Gestalt Therapy. This therapeutic system views a patient with unexpressed guilt as...

A) Dysfunctional
B) Normal
C) Neurotic
D) Having unfinished business

Answer on Page: 173

Question 188 **Section: Psychotherapy**

You are assessing a 21 year old male client whose father is in prison with a release date 10 years from now. The client's mother was killed in a single car accident and he believes she committed suicide. You have no other information in the crash. He has been raised by his father's sister and her husband. He has not completed high school due to excessive absences and has failed the GED twice. You have received the referral due to variety of issues with both teachers and other students in his GED classes. His reported problems include a pattern of deceitful behavior (which was verified by his aunt) which included repeated 1) lying and attempts to dupe others into activities or behaviors for his personal profit, 2) a failure to plan ahead, 3) an instance where he threw a rock through the window of a garage adjacent to school property and an 4) overall lack of remorse regarding his various behaviors which negatively affect and impact others in his life and 5) the use of aliases in order to steal mail order products. The BEST possible diagnosis would be

A) Conduct Disorder
B) Oppositional Defiant Disorder
C) Narcissistic Personality Disorder
D) Antisocial Personality Disorder

Answer on Page: 175

Question 189 **Section: Psychotherapy**

** A cognitive bias is a pattern of "deviation in judgment" often brought out by a particular situation. It is very easy to allow a cognitive bias to affect your perception.

In the following, you have just received a case and are reading the client's previous file. You realize they have had three admissions during the past two years. In two of the admissions they were diagnosed with Bipolar Disorder NOS and in the third, a Major Depressive Disorder. You decide that they are coming into see you for issues relating to their bipolar diagnosis in order to keep them from needing a re-hospitalization. It is very possible, with that decision, that you have just committed a cognitive bias which will interfere with what you can do to assist them. The BEST description of the cognitive bias you may have used is…

A) Anchoring bias
B) Attentional Bias
C) Bandwagon Bias
D) Bias blind spot

Answer on Page: 179

Question 190   **Section: Psychotherapy**

** A cognitive bias is a pattern of "deviation in judgment" often brought out by a particular situation. It is very easy to allow a cognitive bias to affect your perception.

In the following, you have started an admission on a 38 year old female client who was referred to you because of problems in her marriage. She has stated that she has "caught" her husband in 3 extra-marital affairs over the past 18 years and she thinks there are more. She relates that she is often harshly critical of him and that he has recently "moved onto the couch of a male co-worker" because he does not want to come home anymore. When discussing issues related to separation and possible divorce, she becomes adamant that they will "work things out" and the marriage is strong and will continue. She is utilizing a cognitive bias to cope with her fear of future actions. The BEST description of the cognitive bias she is using is...

A) Negativity bias
B) Neglect of probability
C) Normalcy bias
D) Omission bias

Answer on Page: 180

Question 191   **Section: Diagnosis**

The DSM IV TR lists a series of diagnoses which can only be used with children under the age of 18 or which can be given to a child prior to the age of 18. Of the following disorders, which CAN NOT be applied during childhood (Less than 18 years of age)?

A) 299.10 Childhood Disintegrative Disorder
B) 299.00 Autistic Disorder
C) 307.3 Stereotypic Movement Disorder
D) 301.7 Antisocial Personality Disorder

Answer on Page: 180

Question 192   **Section: Diagnosis**

You know the Diagnostic and Statistical Manual uses a Multi-axial system for diagnosis. Axis I is for issues of Major Clinical concern, and Axis II are for personality disorders and mental retardation. Using this system, what information is coded on Axis V...

A) Social Functioning and Assessment

B) Provisional Diagnoses
C) Global Assessment of Functioning
D) None of the Above

Answer on Page: 185

Question 193   Section: Diagnosis

Psychoanalytic theory postulates there are three major
functioning portions of the personality (consciousness). Each
portion has specific duties and acts within specific arenas to
help the client function productively.   The personality portion
which assists the individual in working through the
consequences of their behavior and helps them weigh
outcome measures and costs is known as the …

A) EGO
B) SUPEREGO
C) ID
D) LIBIDO

Answer on Page: 187

Question 194   Section: Diagnosis

The Diagnostic and Statistical Manual of Mental Disorders
(DSM) is used in the United States. All other countries use the
International Classification of Diseases Volume 10 (ICD-10).
The primary purpose of the DSM in our work as clinical social
workers is in…

A) locating the best approach to treatment
B) mapping the etiology of a disorder
C) evaluating a prior diagnosis.
D) Assessing the client

Answer on Page: 190

Question 195   Section: Diagnosis

You are working with a client who has a full scale IQ (FSIQ) of approximately 40. Your BEST diagnosis on Axis II would be that of...

A) Borderline Intellectual Functioning
B) Autism
C) Mild Mental Retardation
D) Moderate Mental Retardation

Answer on Page: 190

Question 196   Section: Diagnosis

You have begun working with a child who has been diagnosed with a conduct disorder. You interpret the world according to Freudian psychoanalytic principles. According to Freud's principles, this child is manifesting a conduct disorder because they **MOST LIKELY** lack;

A) Ego functioning
B) Superego functioning
C) An Authoritarian parent
D) a rigid family structure

Answer on Page: 191

Question 197   Section: Diagnosis

You have a referral on a child who is described as "latency aged". Without looking at the chart, you know the child is between the ages of...

A) Birth to 1 year
B) 1-3 years old.
C) 6-12 years old.
D) 3-6 years old.

Answer on Page: 192

Question 198   **Section: Ethics**

You have been seeing a client for 11 sessions and have been addressing issues including anger, aggression, and impulse control particularly regarding the relationships of people close to him. During a session where you are providing him with psychoeducation concerning aggression as a behavior which is under his voluntary control, he becomes hostile, gets up and leaves. About 4 weeks later you receive a letter from him stating he has started seeing another therapist and you need to release his entire record to him immediately, so he can give it to his new social worker. You believe there is the possibility of serious harm if the record is released to him. You contact him and explain you can release a case summary to the new therapist; however, you cannot release the file to him. He threatens legal action if he does not get the file immediately. In order to keep from committing an ethical violation, you should do which of the following FIRST?

A) Contact an attorney
B) Document the request by the patient and include the reason for non-release
C) Refuse to release the information.
D) Document your concerns about release and then provide the   records to the client.

Answer on Page: 193

Question 199   **Section: Diagnosis**

As an emergency room social worker, you are asked to evaluate an emergency admission. The client is a 46 year old African-American retired soldier who has served three tours in the Middle East in combat. His wife is reporting she called police because her husband and she were watching a television show when a commercial showed a series of explosions. He became very agitated, began shaking uncontrollably and crawled behind his chair and refused to come out. Your MOST LIKELY diagnosis would be...

A) Psychotic Break
B) Acute Panic Attack
C) Adjustment Disorder with mixed emotional features
D) Post Traumatic Stress Disorder

Answer on Page: 194

Question 200   **Section: Assessment**

You HAVE been asked to assess a Hispanic client. During the initial portion of the interview, you realize they are not very proficient in English. You begin to explain confidentiality for informed consent and the client appears to be getting upset and seems very frustrated. Your next BEST action would be to ...

A) Give the client your agency's written policy on client confidentiality
B) Ask them why that are getting angry and frustrated
C) Ask the client to tell you, in their own words, what they heard you say and want they understood.

D) Refer the client to a social worker who is fluent in Spanish.

Answer on Page:198

ANSWERS

Question 101   Section: Psychotherapy

The correct answer is C
Part of the mandate of social work is to meet a client "where they are at." In this case the clients are in crisis. As all parents do, these parents have goals and aspirations for their children and have probably plotted out a "life-story" for their child, including the 'son-in-law' and the 'grandchildren'. This life script is about to be shattered. On some level they are wondering how they are going to be able to share a Thanksgiving dinner in the future with their daughter and her 'wife'. Help them through their despair and disappointment and then provide them access to a support group. They need to build a new future story for their family, and interacting with other parents who have done this task will ultimately be very helpful.

A is INCORRECT
Conversion therapy, sometimes called reparative therapy or reorientation therapy, is one type of sexual orientation change effort that attempts to change the sexual orientation of a person from homosexual or bisexual to heterosexual. These types of therapies have been a source of intense controversy in the United States and other countries. The American Psychiatric Association states that political and moral debates over the integration of gays and lesbians into the mainstream of American society have obscured scientific data about changing sexual orientation "by calling into question the motives and even the character of individuals on both sides of the issue." The most high-profile contemporary advocates of conversion therapy tend to be conservative Christian groups and other religious organizations. The main organization advocating secular forms of conversion therapy is the National Association for Research & Therapy of Homosexuality (NARTH), however, NARTH often partners with religious groups.

The American Psychological Association defines conversion therapy as therapy aimed at changing sexual orientation. The American Psychiatric Association states that conversion therapy is a type of psychiatric treatment "based upon the assumption that homosexuality per se is a mental disorder or based upon the a priori assumption that a patient should change his/her sexual homosexual orientation." Psychologist Douglas Haldeman writes that conversion therapy comprises efforts by mental health professionals and pastoral care providers to convert lesbians and gay men to heterosexuality by techniques including aversive treatments, such as "the application of electric shock to the hands and/or genitals," and "nausea-inducing drugs...administered simultaneously with the presentation of homoerotic stimuli," masturbatory reconditioning, visualization, social skills training, psychoanalytic therapy, and spiritual interventions, such as "prayer and group support and pressure."

Mainstream American medical and scientific organizations have expressed concern over conversion therapy and consider it potentially harmful. The advancement of conversion therapy may cause social harm by disseminating inaccurate views about sexual orientation. The ethics guidelines of major mental health organizations in the United States vary from cautionary statements to recommendations that ethical practitioners refrain from practicing conversion therapy (American Psychiatric Association) or from referring patients to those who do (American Counseling Association).

Reference: *http://en.wikipedia.org/wiki/Conversion_therapy*

B is INCORRECT

Nowhere in the vignette does it state that the girl has problems with her orientation. It appears that she is comfortable and assured. The problem here is with the feelings, aspiration and views of the family.

D is INCORRECT
While every client could ultimately benefit by education, in this situation the primary focus needs to be on alleviating the fear and anxiety caused by their daughter's revelation.

Question 102   **Section: Psychotherapy**

The correct answer is D
Pica is a condition we know little about. Symptoms must occur for at least one month. There is no clear treatment or prognosis. Sometimes Pica lasts for several months and then stops on its own and other times it persists for a lifetime.

Further information:
Pica is a pattern of eating non-food materials (such as dirt or paper).

Causes, incidence, and risk factors
Pica is seen more in young children than adults. Between 10 and 32% of children ages 1 - 6 have these behaviors.

Pica can occur during pregnancy. In some cases, conditions due to a lack of certain nutrients, such as iron deficiency anemia and zinc deficiency, may trigger the unusual cravings. Pica may also occur in adults who crave a certain texture in their mouth.

Symptoms
Children and adults with pica may eat:
Animal feces – Clay – Dirt – Hairballs – Ice – Paint – Sand

This pattern of eating should last at least 1 month to fit the diagnosis of pica.

Signs and tests
There is no single test that confirms pica. However, because pica can occur in people who have lower than normal nutrient levels and poor nutrition (malnutrition), the health care provider should test blood levels of iron and zinc.

Blood tests can also be done to test for anemia. Lead levels should always be checked in children who may have eaten paint or objects covered in lead-paint dust to screen for lead poisoning.

The health care provider should test for infection if the person has been eating contaminated soil or animal waste.

Treatment
Treatment should first address any missing nutrients or other medical problems, such as lead exposure. Treatment involves behavioral, environmental, and family educational approaches. Other successful treatments include associating the pica behavior with bad consequences or punishment (mild aversion therapy) followed by positive reinforcement for eating the right foods.

Medications may help reduce the abnormal eating behavior, if pica occurs as part of a developmental disorder such as mental retardation.

Expectations (prognosis)
Treatment success varies. In many cases, the disorder lasts several months, then disappears on its own. In some cases, it may continue into the teen years or adulthood, especially when it occurs with developmental disorders.

Complications

- *Bezoar (a mass of indigestible material trapped inside the body, usually in the stomach)*
- *Infection*
- *Intestinal obstruction*
- *Lead poisoning*
- *Malnutrition*

Prevention
There is no specific prevention. Getting enough nutrition may help.

References
1. Boris NW, Dalton R. Vegetative disorders. In: Kliegman RM, Behrman RE, Jenson HB, Stanton BF, eds. Nelson Textbook of Pediatrics. 18th ed. Philadelphia, Pa: Saunders Elsevier; 2007:chap 22.
2. Brittenham GM. Disorders of iron metabolism: Iron deficiency and iron overload. In: Hoffman R, Benz EJ, Shattil SS, et al, eds.Hematology: Basic Principles and Practice. 5th ed. Philadelphia, Pa: Elsevier Churchill Livingstone; 2008:chap 36.
Review Date: 2/28/2010.

Question 103   Section: Psychotherapy

The correct answer is B
Jayne could clearly benefit from individual therapy in order to examine her choices and to become aware of their consequences. She will also need help in coping with the effects her parents' divorce had on her and the current pressure it puts on her. Remember, the yelling began at age 12 and a half, just when she was starting into the Erickson Stage of Identity vs. Role Confusion. Up to that point in time she

[78]

perceived her family live as stable, but just as she begins to enter a very difficult stage of development, her family life crumbles and she not only has to wrestle with "How am I different from my parents?" and "who am I?", but she has to do it with the foundation of her world split in two.

The parent also need help to keep themselves from doing even more damage to Jayne. They need to understand that their new situation (divorce) is their "normal" situation and they need help in understanding how to cope with their new situation as well as strategies for healing and rebuilding their lives.

A is INCORRECT
This approach would probably help Jayne in the long run, as her current peer group appears to be Detention Center Bound, but it does nothing to address the needs of the parents or multi-family unit.

C is INCORRECT
Continuing Individual therapy = YES; Telling the Parents is a stage she will grow out of = NO. Our society takes illegal drug use very seriously. A conviction can bar a child from entering college and certain Felony Drug Charges make a person unable to get Federal Financial Aid for college. Also Prior drug arrests will limit the choices of the child in employment and career goals including Military Service in most branches. Drug use can have a devastating effect on a child's future plans.

D is INCORRECT
I am all for using the resources offered by your Church, Synagogue, Mosque, or Temple, however, the standard bias that "these kids behavior better" is unproven, and this answer does not address the needs of the family. Once you achieve progress on other goals, this would be a rather good choice.

Question 104 **Section: ETHICS**

The correct answer is B

Because it is a first session and you do not know the client, it is important you make safety your first concern. You do not know if they will show up alone or with other people, you do not know there mental state and you do not know if there are other aspects of their live that could harm the counseling relationship. The first aspect of the question touches upon the possibility of rape or sexual violence, however, the question does not address the sex of the client. Even if it was a male social worker and the client were a female, there would be no way to dispute a charge of sexually inappropriate behavior made by the client if no one was there. Another possibility: what if the client was a female and domestic violence survivor and was stalked by her ex-partner. You could get injured or killed in an altercation.

A is INCORRECT

While you may find a sympathetic co-worker, you really need to complete initial assessments in a place and at a time when the entire staff is there. It is the most violate part of the therapeutic process and the time when you know the least about the client.

C is INCORRECT

Always think about your safety. One of the ways you become an experienced and well-seasoned social worker is to remain alive. Death and severe injury generally limit your career.

D is INCORRECT

This is a HIPAA violation and can get you sued, reprimanded, fired and have your license revoked.

Question 105 **Section: ETHICS**

The correct answer is D
{Test Strategy: You must answer the questions with ONLY the information given.} Without a release or specific permission, you can not acknowledge that Margaret is your client, let alone appointment times and other information regarding the sessions. A polite but firm, "I can neither confirm nor deny that the person you are calling about is a client. I am sorry I cannot be of assistance to you." usually does the trick. If they keep asking, keep repeating this phrase until they hang up.

HINT: early in my career I worked on a locked, psychiatric facility that functioned as a multi-county intake for indigent psychiatric clients. We had this simple message types out and posted above the phone. We were instructed to simply repeat the message until the caller 'got the point.' It worked!

A is INCORRECT
You have just breached confidentiality. Now the caller, who may or may not be the husband knows Margaret is receiving mental health services, but also knows when and where she will be. If he is a stalker, or dangerous, you have placed both yourself and your client in danger.

B is INCORRECT
You have just acknowledged Margaret as your client and let 'someone' know she is receiving mental health services.

C is INCORRECT
See the answer for A!

Question 106 **Section: CLINICAL**

The correct answer is C
Alopecia - means loss of hair from the head or body. Think BALDNESS. While not a psychotic symptoms, men suffering from this often act in ways that seem psychotic (smile) in order to keep their hair.

A is INCORRECT
DELUSIONS ARE a symptom of psychosis! They are a false belief that cannot be explained by the client's culture, education or past experience.

B is INCORRECT
NEGATIVE SYMPTOMS are a symptom of psychosis! They include a marked reduction in fluency of speech and a loss of the will to do things. (Known as AVOLITION)

D is INCORRECT
DISORGANIZED SPEECH is a symptom of psychosis! This includes speech where the mental associations are governed by puns, rhymes, and other rules that the listener does not know. In order to be considered disorganized speech, it must significantly interfere with communication.

Question 107 **Section: CLINICAL**

The Correct answer is D
Negative symptoms are deficits of normal emotional responses or of other thought processes, and respond less well to medication. They commonly include flat or blunted affect and emotion, poverty of speech (alogia), inability to experience pleasure (anhedonia), lack of desire to form relationships (asociality), and lack of motivation (avolition). Research suggests that negative symptoms contribute more to poor

quality of life, functional disability, and the burden on others than do positive symptoms. People with prominent negative symptoms often have a history of poor adjustment before the onset of illness, and response to medication is often limited.

Ref: http://en.wikipedia.org/wiki/Schizophrenia

A is INCORRECT
It is only one of a number of NEGATIVE SYMPTOMS.

B is INCORRECT
It is only one of a number of NEGATIVE SYMPTOMS.

C is INCORRECT
It is only one of a number of NEGATIVE SYMPTOMS.

Question 108   Section: CLINICAL

The correct answer is D
A bizarre delusion is something that is so far from usual life experiences that if told to most people, they would not understand it and would probably regard the event to have been unlikely to occur.

A is INCORRECT
Disorganized thought can be seen in certain subtypes of schizophrenia. An example would be, "thought blocking". When a person stops abruptly in the middle of a thought, then states the feel the thought has been taken or plucked out of their head, and then start making up unintelligible words.

B is INCORRECT
A False Belief is often bizarre and unusual, however, the power to which one holds onto a false belief is much less than the power to which someone clings to a delusion. A false belief

may be able to be shaken, but a delusion will persist, sometimes even after the client is stabilized on medication.

"ELVIS is ALIVE and living in Newark NJ!" is an example of a false belief.

C is INCORRECT
A Hallucination is a false perception in the absence of any sensory stimulus that is related to the event. If someone is sitting next to you at STARBUCKS and you perceive them as an alien invader, you are DELUSIONAL. If NOONE is sitting next to you at STARBUCKS and you perceive an alien invader there, you are HALLUCINATING.

Question 109   Section: CLINICAL

The correct answer is D
Unless the employment history specifically deals with a precipitating factor of the illness it is probably irrelevant. Now, it is quite possible that an event that occurred in the employment arena was a PRECIPITATING FACTOR, but the employment story as a whole is not a direct factor.

A is INCORRECT
Because duration of symptoms is EXTREMELY IMPORTANT in diagnosing issues. Length of time of current episodes and previous episodes are major markers for diagnosis. If duration of illness is less than six months (in general) it is more likely to be a non-chronic condition, but a duration longer than six months tends to be a indicate more chronic conditions. NOTE: Please DO NOT diagnosis someone as schizophrenic with less than six months data or observation. It causes concern and confusion to the therapist that follows you. Be conservative! A Brief Psychotic Reaction or a Reactive Psychosis is more reasonable than schizophrenia.

B is INCORRECT
Precipitating Factors are EXTREMELY IMPORTANT in diagnosis. Emotion distress, severe stress, chronic medical conditions, postpartum depression, and drug use can all look like PSYCHOSIS. Remember, sometimes a brief reactive psychosis is occasionally very function at dealing with serious issues and in allowing the client to "Save themselves" when all other tools fail.

C is INCORRECT
Premorbid Personality is EXTREMELY IMPORTANT to diagnosis. People who are happy, pleasant and optimistic and then experience a psychotic reaction would lead you along a different path of inquiry than someone who is depressed, sad and hostile. It is good to remember that all behavior is functional on some level.

Question 110 Section: CLINICAL

The correct answer is C
Family Illness is not an exclusion for schizophrenia

A is INCORRECT
Symptoms of Psychosis can be mimicked. Abuse of street drugs including cocaine, alcohol, stimulants can cause symptoms of psychosis. Some prescription medicines including adreno-corticosteroids can produce symptoms of psychosis.

B is INCORRECT
Mood disorders can often mimic psychosis or can move a person into a psychotic state. Extreme depression, mania, manic episodes can all cause psychotic-like symptoms.

D is INCORECT

Certain medical conditions can cause PSYCHOSIS. These include hypothyroidism and LUPUS. Always rule out possible medical causes before making a diagnosis.

Question 111   **Section: CLINICAL**

The correct answer is D

A is INCORRECT (When Chosen ALONE)
We know that schizophrenia has a familial component. It tends to run in families. This may indicate a genetic linkage, but the problem is far too complex, and our knowledge of genetic expression is far too meager to fully understand it. If a close relative (Mother, Father, sister, brother) the risk of schizophrenia increases markedly. A less close relative (Uncle, cousin, nephew, niece) and the risk is higher than normal, but not as elevated as a close relative risk.

B is INCORRECT (When Chosen ALONE)
If a client has a history of positive response to lithium in their past, it is most likely the psychotic state is due to a mood disorder, and not schizophrenia.

C is INCORRECT (When Chosen Alone)
Onset of schizophrenia occurs as early as mid teen and on into the middle 20's. It is rather rare for it to develop later in life. If onset of illness is after age 40, you should be looking at a mood disorder or a delusional disorder. Remember, this is only a guideline, schizophrenia can manifest itself in the later years.

Question 112   **Section: CLINICAL**

The correct answer is C
Schizophrenia affects about 1% of the adult population. Adequate treatment almost always requires neuroleptic

medications which can have very severe side effects, including Tardive Dyskinesia, and usually must be taken for the rest of a patient's life, or symptoms will return.

A is INCORRECT

5% is too high a figure. The CHRONICITY of Schizophrenia (How chronic it is) tends to be lifelong. Once symptoms starts, it is very likely that the person will continue to have symptoms of the disorder for the rest of their life, which will need to be controlled with medications.

B is INCORRECT

5% is too high a figure. However, the second half of this answer is accurate, symptoms tend to be lifelong. (High CHRONICITY)

D is INCORRECT

While the percentage is correct, the impact on social and work function is usually profound. The disorder is lifelong, usually requires medication, symptoms can re-occur and adjustment can be extremely difficult for the patient.

Question 113   Section: CLINICAL

The correct answer is B

Distractibility and disorientation which causes or contributes to material impairment of work, social interactions, studying, or the ability to provide self-care all fall under the rubric of COGNITIVE DYSFUNCTION.

A is INCORRECT

Often the patient with schizophrenia will not believe they are ill and will refuse to accept medications. This inability to accept their condition and accept the changes that will occur due to their condition often lead to major problems.

C is INCORRECT
Dysphoria is a more global term used to cover anxiety, anger, disgust, depression and any other negative emotional set a client presents with.

D is INCORRECT
All three are symptoms of schizophrenia.

Question 114   Section: CLINICAL

The correct answer is D
Residual Schizophrenia is used to diagnose a person when they have had previous episodes and are currently in a temporary remission. Episodic means they are still prone to full episodes and Interepisode defines the condition of still showing some negative symptoms between episodes.

A is INCORRECT
This set of symptoms defines a Schizophrenic diagnosis that would be described as Catatonic Type. The key points are the catalepsy and marked negative symptoms.

B is INCORRECT
This set of symptoms is too vague to classify and should probably be listed as Schizophrenia, Undifferentiated Type.

C is INCORRECT
This set of symptoms describes Schizophrenia, Disorganized type. The important features being; talk gibberish, neglect their appearance and neglect their hygiene.

Question 115   Section: CLINICAL

The correct answer is D
All of the answers are correct. No particular social class or race is affected more by mood disorders or is shielded from the affects of mood disorders. People without a "significant other", or who are single, widowed, divorced show a higher prevalence of mood disorders. While women have a higher rate of mood disorders than men, the occurrence of mood disorders is increasing throughout the general population.

A is INCORRECT (When chosen alone)
Women do have almost twice the rate of mood disorders as men. We need to remember that the data used by the DSM IV was collected primarily in the United States and may not translate well into other countries. My suspicion is that the difference between men and women in this country is related to the different ways men and women are socialized as well as physiological issues.

B is INCORRECT (when chosen alone)
Social class and race do not appear to have a serious impact on the prevalence of mood disorders.

C is INCORRECT (When chosen alone)
Single individuals seem to have more problems with mood disorders than married couples. This could be due to the stress of living alone or is could be that there is no one to notice the beginning of the mood disorder so the disorder becomes worse before help is sought.

Question 116   Section: CLINICAL

The correct answer is B

The diagnosis of mood disorder is very complicated and requires a tremendous amount of information gathered from family, friends, patient, patient records, past hospitalizations and any other information source you can find. If you are going to diagnose a mood disorder, (and do it properly) you should spend hours collecting data, more hours organizing and sifting through the data, create a chart of all the data and then use the diagnostic trees in the back of the DSM IV-TR.

A is INCORRECT
This would be more accurately described as 296.4 Bipolar Disorder I, Most Recent Episode Manic

C is INCORRECT
A person who presented with hypomanic episodes would probably not be diagnoses as a Bipolar Disorder. They may have a mood disorder of unspecified type or you may not have enough information to make a diagnosis.

D is INCORRECT
Probably not! Alcoholism is diagnosed in as many as 30% of Mood Disorders. It is often assumed that alcoholics are self-medicating bipolar disorders. This may be common wisdom, but do not let it lead you away from the data. If you do not have enough information, you need to gather more data.

Question 117   Section: CLINICAL

The correct answer is C
Bipolar I and II are very similar and have almost identical criteria. The distinction between the two deals with the amount of discomfort or disability caused by the "High" phase. In Type II, the High phase never leads to hospitalization and the episodes are more "hypomanic".

A is INCORRECT
Both Types I and Type II have depressive symptoms interspersed among "High" phases.

B is INCORRECT
Both Types I and Type II have depressive symptoms interspersed among "High" phases.

D is INCORRECT
Bipolar Type I is characterized by the overall disability and hurt caused to the client by BOTH the "High" phase and the depressive phase.

Question 118   Section: CLINICAL

The correct answer is A
All six symptoms are classic for a hypomanic episode. The important pieces are: NO psychosis and NO Hospitalization needed. Other symptoms would include if the episode DID NOT markedly interfere with work or social functioning. The final qualifier is the episode is NOT CAUSED by a general medical condition, substance use or reactions to prescription medications.

B is INCORRECT
Mixed Episodes CAUSE psychotic features require hospitalization and markedly impair social, work or personal functioning.

C is INCORRECT
In the Manic Episode the psychotic symptoms are FLORID, which mean they "shine in the night", so to speak. The average person would realize something was wrong even if they did not know them

D is INCORRECT

The criteria for a depressive episode include a period of time of at least 2 weeks where the patient feels depressed (to the point of not being able to enjoy life) and has problems with eating, sleeping, loss of energy, feelings of guilt, trouble concentrating or thoughts about death.

Question 119   Section: CLINICAL

The correct answer is A

All of these features are part of the ATYPICAL Features specifier.

B is INCORRECT

Melancholic Features are specified by symptoms of classic depression. The patient will wake early and feel worse as the day gets later. They lose appetite and weight; they feel guilty and are either agitated or functioning "slowly". When something good happens for them, they do not feel better

C is INCORRECT

Catatonic Features are specified when the client either has excessive motor activity or extreme inactivity. Remember, all catatonic behaviors deal with some type of motor activity.

D is INCORRECT

Postpartum Onset deals with symptoms that occur AFTER the Birth or Miscarriage of a child. (Abortion would be considered a miscarriage for the purpose of this discussion.) The onset of symptoms usually occurs within a month of the incident, but can be delayed.

Question 120   Section: CLINICAL

The correct answer is D

All of these Disorders have depressive and/or manic features that can confuse the clinician who HAS NOT gathered a detailed and extensive history.

A is INCORRECT (When chosen alone)
Vascular Dementia is a Cognitive Disorder. Like Dementia of the Alzheimer's Type, they can be accompanied by delirium, depression, anxiety and extremely altered mood.

B is INCORRECT (When chosen alone)
Of the 10 specific personality disorders, Borderline, Avoidant, Histrionic and Dependent all exhibit signs of altered mood which can be mistaken for other problems if you do not have enough information.

C is INCORRECT (When chosen alone)
Grief and sadness when dealing with the death of a loved one can appear very severe. When evaluating a person who appears to have a mood disorder two or more months after the death of a loved one, it is generally a good idea to find out about the length and depth of the relationship and any other factors surrounding the interactions. People who have been married for 30 or more years should be expected to present with great depression, as do parents who have lost a child.

Question 121   Section: CULTURAL

The correct answer is B
Look at each new client as an opportunity to expand your knowledge and experience. Start with some research on the internet and then try to find other people from the culture and ask questions. Every culture is incredibly complex. Also, when counseling a person with a very different cultural background, do not be afraid to let them know about your lack of knowledge.

As the therapist, you are there to 'guide' the session and allow growth; you are not there to be the omnipotent know-it-all.

A is INCORRECT
The difference between A and B is subtle. Once you start counseling, you can certainly ask the client about aspects of their culture. The portion of counseling that is a combined effort will allow this. But, they are not your social-cultural teacher, they are your client. You need to respect that boundary. The job of learning about their culture falls squarely on your shoulders and not theirs.

C is INCORRECT
Every patient, whether they are from a different culture or not should be a learning experience for you. Indifference in the face of learning will make you a mediocre to bad therapist.

HINT: Once you feel like you know enough, you are probably at your most ignorant and need to redouble your efforts to learn more.

D is INCORRECT
Only do this if there appears to be NO WAY of connecting with and creating a therapeutic bond with a client. There are rare times when someone is from a sufficiently different culture that you will not be able to reach them. However, do not think that being able to work with someone is the same as being able to work well with them. I worked at a practice years ago that had some "Christian Counselors." In many ways their style of counseling was more like that of a clergyman or minister. A client I was referred wanted one of these counselors but there were no appointments so he agreed to see me. After three sessions, I transferred him to a Christian Counselor as the first appointment became available. He was from a specific branch of Protestantism called "**FOURSQUARE**" and his religious

belief systems were so ingrained into his life that it was clear he should be helped by someone who could "focus the message" of therapy through the specific lens he needed. Upon reflection, I wasted three of his insurance-allotted twelve sessions.

NOTE: When dealing with people who have been incarcerated in the State or Federal Prison system for any length of time, be especially sensitive to the "prison culture" from which they come. Prison has a very different culture that overrides race, ethnicity and personality. In order to survive (emotionally, mentally or even physically) in you need to adapt to this culture and accept it. It can take years to "throw off" this cultural blanket after a person is released.

Question 122   Section: CULTURAL

The correct answer is D
Think of this situation from the viewpoint of the need for services. Your client's primary need is legal assistance. If he has an immigration problem it is serious and he should have legal representation during his involvement. This situation could have repercussions for his girlfriend and their baby.

A is INCORRECT
You are a clinician, not an attorney. The unauthorized practice of law is a felony. This answer hinges on the word "truth". You do not know what the truth is. What the client believes is a false statement on his application may be nothing, a technicality or something very serious. These are all questions for a lawyer to deal with. You are under no obligation to get him to "turn himself in" because there is no clear indication that a "crime" has been committed.

B is INCORRECT

Once again, you are not an attorney. No crime has been committed that you know of. It would be inappropriate for you to make a judgment on your client's legal status. Immigration is a "hot button" topic and feelings tend to run high around immigration issues. Be sure to keep your cool and not get swept away in the hype.

C is INCORRECT
There is a clearly identified need. You cannot ignore it. You must assist the client in understanding his problem and should make a clear referral. If you do not know a lawyer who deals in immigration law, USE THE PHONE BOOK. Also, other immigration resources include your local Catholic Social Services (it does not matter if your client is Catholic) and in larger metropolitan areas, the local Jewish Social Services Agency, once again, the client does not have to be Jewish to access Jewish Social Services.

Question 123   Section: CULTURAL

The correct answer is B
It is apparent from the interaction that the parents are ashamed and embarrassed by the current situation. Like most people, this is not the "story" they have written for their lives. Their story included a man-women marriage, grandkids and time spent with their son's new family. While grandchildren are possible, the parents cannot see anything currently except their pain and loss at their "story " changing. As a therapist, start with a non-judgmental attitude and proceed with helping the parent accept their new roles. Their disappointment will be directed at their son, however, the root cause of their disappointment is the loss of their "dream" or their projection for the future.

A is INCORRECT

Regardless of your personal belief systems, Reparation therapy is considered by all National counseling Agencies as UNETHICAL TREATMENT and could result in the loss of your license. Regardless of your belief system, the client always has the right to direct the course of therapy. If your viewpoints get in the way, you may need to make a referral to another counselor.

C is INCORRECT
This is a clear statement of FACT.

D is INCORRECT
You should choose this option ONLY if you are planning the leave the field as a licensed therapist. It would be a great way to end your career.

Question 124   Section: CULTURAL

The correct answer is C
It is a standard fixture of Asian Culture that outsiders should not be involved. There is a very long standing streak of Xenophobia in some Asian cultures. Regardless of how your client feels about his problems, his family is likely to feel shame and embarrassment at his "going to an outsider" to seek help. Asian culture also puts a very high priority on "Handling Your Own Problems" and "Bear your own problems without complaining". These are all issues that you need to keep in your consciousness when working with a 1st or 2nd generation Asian American.

A is INCORRECT
Almost no one has problems understanding the eligibility requirements for psychotherapy. The only eligibility

requirement I am aware of it showing up, physically, while we try to reach you emotionally.

B is INCORRECT
This may be a secondary issue but it is certainly not reserved for Asian American as a group. Most people feel a little shame at going to therapy because we are all taught that we need to handle ourselves. This is part of the American "Pull yourself up by your bootstraps" MYTH.

D is INCORRECT
For obvious reasons (smile)

Question 125   Section: CULTURAL

The correct answer is A
Amok – is a dissociative episode: period of brooding followed by an outburst of violent, aggressive or homicidal behavior directed at people and objects. Episode is precipitated by a perceived slight or insult. Episode is often accompanied by persecutory ideas, automatism, amnesia, exhaustion, and a return to premorbid state following the episode. Originally described in Malaysia. Similar episodes are found in Laos, Philippines, Polynesia, Papua New Guinea, Puerto Rico (mal de pelea), and among the Navajo (iich'aa)

If he was from West Africa or Haiti you would call this same behavior: boufée delirante - a cultural interaction from West Africa and Haiti. Sudden outburst of agitated and aggressive behavior, marked confusion, and psychomotor excitement. Sometimes accompanied by visual and auditory hallucinations or paranoid ideation. It may resemble a brief psychotic disorder.

B is INCORRECT

Because he is from New Guinea, it should be treated as a cultural syndrome and not as a psychotic disorder.

C is INCORRECT
dhat - folk diagnostic term used in India to refer to severe anxiety and hypochondriacal concerns associated with the discharge of semen, whitish discoloration of the urine, and feelings of weakness and exhaustion.

D is INCORRECT
Hwa-byung - Korean folk syndrome literally translated into English as "anger syndrome" and attributed to the suppression of anger. The symptoms include insomnia, fatigue, panic, fear of impending death, dysphoric affect, indigestion, anorexia, dyspnea, palpitations, generalized aches and pains.

CLINCIAL NOTE: You do not have to memorize all the different cultural syndromes. Just be aware when assessing a person from another culture or country that behavior we might consider to be problematic is culturally acceptable.

Question 126   Section: CLINICAL

The correct answer is C
Autistic fantasy occurs when a client copes with emotional conflict or internal/external stressors by excessively daydreaming, instead of seeking human relationships. Isolation is a more effective strategy for them than meeting and making new friends. When dealing with this kind of defense mechanism, probably your most effective strategy would be to give homework assignments that require the client to go into the community and do a specific task, which may involve other people. Also realize that part of the isolation may be due to poorly developed social skills and some

"Direct Interaction" training may be required as a way of teaching her how to interact with others

A is INCORRECT
Rationalization occurs when the client copes with emotional conflict or internal/external stressors by concealing the true motivations for his or her own thoughts, actions, or feelings through the elaboration of reassuring or self-serving but incorrect explanations.

B is INCORRECT
projection occurs when a client copes with emotional conflict or internal/external stressors by falsely attributing to another his or her own unacceptable feelings, impulses, or thoughts.

D is INCORRECT
devaluation occurs when a client copes with emotional conflict or internal/external stressors by attributing exaggerated negative qualities to self or others

Question 127   Section: CLINICAL

The correct answer is B
idealization is used when the client copes with emotional conflict either internal or external, and internal/external stressors by attributing exaggerated positive qualities to others. It is often easier to see the world as perfect rather than perceive it as it is. This may be caused by a projection Saheed is using on the world, or it may cover up feelings of insecurity or even fear. If you believe everyone is great, you don't have to worry about them trying to hurt you, because they wouldn't. This defense mechanism is probably covering up a great deal of hurt and disappointment, so, as a therapist, I would not want to take it away very quickly. I would want to

fully explore the entire underbelly of the issue before I worked with Saheed to surrender this set of protections.

A is INCORRECT
Intellectualization is used by a client to cope with emotional conflict or internal/external stressors by the excessive use of abstract thinking or the making of generalizations to control or minimize disturbing feelings. This is often a very difficult defense mechanism to overcome because the individual will have probably learned some basic logic skills and will fight to maintain this perception. This is a defense mechanism that allows the user to feel "in control" because of its power at evading issues using logic. This is a defense mechanism that could take many sessions to confront fully.

C is INCORRECT
Humor is used to avoid problems. The client will use this to cope with almost all situations. They tend to emphasize the amusing or ironic aspects of the conflict or stressors. This is also a difficult mechanism to overcome. It can be used in many different situations to repel unwanted contact and to control a situation. The entire cast of Seinfeld is a glowing (if not somewhat exaggerated) example of people who are seriously maladaptive and use humor to avoid coping with their problems.

D is INCORRECT
Isolation of affect is a mechanism that allows the client to cope with emotional conflict or internal/ external stressors by separating their ideas from the feelings associated with them. Social skills training and changing expectations are both ways to deal with this defense mechanism in therapy.

Question 128   Section: CLINICAL

The correct answer is B

affiliation occurs when the client copes with emotional conflict or internal/ or external stress by turning to others for help or support. They will often share their problems with others. They usually do not try to make someone else responsible for their problems. It is important to note that ego defense mechanisms are neutral, and the pathology lies in how they are used. In this situation, there is no clear indication that her use of this mechanisms interferes with her social, emotional, or occupational functioning. Therefore there is no identified problem. It is clear that her family does not understand or like her responses, and this may indicate the need to educate the mother and father about the mechanism.

A is INCORRECT

acting out occurs when the client copes with emotional conflict or internal/external stress by actions rather than reflections or feelings. This definition is broader than the original concept of the acting out of transference, feelings or wishes during psychotherapy. This is intended to include behavior arising both within the psychotherapeutic transference as well as outside the dynamic relationship. Sometimes acting out is "defensive". This should not be confused with "bad behavior". It is defensive acting out because there is evidence that the behavior is related to emotional conflicts.

C is INCORRECT

altruism occurs when the client copes with emotional conflict or internal/external stress by dedicating themselves to the needs of others and to meet the needs of others. Unlike the self-sacrifice sometimes characteristic of reaction formation, the individual receives gratification either vicariously or from the response of others. This may be part of the underpinning of the Munchausen's' Syndrome by Proxy.

D is INCORRECT
anticipation occurs when the client cope with emotional conflict or internal/external stress by experiencing emotional reactions in advance of, or anticipating consequences of, possible future events and considering realistic, alternative responses or solutions.

Question 129   Section: CLINICAL

The correct answer is B
Projective identification is a form of projection in which the client copes with emotional conflict or internal/external stressors by falsely attributing his or her own unacceptable feelings, impulses, or thoughts to someone else Unlike simple projection, the client does not fully deny his projection and often remains aware of his or her own affects or impulses, however they often falsely attribute then as justifiable reactions to the other persons behavior. Often, the client will induce or create the impulse in others, for the very feelings they mistakenly believe exist, which causes further problems in deciding who did what to whom first.

A is INCORRECT
passive aggression occurs when the client copes with emotional conflict or internal/external stress by indirectly and unassertively expressing aggression toward others. Often they present with a façade of overt compliance which masks serious covert resistance, hostility and resentment. Passive aggression often exhibits itself in response to demands for independence, freedom of action and/or performance of non-dependent behavior. It is often seen in situations where a person in a

subordinate position has no other safe method of expressing their assertiveness more openly and independently.

C is INCORRECT
reaction formation occurs when the client copes with emotional conflict or internal/external stress by substituting behavior, thoughts, or feelings that are diametrically opposed to their own unacceptable feelings or thoughts. You will often see the client repress these unacceptable feelings as a method of achieving cognitive consonance.

D is INCORRECT
repression occurs when the client copes with emotional conflict or internal/ external stress by expelling or pushing disturbing wishes, thoughts, or experiences from their conscious awareness. Often the feelings associated with the disturbing wishes, etc, remain in the conscious realm of the client, therefore causing emotional problems, while the actual associated ideas are pushed out of the conscious "light".

Question 130   Section: CLINICAL

The correct answer is C
Sublimation occurs when the individual copes with emotional conflict or internal/external stress by channeling potentially maladaptive feelings and impulses into socially acceptable behavior. Instead of venting his anger towards his daughter he sublimates it into "spreading the word" of his views to different churches.

A is INCORRECT
self-assertion occurs when the client copes with emotional conflict or stress by expressing their feelings and thoughts directly, in a non- coercive or non-manipulative manner.

B is INCORRECT

self-observation occurs when the client copes with emotional conflict or stress by reflecting on their own thoughts, feelings, motivation, and behavior, and responding appropriately.

D is INCORRECT

Suppression occurs when a client copes with emotional conflict or internal/external stress by intentionally avoiding thinking about disturbing problems, wishes, feelings, or experiences.

Question 131   Section: CLINICAL

The correct answer is D

The "help-rejecting" client copes with emotional conflict or internal/external stressors by complaining or making repetitious requests for help that mask or disguise buried feelings of hostility or reproach toward others.   They then reject suggestions, advice and offers of help. Their complaints can be physical in nature or psychological.   Their secondary payback appears to be a self-reinforcing loop of "I can't be helped and I can't change my environment, so I am justified in feeling anxious and pressured."

This particular ego-defense mechanism can be approached with basic reality therapy; "What do you want?"; "Are you getting what you want?"; "Is what you're getting making you happy?"

This approach transfers the onus of responsibility for the problems back on the client and renders the defense mechanism avoid. At this point they will either begin to change or will find a therapist who wants to play their "game.'

A is INCORRECT

Denial is used by the client to cope with emotional conflict or internal/external stress by refusing to acknowledge painful aspects of their external reality or of their subjective experience. Usually this external reality of subjective experience is apparent to others.

B is INCORRECT
Displacement manifests itself when the client copes with emotional conflict or internal/external stress by transferring feelings about one object onto another object. Usually the object the feelings are transferred to is less threatening or scary than the object avoided.
(It is safe to yell at your children and may be dangerous to yell at your boss, even though the boss is causing you stress.)

C is INCORRECT
Dissociation is seen when the client copes with emotional conflict or internal/external stress with a breakdown in their integration of the functions of consciousness, memory, perception of self, the environment, and/or sensory-motor behavior.

Question 132   Section: CLINICAL

The correct answer is B
Emotional reasoning is a thinking error where you ASSUME that your negative feelings are TRUE, without any direct evidence to support them. This thinking error has an "emotional payoff". The payoff comes in the form of you not having to review your feelings and compare them to the accurate facts. You get to maintain your belief system without putting any energy into change. You also are able to avoid any real criticism of your refusal to change.

A is INCORRECT

Entitlement is the thinking error where you BELIEVE you have suffered and that LIFE now OWES you. It allows you to cope with mistakes by believing that people should cut you some slack because you are a victim and they should understand that you only made the mistake BECAUSE you are A VICTIM. This thinking error allows you to relieve yourself of any responsibility or guilt for your actions.

C is INCORRECT
Fortune telling is the thinking error where you BELIEVE you possess the power to see the future and the future is BAD. Because it is always bad, there is no particular reason to change your behavior...because it will not matter. You feel anyone who is optimistic or has hope for the future is simply uninformed.

D is INCORRECT
Externalization is the thinking error that allows you to BELIEVE that all human suffering is caused by external events and the only way you can control your life is to control all events in your life. This thinking error allows you to claim yourself as a victim of circumstance and removes your need to change, because you are not in control anyway.

Question 133   Section: CLINICAL

The correct answer is C
Jumping to conclusions is a thinking error or pattern of erroneous thought which allows the adolescent to interpret a situation negatively, regardless of any external evidence to support their beliefs. This allows Tommy to always be right because he does not have to gather information or ask others for feedback.

A is INCORRECT

Image is a thinking error which occurs when the client is trying to copy other people because they do not feel they have a "true self." They do not know who they are and therefore will mimic other people. As a clinician you have to be careful about this error because it closely parallels the conflict in the Ericksonian Stage of Identity VS Role Confusion. Some copying behavior is to be expected in adolescents, however, when it becomes the primary mechanism, you will begin to see problems. If Tommy were using IMAGE he would be very involved in something and dressing or acting like that "something" all the time.

B is INCORRECT
When your client is catastrophizing, they only see the worst of everything. They will take any negative and stretch it to the farthest ends of perception. This thinking error allows the client to stop trying because they will never be successful. It allows them to cease trying. If Tommy were catastrophizing, he would talk about how bad it was going to each of the events he was invited to.

D is INCORRECT
The client who uses MIND READING actively believes they know what other people are thinking by their actions and what the other person thinks about them is bad. They do not bother to ask the person whose "mind" they are reading for clarification. This allows them to plead a lack of control in their lives and they should not be held responsible. If Tommy were MIND READING, he would be telling you "his parents hate him" or "he knows they are mad at him."

Question 134   Section: CLINICAL

The correct answer is B

Using the victim stance allows you to blame other people for what has happened to you. Your primary behavioral mechanism is to "point fingers at others" and "generate excuses" for your lack of success. The pay-off for this type of behavior is the ability to NOT ACCEPT responsibility for your life. There is no need to put in the hard work of actually determining why you are "where you are".

Other examples of statements that show this thinking error are:

1) The thief who says, "He (the victim) is the real criminal here. His watch only cost $75 and the court is making me pay restitution of $250.

2) I do what I do because my father was a drunk. If he had cared about me and stopped drinking, I would not be like I am.

3) My boss pays me minimum wage. I broke into his car because I needed some extra money. If people are going to pay such low wages, they got to expect I will have to steal to survive."

A is INCORRECT

The "Good person" stance is a thinking error that belongs to a class of BLACK and WHITE views of the world. You often see this type of behavior in people who have been diagnosed with a personality disorder.

You are the good guy, no matter what you do. You see all behavior in terms of you being in the "right" and other people being in the "wrong". There is no GREY in your universal view. You actively ignore anything which does not fit nicely into your world view.

C is INCORRECT

The "Lack-of-time" stance is a thinking error which focused only on the HERE and NOW. The person who used this stance will refuse to look at the past and will not be willing to explain past behaviors. They only are interested in their current needs and wants. These people often expect to be a big success without any effort. Common statements you may hear during a session are "You only live once" and "if I don't get it now, I may never get it."

D is INCORRECT
This thinking error has a lot in common with the ego defense mechanism of ENTITLEMENT. You believe that there is no one in the world like you, or that your experiences are unique among people and therefore you have a right to do what you want because the rules don't apply to you. This also plays into the feelings of superiority of your feelings because "you believe you will never get caught."

Question 135   Section: CLINICAL

The correct answer is A
The fragmented personality thinking error is common in persons with antisocial features. It is a method where they can interpersonal conflict by separating themselves into two personality sets. They have a core belief that they are a good person and therefore could do no wrong. If they do something exploitive or hurtful they can justify it by making the logical leap: "If I am a good person and I hurt someone, they must have done something to deserve it, because I would not hurt them for no reason. They caused it. It has nothing to do with whether or not I am a good person." This thinking error allows them to refuse to look at the inconsistency between their beliefs and actions.

B IS INCORRECT

Justifying is also an externalizing thinking error. It allows the user to place all blame outside of them and therefore be able to avoid responsibility. Statements you may hear which could clue you in on this error would include: "He yelled at me so I had a right to hit him."; "She was mean to me so I broke her pottery."

C is INCORRECT
Fronting occurs when the client creates a persona which they use to try to convince you they are something or someone they are not. This error is similar to a conscious splitting where they can deny behaviors they have committed by refusing or denying they committed the behaviors. This error responds well to a simple statement that you know they are fronting and they should stop.

D IS INCORRECT
A person using the thinking error "Grandiosity" often has an exaggerated sense of self-importance or ability. They often feel they are the best or the best at doing something. They refuse to process any of their actions which could conflict with this thinking pattern. This client is minimizing or maximizing the significance of an issue, and it justifies not solving the problem.

Statements you may hear from a client involved in this thinking error may include:

> "I hate school; I could run the classroom better than that stupid teacher."

> "Coach is stupid; I am a better player than him. I should be playing Quarterback!"

Question 136   Section: ETHICAL

The correct answer is D

This is a very complex situation. The answer here is not so much an ethical consideration as it is a concern for you and your current licensure status. In the state of Florida, you are considered to be a licensed individual. However you are licensed as a Clinical Social Worker intern. In other states you would be licensed as a Master Social Worker. Both of these licensure designations are non-independent. Which means, in order for you to work, your license is tied to, and subordinate to, an Independent License, held by your Licensed Clinical Social Work Supervisor. Your license is not recognized as a license to practice independently. Assuming the information you have is correct, the ex-wife carries an independent license. The short answer here is that regardless of your expertise, regardless of your experience, and regardless of your competency, your license is not as powerful as the license of an independent clinical social worker. In any possible confrontation you will be seen as a subordinate, and as an intern. Numerous situations involving the custody arrangements of children become very contentious between all parties. There is a high probability that if you continue with this case you will be involved in some contentious situation with both parties. It would be very easy for the ex-wife to "pull rank on you" in a licensure sense. It would be quite possible for you to injure your career or possibly your chance at independent licensure status if you were to continue working with this case. The most appropriate thing to do would be to turn the case over to your agency and have them assign a licensed professional.

A is INCORRECT.
While there is no specific ethical violation for seeing this couple in therapy, there is nothing positive that can come out of it for you. All relationships, as they breakup, can become volatile. People become angry and are looking for resolution and retribution. Whether you like it or not, there is a form of bigotry among licensed professionals. Fully independent licenses are

more powerful than intern licenses. And if a confrontation were to occur you would be placing your subordinate license against an independent license. Chances are very good you would lose. Even if you did not lose, you could end up in the middle of an investigation that could take several months to sort out all the particulars. The best thing you can do is to refer this back to your agency and walk away.

B is INCORRECT
The largest problem you will have been the situation, if you want to continue to provide services, would be to place yourself in an adversarial position between this divorcing couple. This would allow you to be triangulated between the two parties. If you were to choose to provide services to the husband only and ask that the month the wife receive a separate therapist, you would only be exacerbated the triangulation. You would also allow the couple to continue their fight through two different proxies, yourself and the other therapist.

C is INCORRECT
Whether the ex-wife wants a licensed clinician because she feels they would be able to better handle the situation, or because they felt that they might have more control over the clinician, it is highly unlikely that the wife is going on accept you as a clinical peer. She will probably see you as inferior in training and skill. No good can come to you in providing services in the situation. Refer the case back to your agency and walk away.

Question 137   Section: ETHICAL

The correct answer is B
This is a very complex situation. Your primary ethical responsibility is to the client.   It is to ensure they receive the correct and appropriate information they require to make

appropriate decisions for their adult child. You need to supply her with the correct information as well as interfering with the other MSW providing her with incorrect information. Needless to say, this should be done with tact. Something like, "I am not sure that is correct. I have called ... And was given different information." As long as you can quote the source of your information, and the time frame in which your information was gathered, you should be alright. If you keep the exchange professional, and do not let your irritation takeover, the mother will figure out who has the most correct information.

A is INCORRECT
if you simply ignore the incorrect information being given by the other professional, to the mother, you run the risk of allowing mother to leave the meeting with incorrect information which may well cause problems for your client, the traumatic brain injury adult female. You have to accept responsibility for ensuring in that mother gets the correct information. As a social worker, there are many times when you will have to be confrontational. The trick is to be confrontational in a tactful manner, this is professional, and ensures that all parties grow and learn from the experience.

C is INCORRECT
While at first glance, this may seem like the best answer, it is not. This answer allows you to avoid a confrontation with the other professional. Many times in your work you will have to be confrontational. You are, after all, at your core, an advocate for your clients. The danger in answering this way is that you run the risk of allowing the mother to leave the conference with inaccurate information. And if the mother does not reschedule, or reschedules and does not show up she may well have left the conference with inaccurate information. Your job is to make sure that she has the accurate information she needs.

D is INCORRECT

In any exchange, as a social worker you must maintain a professional demeanor. During the conference with the mother, your personal feelings are irrelevant. You have a mandate, as a social worker, to provide the client was accurate and appropriate information. There is no room for personal feelings, at this point in time.

This is not to say that your feelings are unimportant. Or that you should not feel hurt, angry, slighted or anyone of a number of other feelings. It simply means that as a professional social worker you need to separate your personal feelings from your professional work. There will be plenty of time, at a later date, to deal with the situation and your feelings.

Question 138   Section: ETHICAL

The correct answer is C

The secretary of the agency, since they are the representative for the agency the client is currently involved with, should contact the caller and instruct her that all information requests need to be in writing. Also the release of all information needs to be done after an informed consent for release information is provided by the client. Regardless of the involvement of the Department of children and families with your client, your primary goal is to facilitate growth and protect their confidentiality. Also because you have no involvement with the child and you know the child is a safe location. There is no particular information you have to give to the Department of family services.

A is INCORRECT

whether or not Judy is from the Department of Children and Family services, without proper authorization she has no access to the information that you have gathered on your client. If indeed, there is a court hearing or court involvement on this client, or her child, the attorney for DCF will be able to submit to you a subpoena asking for information and requesting your presence at a deposition or a hearing. Remember that all people, regardless of their position or station, who wish to have access to information on your clients, must come through standard channels. Your client drives therapy; your client also drives control of information. Your client is the only person who can determine what information is released, unless there is a court order, or a subpoena.

B is INCORRECT
technically the client belongs to the agency, or the drop in center. And you are the therapist. This is not a private practice client. You have no responsibility to return the call to Judy and give her the information. This is a task the agency should do. The agency may not be used to dealing with the department children and family, they may not be used to dealing with any outside agency. The agency must however, have policies and procedures for the release of confidential information.

D is INCORRECT
This answer is not correct, because it can leave your client open to some problems. If your client is indeed involved with the court systems, at some point in time you will probably have to interface with them. There is no benefit to your client for angering or frustrating the court system. However, you need to keep in mind that all information can only be released to specific channels, with specific agreements and paperwork. While no one could probably fault to you, for throwing away the number and not returning the call, you could end up causing your client grief and undermining your client's position on an issue that is very important to your client.

Question 139   Section: ETHICAL

The correct answer is A

Ethics are messy and they often seem like little things that will have no great consequence. However, they shape who we are. The data gathered indicates a diagnosis of Adjustment Disorder. It could, with exaggeration and a blind eye be morphed into PTSD, but at what cost to the client. An adjustment disorder is considered to be short-term, PTSD is often considered chronic. If you frame the problem as an adjustment disorder the client learns that when things happen to them they may have a reaction, but the situation is able to be overcome. They are likely to adopt that attitude. If you frame it as PTSD, they may frame it as chronic and invasive and accept it as a permanent part of themselves. They may come to identify with it and it may damage "who they are." These are not trivial things we deal with each day. Your need to get paid can never overshadow your client's long-term health. If the parents really want the girl to see you, they may be able to make arrangements. Remember, you are a therapist and clinician, not a savior.

B is INCORRECT

The moment you decide to give a diagnosis that is acceptable to an insurance company, rather than to the "truth" of the situation, you have bastardized yourself and your profession. We all work alone. No-one really knows what goes on in our offices or our heads. It is human nature (and very easy) to justify situations which we would not originally agree to do. As a rule of thumb, before you do something like this, ask yourself if you would be comfortable standing in a group of your peers and telling them you did this.

C is INCORRECT

The only thing more compromising than deciding to give a false or unsubstantiated diagnosis is to bring others into the situation and collaborate. You are not only willing to ignore your ethics but are also willing to talk other people into thing which are inappropriate. Realize, that while proving it may be very difficult and the possibility of being caught is remote, your behavior could be construed as insurance fraud.

D) You have already decided you cannot take on any more pro bono clients. You should have made this decision as a matter of workload versus money. If you do decide to change the decision and take on the client, be sure you are doing it for appropriate reasons and not to fulfill a need in yourself to be a savior or to try to "rescue" someone. This is the fast track to burnout.

Question 140   Section: ETHICAL

The correct answer is B
you must always remember that you are driven by the needs, and the wants of the client. The client is allowed to determine their status, their intervention, and every other aspect of treatment. You cannot force a client to do anything, except under very specialized circumstances. You are under no obligation to get the client to sign any financial paperwork. If the client refused to sign and your agency decides to terminate services, that situation is beyond your control. By the way, writing refused across the signature line indicates very clearly that you gave the client the option and the client chose to decline. It also proves you presented the paperwork to the client.

A is INCORRECT
demanding the client to sign anything could be seen as coercive. It could be declared unethical by your license board,

and certainly not in the best interest of the client. Your client has the right to determine the future. They have the right to make their financial decisions. It should also be noted that failure on the part of your agency to ensure that the financial paperwork was completed properly before seeing the client is not your mess to clean up.

C is INCORRECT
this would most certainly be seen as coercive. It also robs the client of their right to make a decision. While you probably cannot refuse to bring the paperwork to the client, without the risk of getting reprimanded or fired by the agency, the fact that you're asked to do something that should be done by administration, should make you think deeply. Why is your agency putting you in this position.

D is INCORRECT
while this certainly could be viewed as an ethical move on your part, it may cause problems with your employment with the agency down the road. Like most situations in life this situation has a formal and informal aspect. The informal aspect is to get paid. The formal aspect is to use your relationship with the client as a method of ensuring payment. If you refuse to do this, the company will probably fall back upon the belief that you were "simply asked to do a simple job" and that the company was not trying to take advantage of anybody. They would've been probably begun to question your loyalty to the company and may even ask you why you thought the company was trying to take advantage of anybody. It is a no-win situation for you. The best response is to present the paperwork to the client and if they refuse to sign it, explain to them how to do so appropriately.

Question 141   Section: CLINICAL

The correct answer is C
The DSM-IV classifies four distinct levels of mental retardation. These are (from most debilitating to least) Profound, Severe, Moderate, Mild.   Individuals with an IQ range of 35-55 are classified as having MODERATE Mental Retardation. They are generally able to learn communication skills during childhood. They can learn to carry out self-care and work tasks with moderate supervision and can often live a rather independent life in a supervised environment like a group home. Of the entire population of individuals with mental retardation, about 10% are classified as in this range.

A is INCORRECT
An IQ score between 20-40 generally indicate severe mental retardation. This group of individuals make up about 3-4% of the population of individuals who suffer from Mental Retardation. They may learn to master basic self-care skills and very basic communication skills; however they will never achieve self-sufficiency. These individuals may be able to live in a group home with constant supervision.

B is INCORRECT
Approximately 85% of the mentally retarded population is in the mildly retarded category. Their IQ score ranges from 50-75, and they can often acquire academic skills up to the 6th grade level. They can become fairly self-sufficient and in some cases live independently, with community and social support.

D is INCORRECT
Only 1-2% of the mentally retarded population is classified as profoundly retarded. Profoundly retarded individuals have IQ scores under 20-25. They may be able to develop basic self-care and communication skills with appropriate support and

training. Their retardation is often caused by an accompanying neurological disorder. The profoundly retarded need a high level of structure and supervision.

The American Association on Mental Retardation (AAMR) has developed another widely accepted diagnostic classification system for mental retardation. The AAMR classification system focuses on the capabilities of the retarded individual rather than on the limitations. The categories describe the level of support required. They are: intermittent support, limited support, extensive support, and pervasive support. To some extent, the AAMR classification mirrors the DSM-IV classification. Intermittent support, for example, is support needed only occasionally, perhaps during times of stress or crisis. It is the type of support typically required for most mildly retarded individuals. At the other end of the spectrum, pervasive support, or life-long, daily support for most adaptive areas, would be required for profoundly retarded individuals.

Ref:http://medical-dictionary.thefreedictionary.com/
Moderate+mental+retardation

Question 142   Section: CLINICAL

The correct answer is B
Brain Lateralization Theory is the idea that the two halves of the brain's cerebral cortex -- left and right -- execute different functions. The lateralization theory -- developed by Nobel-prize-winners Roger Sperry and Robert Ornstein -- helps us to understand our behavior, our personality, our creativity, and our ability to use the proper mode of thinking when performing particular tasks. (The cerebral cortex is a part of the brain that exists only in humans and higher mammals, to manage our sophisticated intellect.)

The two halves ("hemispheres") are joined by the Corpus Collosum. This is a bundle of more than 200 million nerve fibers which transmit data from one hemisphere to the other so that the two halves can communicate. Although this nerve connection would seem to be vital, it is severed in a surgical procedure for some people who have epilepsy. The corpus collosum is up to 40 percent larger in women than it is in men.

We can specify the functions of the two hemispheres. (The following descriptions apply to right-handed people; for left-handed people, this information is reversed; for example, it is the right hemisphere which processes analytical thought.)

The left hemisphere specializes in analytical thought. The left hemisphere deals with hard facts: abstractions, structure, discipline and rules, time sequences, mathematics, categorizing, logic and rationality and deductive reasoning, knowledge, details, definitions, planning and goals, words (written and spoken and heard), productivity and efficiency, science and technology, stability, extraversion, physical activity, and the right side of the body. The left hemisphere is emphasized in our educational system and in our society in general, for better or for worse; as Marshall McLuhan speculated, "The day when bureaucracy becomes right hemisphere will be utopia."

The right hemisphere specializes in the "softer" aspects of life. This includes intuition, feelings and sensitivity, emotions, daydreaming and visualizing, creativity (including art and music), color, spatial awareness, first impressions, rhythm, spontaneity and impulsiveness, the physical senses, risk-taking, flexibility and variety, learning by experience, relationships, mysticism, play and sports, introversion, humor, motor skills, the left side of the body, and a holistic way of perception that recognizes patterns and similarities and then synthesizes those elements into new forms.

Ref::http://www.theoderoftime.com/politics/cemetery/
stout/h/brain-la.htm

A is INCORRECT
This is a "made up" phrase

C is INCORRECT
This is a "made up" phrase

D is INCORRECT
This is a "made up" phrase

Question 143   Section: CLINICAL

The Correct Answer is A
An EEG is an ElectroEncephaloGraph, and is used to measure alpha waves activity in the brain. These waves occur when we are both alert and relaxed. These waves decrease with concentrated or busy activity. They have been studied in depression and relaxation.

B is INCORRECT
I don't know what this one is but if you ever find something that does this, please forward it to me. It could provide information for many dissertations.

C is INCORRECT
The concept of Mental Retardation caused by an extra chromosome is known as Trisomy 21. It goes by the common name of Down's Syndrome.

D is INCORRECT
Not directly! We definitely could benefit from knowing more about the physiology of our bodies, but that research is probably 20 years off.

Question 144   Section: CLINICAL

The Correct Answer is A

Smoking is linked to lower birth weights and premature birth rates. Children born to women who smoke are at risk for the following other possibilities as well: 1) "According to Marjorie Greenfield, M.D. at DrSpock.com, an overabundance of red blood cells in the fetus can cause a thickening of the blood, thus blocking blood flow. The carbon monoxide that is created when tobacco smoke is consumed displaces oxygen in the blood. This displacement can cause the fetus to produce more red blood cells to compensate for the lack of sufficient oxygen."

2) Nicotine is believed to contribute to behavioral and nervous disorders in newborn babies. This comes from the hypothesis that nicotine affects the production of neurotransmitters in the brain. Serotonin and dopamine are replaced by nicotine which causes withdraw symptoms after the baby is born.

3) Fetal Thyroid Damage - The thyroid gland, which begins to develop by the 12th week of gestation, is responsible for metabolism and growth rates. Smoking affects thyroid development in fetuses, which seems to cause neuron damage. This damage was seen as contributing to the potential for debilitating mental conditions such as retardation. This effect is caused by both first-hand and second-hand smoke.

Reference: http://www.ehow.com/about_5292686_effects-smoking-fetus.html

B is INCORRECT

There are many causes of mental retardation, including Trisomy 21, Anoxia, Alcohol Abuse and a variety of abused substances. Given our current store of knowledge, smoking is not a primary cause of mental retardation.

C is INCORRECT

There is no direct correlation in the research showing a link between muscle tone at birth and smoking.

D is INCORRECT

Tay Sachs is a genetic disorder which tends to show itself in Eastern European populations and their descendants, especially Ashkenazic Jews. It is initially debilitating and finally fatal in all cases by age 6-7. The only "cure" is the testing of the parents for the recessive trait and genetic counseling regarding transmission of the double recessive gene during conception.

Question 145   Section: CLINICAL

The Correct Answer is D

These parents show a permissive style of parenting. Permissive parents, sometimes referred to as indulgent parents, have very few demands to make of their children. These parents rarely discipline their children because they have relatively low expectations of maturity and self-control. According to Baumrind, permissive parents "are more responsive than they are demanding. They are nontraditional and lenient, do not require mature behavior, allow considerable self-regulation, and avoid confrontation" (1991). Permissive parents are generally nurturing and communicative with their children, often taking on the status of a friend more than that of a parent.

Baumrind found the impact of permissive parenting often results in children who rank low in happiness and self-regulation. These children are more likely to experience problems with authority and tend to perform poorly in school.

A is INCORRECT

In this style of parenting, children are expected to follow the strict rules established by the parents. Failure to follow such rules usually results in punishment. Authoritarian parents fail to explain the reasoning behind these rules. If asked to explain, the parent might simply reply, "Because I said so." These parents have high demands, but are not responsive to their children. According to Baumrind, these parents "are obedience- and status-oriented, and expect their orders to be obeyed without explanation" (1991).

B is INCORRECT
Like authoritarian parents, those with an authoritative parenting style establish rules and guidelines that their children are expected to follow. However, this parenting style is much more democratic. Authoritative parents are responsive to their children and willing to listen to questions. When children fail to meet the expectations, these parents are more nurturing and forgiving rather than punishing. Baumrind suggests that these parents "monitor and impart clear standards for their children's conduct. They are assertive, but not intrusive and restrictive. Their disciplinary methods are supportive, rather than punitive. They want their children to be assertive, as well as socially responsible, and self-regulated as well as cooperative" (1991).
Baumrind found the impact of authoritive parenting styles tend to result in children who are happy, capable and successful (Maccoby, 1992).

C is INCORRECT
An uninvolved parenting style is characterized by few demands, low responsiveness and little communication. While these parents fulfill the child's basic needs, they are generally detached from their child's life. In extreme cases, these parents may even reject or neglect the needs of their children.
Baumrind found the impact of uninvolved parenting styles rank lowest across all life domains. These children tend to lack self-control, have low self-esteem and are less competent than their peers.
http://psychology.about.com/od/developmentalpsychology/a/pa
renting-style.htm

Question 146   Section: HUMAN DIVERSITY

The Correct Answer is A
The primary tenet of Social Work is the right of client self-determination. Even if the client does not agree with you, or chooses to live in a manner which you consider to be inappropriate or degrading. As long as they are not a danger to themselves or others, they are free to make their own decisions.

B is INCORRECT
If she asked you to do this, you should comply. She would be directing her behavior, however, this is not a part of the question and cannot be assumed.

C is INCORRECT
There is nothing in the scenario that tells you about her family.

D is INCORRECT
You should do this with her or after she leaves, and be ready to suggest alternatives when she comes by again. Except in very extreme circumstances, you are required to allow the client the right of self-control and choice.

Question 147   Section: CLINICAL

The correct answer is A
-- School Age: 6 to 12 Years
-- Ego Development Outcome: Industry vs. Inferiority
-- Basic Strengths: Method and Competence
During this stage, often called the Latency, we are capable of learning, creating and accomplishing numerous new skills and knowledge, thus developing a sense of industry. This is also a very social stage of development and if we experience unresolved feelings of inadequacy and inferiority among our

peers, we can have serious problems in terms of competence and self-esteem.

As the world expands a bit, our most significant relationship is with the school and neighborhood. Parents are no longer the complete authorities they once were, although they are still important.

http://www.learningplaceonline.com/stages/organize/Erikson.htm

B is INCORRECT

-- Young adulthood: 18 to 35

-- Ego Development Outcome: Intimacy and Solidarity vs Isolation

-- Basic Strengths: Affiliation and Love

In the initial stage of being an adult we seek one or more companions and love. As we try to find mutually satisfying relationships, primarily through marriage and friends, we generally also begin to start a family, though this age has been pushed back for many couples who today don't start their families until their late thirties. If negotiating this stage is successful, we can experience intimacy on a deep level. If we're not successful, isolation and distance from others may occur. And when we don't find it easy to create satisfying relationships, our world can begin to shrink as, in defense, we can feel superior to others.

Our significant relationships are with marital partners and friends.

http://www.webster.edu/~woolflm/lrerikson.html

C is INCORRECT

The final stage of Erikson's (1982) theory is later adulthood (age 60 years and older). The crisis represented by this last life stage is integrity versus despair. Erikson (1982) proposes that this stage begins when the individual experiences a sense of mortality. This may be in response to retirement, the death of a spouse or close friends, or may simply result from changing social roles. No matter what the cause, this sense of mortality precipitates the final life crisis. The final life crisis manifests itself as a review of the individual1s life-career. Similar to Butler's (1963) life review, individuals review their life-career to determine if it was a success or failure. According to Erikson (1982), this reminiscence or introspection is most productive when experienced with significant others. The outcome of this life-career reminiscence can be either positive or negative. Ego integrity is the result of the positive resolution of the final life crisis. Ego integrity is viewed as the key to harmonious personality development; the individual views their whole of life with satisfaction and contentment. The ego quality that emerges from a positive resolution is wisdom. Erikson (1982) defines wisdom as a kind of "informed and detached concern with life itself in the face of death itself" (p. 61). Conversely, despair is the result of the negative resolution or lack of resolution of the final life crisis. This negative resolution manifests itself as a fear of death, a sense that life is too short, and depression. Despair is the last dystonic element in Erikson's (1959, 1982) theory. Reference: http://www.webster.edu/~woolflm/lrerikson.html

D is INCORRECT
-- Adolescence: 12 to 18 Years
-- Ego Development Outcome: Identity vs. Role Confusion
-- Basic Strengths: Devotion and Fidelity

Up to this stage, according to Erikson, development mostly depends upon what is done to us. From here on out, development depends primarily upon what we do. And while adolescence is a stage at which we are neither a child nor an adult, life is definitely getting more complex as we attempt to find our own identity, struggle with social interactions, and grapple with moral issues.

Our task is to discover who we are as individuals separate from our family of origin and as members of a wider society. Unfortunately, for those around us, in this process many of us go into a period of withdrawing from responsibilities, which Erikson called a "moratorium." And if we are unsuccessful in navigating this stage, we will experience role confusion and upheaval.

A significant task for us is to establish a philosophy of life and in this process we tend to think in terms of ideals, which are conflict free, rather than reality, which is not. The problem is that we don't have much experience and find it easy to substitute ideals for experience. However, we can also develop strong devotion to friends and causes. It is no surprise, that our most significant relationships are with peer groups.

Reference: http://www.learningplaceonline.com/stages/organiz e/Erikson.htm

Question 148   Section: CLINICAL

The correct answer is B

Boundaries lead to differentiation of roles and tasks in a community setting. In general, boundaries are a very good thing to help individuals to structure their relationships. Some level of boundaries are essential to proper development. Enmeshment is a lack of boundaries and an intermingling of roles and responsibilities. This often leads to confusion and conflict.

A is INCORRECT
Lack of boundaries would create more enmeshment

C is INCORRECT
Boundaries should always change a level of enmeshment

D is INCORRECT
Differentiation is a the opposite side of the enmeshment coin

Question 149   Section: CLINICAL

The correct answer is C
Cognitive dissonance is an uncomfortable feeling caused by holding conflicting ideas simultaneously. The theory of cognitive dissonance proposes that people have a motivational drive to reduce dissonance. They do this by changing their attitudes, beliefs, and actions. Dissonance is reduced by justifying, blaming, and denying. It is one of the most influential and extensively studied theories in social psychology. A closely related term, cognitive disequilibrium, was coined, by Jean Piaget to refer to the experience of a discrepancy between something new and something already known or believed.
Reference: http://en.wikipedia.org/wiki/Cognitive_dissonance

A is INCORRECT
Dissociation is a partial or complete disruption of the normal integration of a person's conscious or psychological functioning. Dissociation can be a response to trauma or drugs and perhaps allows the mind to distance itself from experiences that are too much for the psyche to process at that time. Dissociative disruptions can affect any aspect of a person's functioning. Although some dissociative disruptions involve amnesia, the vast majority of dissociative events do not. Since dissociations are normally unanticipated, they are typically experienced as startling, autonomous intrusions into the person's usual ways of responding or functioning. Due to their unexpected and largely inexplicable nature, they tend to be quite unsettling.
Reference: http://en.wikipedia.org/wiki/Dissociation

B is INCORRECT

Acculturation is the exchange of cultural features that results when groups of individuals having different cultures come into continuous first hand contact. The original cultural patterns of either or both groups may be altered, but the groups remain.
Reference: http://en.wikipedia.org/wiki/Acculturation

D is INCORRECT

In developmental psychology - particularly analytical psychology - individuation is the process through which a person becomes his/her 'true self'. Hence it is the process whereby the innate elements of personality; the different experiences of a person's life and the different aspects and components of the immature psyche become integrated over time into a well-functioning whole. Individuation might thus be summarized as the stabilizing of the personality.
Reference: http://en.wikipedia.org/wiki/Individuation

Question 150   Section: ETHICS

The correct answer is C
There is no indication that the professionals involved made any mistakes in their assessment of the mental state of Poddar or in understanding what he was capable of doing.

A brief description of the case follows:
On October 27, 1969, Prosenjit Poddar killed Tatiana Tarasoff. Tatiana's parents alleged that two months earlier Poddar confided his intention to kill Tatiana to Dr. Lawrence Moore, a psychologist employed by the Cowell Memorial Hospital at the University of California at Berkeley. Dr. Moore requested the campus police detain Poddar, and after a brief detention, they released him when they decided he appeared rational. Tatiana's parents have further stated that Dr. Harvey

Powelson, Moore's superior, then directed that no further action be taken to detain Poddar. No one warned Tatiana of Poddar's threats.

A is INCORRECT
Malpractice liability is directly affected by the Tarasoff case. You, as a mental health professional, have a DUTY to warn someone of a threat against their person or safety; thus allowing them to determine the credibility of the threat.

B is INCORRECT
Tarasoff directly defines the limits of Privileged communication. If your client threatens someone you can identify and you feel the threat is credible, then that part of the conversation with your client is no longer privileged and you have a duty to warn the person threatened.

D is INCORRECT
Tarasoff directly impacts what information can and cannot remain protected and confidential.

Question 151   Section: CLINICAL

The Correct answer is B
Diagnostic criteria for 301.83 Borderline Personality Disorder :
A pervasive pattern of instability of interpersonal relationships, self-image, and affects, and marked impulsivity beginning by early adulthood and present in a variety of contexts, as indicated by five (or more) of the following:
(1) frantic efforts to avoid real or imagined abandonment.
   Note: Do not include suicidal or self-mutilating behavior covered in Criterion 5.
(2) a pattern of unstable and intense interpersonal relationships characterized by alternating between extremes of idealization and devaluation

(3) identity disturbance: markedly and persistently unstable self- image or sense of self

(4) impulsivity in at least two areas that are potentially self-damaging (e.g., spending, sex, Substance Abuse, reckless driving, binge eating).

Note: Do not include suicidal or self-mutilating behavior covered in Criterion 5.

(5) recurrent suicidal behavior, gestures, or threats, or self-mutilating behavior

(6) affective instability due to a marked reactivity of mood (e.g., intense episodic dysphoria, irritability, or anxiety usually lasting a few hours and only rarely more than a few days)

(7) chronic feelings of emptiness

(8) inappropriate, intense anger or difficulty controlling anger (e.g., frequent displays of temper, constant anger, recurrent physical fights)

(9) transient, stress-related paranoid ideation or severe dissociative symptoms

A is INCORRECT

This behavioral set corresponds to the diagnostic criteria for 301.50 Histrionic Personality Disorder. A pervasive pattern of excessive emotionality and attention seeking, beginning by early adulthood and present in a variety of contexts,

C is INCORRECT

This behavioral set corresponds to the diagnostic criteria for 301.81 Narcissistic Personality Disorder. A pervasive pattern of grandiosity (in fantasy or behavior), need for admiration, and lack of empathy, beginning by early adulthood and present in a variety of contexts. Grandiosity is defined as inflated self-esteem or self-worth, usually manifested as content of thinking or talk with themes reflecting the patient's belief that he or she is the greatest or has special attributes or abilities.

D is INCORRECT
This behavioral set corresponds to the diagnostic criteria for 301.6 Dependent Personality Disorder. A pervasive and excessive need to be taken care of that leads to submissive and clinging behavior and fears of separation, beginning by early adulthood and present in a variety of contexts.

Question 152   Section: CLINICAL

The correct answer is B
Ontogenesis is defined as the process of an individual organism growing organically; a purely biological unfolding of events involved in an organism changing gradually from a simple to a more complex level. In psychoanalysis it is the process during which personality and sexual behavior mature through a series of stages: first oral stage and then anal stage and then phallic stage and then latency stage and finally genital stage.
Ref: http://www.thefreedictionary.com/ontogenesis

A is INCORRECT
Any word ending in -GENESIS described a process of creation or growth throughout a set period of time. Stimulation of an emotional state or arousal occurs from environmental and internal cues and is regarded as a response mechanism.

C is INCORRECT
It defines a symptom.

D is INCORRECT
Understanding the perceptions of your client and their interactions with their family are both extremely important to counseling. However, this answer deals with the "present" and ONTOGENESIS deals with the complete spectrum.

Question 153 Section: CLINICAL

The correct answer is B
Schizophreniform disorder replicates the Schizophrenia criteria but the duration symptoms exist are present between one and six months. Because you have no prior history of any symptoms, you cannot diagnose schizophrenia.

A is INCORRECT
The schizoid personality disorder is not related schizophrenia, even though it uses the same root word. Schizoid Personality Disorder is characterized by a long-standing pattern of detachment from social relationships. A person with schizoid personality disorder often has difficulty expression emotions and does so typically in very restricted range, especially when communicating with others

C is INCORRECT
A diagnosis of schizophrenia requires at least 2 of the following symptoms:, which must be present for a period of time of more than 6 months.

-Delusions
-Hallucinations
-Disorganized speech (e.g., frequent derailment or incoherence)

-Grossly disorganized or catatonic behavior
-Negative symptoms (e.g., a "flattening" of one's emotions, alogia, avolition)
(Only one symptom is required if delusions are bizarre or hallucinations consist of a voice keeping up a running commentary on the person's behavior or thoughts, or two or more voices conversing with each other.)

D is INCORRECT
Schizophrenia, undifferentiated Type is a category of schizophrenia in which we place individuals with symptoms that are not compatible with the other categories of schizophrenia. (I have always thought this diagnosis should be called Schizophrenia NOS)

Question 154   Section: ETHICS

The correct answer is D
Once you begin an intake you have an ethical obligation to assist the client. This obligation can be fulfilled by seeing the client for free (pro bono) or by reducing your fees (sliding scale) or by assuring a referral and a linkage (making sure the referral agency is contacted). The one thing you cannot do is to leave them stranded.

A is INCORRECT
This would be the same as throwing them out of your office. It could also be construed as client abandonment. Failure to pay does not give you the right to terminate services without an appropriate referral.

B is INCORRECT
This answer smacks of coercion and manipulation. You need to respect what the client brings to the table. They may not be good money managers, but helping them figure out how to

borrow money to see you would probably put you on the wrong side of an ethical complaint.

C is INCORRECT
This answer is analogous to C

Question 155   Section: CLINICAL

The Correct answer is C
The cognitive damage that is done by sexual abuse often leads to inappropriate and unstable relations. This may be due to the damage to normal societal boundaries. It may also be due to the feeling of being unprotected, and "out-of-control" which are part of the pattern of sexual abuse. Without healthy boundaries and healthy interactions with adults during the formative years, children are doomed to a life of discontent and disaster in their primary relationships.

A is INCORRECT.
While sexual dysfunction may occur as an adjunct to their abuse, it is not as highly correlated with sexual abuse as answer c. There are many causes of sexual dysfunction, and in reality, the term sexual dysfunction is too broad to be useful in this context.

B is INCORRECT
There is no direct correlation with alcohol abuse, alcoholism and sexual abuse survivors. While, it is possible that, alcohol may be used to cope with the stress and intrusive thoughts surrounding sexual trauma, it would most likely only become a problem if it were the primary escape mechanism used by the individual.

D is INCORRECT

While this is a possible outcome, there is not a high degree of correlation between this response and sexual abuse. That is to say; not everyone who is abused replicates the pattern.

Question 156   Section: CLINICAL

The correct answer is B

Dysthymia is a subcategory of depression. It is usually long-term, low level (not completely debilitating) and is experiences for years.

Clients with dysthymia will often display a low, dark, or sad mood on most days for at least 2 years. When dysthymia is diagnosed in children, it is possible the depression will present as irritability. You will almost always see two or more of the following symptoms present during the duration of the dysthymic state. These include 1) Feelings of hopelessness 2) Too little or too much sleep 3) Low energy or fatigue 4) Low self-esteem 5) Poor appetite or overeating and 6) Poor concentration. Also your client with dysthymia will have a negative self-view and will perceive their future as discouraging, as well as taking a dim view of other peoples life and life events.

A is INCORRECT

Hallucinations are more closely associated with psychotic disorders. A note of concern when dealing with olfactory hallucinations; olfactory means "sense of smell" and these types of hallucinations tend to be rare. They also have a tentative relationship with certain types of brain tumors. If you have a client complaining of olfactory hallucinations, it would be good practice to refer them for a diagnostic evaluation by a neurologist.

C is INCORRECT

These symptoms represent drug dependency or drug abuse. Most substance abusers who deal with stimulants will not present with a pattern of dysthymia.

D) is INCORRECT
These symptoms more closely resemble Post Traumatic Stress Disorder and are not specifically tied to Dysthymia.

Question 157   Section: CLINICAL

The correct answer is A
The primary diagnostic issues with PTSD are the identification of the trauma incident, the presence of intrusive thoughts and flashbacks, and the time-frame of greater than 1 month of symptoms.

B is INCORRECT
There is no real value, from a clinical perspective, of knowing the length of time between the trauma and the onset of symptoms. Many of our ego defense mechanisms allow or create the suppression, denial or refusal of accepting what has occurred to us. These processes can skew the length of time between event and response.

C is INCORRECT
Somatization, the occurrence of tactile or physical symptoms, does not play a role in the diagnosis of PTSD or Acute Stress Disorder.

D is INCORRECT
The degree of trauma is individualized to each person. Some situations, which may cause you great trauma, may hardly impact someone else.

Question 158   Section: CLINICAL

The correct answer is D
While SSRI's tend to be excellent medications with less side effects than their predecessor, Tricyclics and MAOI's, they are NOT side-effect free. One of the most disturbing side-effects to some men is the sexual dysfunction which can express itself in a range from mild impairment to complete impairment. Males, age 18 to 45, on average, do not respond well to problems involving sexual dysfunction.

A is INCORRECT
NMS is a life- threatening neurological disorder most often caused by an adverse reaction to neuroleptic or antipsychotic drugs. It generally presents with muscle rigidity, fever, autonomic instability and cognitive changes such as delirium, and is associated with elevated creatine phosphokinase. (Thus, blood tests will show if it is present)

B is INCORRECT
All SSRI's are covered by all major insurance plans. They have been around long enough that almost all of them are available in a 'generic' formulation

C is INCORRECT
Some people experience a mild "compression of affect", where they describe feeling 'non-depressed but also not happy". This side effect will often go away over time.

Question 159   Section: Ethical

The correct answer is D
You bear responsibility because you are the supervisor. The intake worker bears responsibility because they are the direct service person and they failed to report back after making a

clinically incorrect decision. The agency employs you both and therefore shares liability.

A is INCORRECT
While you bear responsibility because you failed to follow-up, you may well have born responsibility even if you followed up and did not correct the problem.

B is INCORRECT
The intake worker failed to follow your directive, made a bad decision on their own, then failed to report their decision to you. They bear responsibility, however they are not the only one.

C is INCORRECT
The agency bears responsibility because it is the focal point of the issue and provides the service. They however share responsibility with multiple other people. This situation represents a complete breakdown of emergency protocol and a young girl died for it.

Question 160   Section: Ethical

The correct answer is A
Your primary obligation is to your client. We are a client centered professional. If your obligation to your client is in opposition to your agency, you need to bite the bullet and take the disapproval of your agency.

B is INCORRECT
Social advocacy is secondary to your client concerns

C is INCORRECT
Client centered only, first and foremost

D is INCORRECT

Social advocacy is always secondary to the needs of your client. You never sacrifice your client on the altar of societal need.

Question 161   Section: Clinical

The correct answer is C
Patients with depression have a greater probability of suicidal behavior than patients without depression, generally speaking, however, there is no clear indication of suicidal thoughts or ideations, but there has been no concrete indications they are not present and just not being brought up by the client. Without further data from the patient and therapy, there should be no change in your level of concern about suicidal potential.

A is INCORRECT
There is no indication of any increase in risk factors or issues. In fact, the information given would lead you to believe suicide has not been a central topic in therapy. There is no information presented that would allow you to assess, let alone alter, your assessment of suicidal potential.

B is INCORRECT
There is no indication of a decrease in any factors, risk or otherwise.

D is INCORRECT
While SSRI's tend to be appropriate medications for depression, there is the possibility of increased suicidal potential on SSRI's. Whether a client is on SSRI's or not, should not cause you to alter your suicidal assessment. Only data and facts should allow you to alter your suicidal assessment.

Question 162   Section: Clinical

The correct answer is D
One of the myths of suicide is the belief that talking about it will plant the idea. This is a MYTH. People who are contemplating suicide are in need of immediate intervention. By discussing the situation openly you are removing the societal TABOO that "we don't talk about that." The "trick" is not to be judgmental. It is much easier for a therapist to have a dialogue with a client if they have had the dialogue with themselves.

Personal Hint: My belief is that almost everyone has thought about suicide at some point. Making peace with this fact makes being non-judgmental, all the more, simple. Taboos need to be confronted directly. In my experience, when a person is contemplating suicide, they have run out of internal options. They have become "tunnel-visioned" and are unable to see opportunities. It has always been helpful to me to try to walk them through options, even if they have already dismissed them, because a new insight might occur.

A is INCORRECT
It is always a good idea to gather as much information as you can, and the genogram and eco-map will gather a lot if information, you must first confront he suicidal possibilities directly. This is a question that requires an "order of precedent"

B is INCORRECT
Once again, not a bad idea, but not the first thing you need to attend to.

C is INCORRECT
This is ABSOLUTELY WRONG in all circumstances. Never avoid talking to someone about suicide. Often people who contemplate suicide will feel their thoughts and ideas are too

strange to talk about. Remember, suicide is a process that continues when there is isolation, failure of coping mechanisms, and a very negative internal dialogue. If your client believes you will not want to talk about suicide, they will not talk openly. Discussing suicide normalizes their thought processes and allows them to talk about their feelings. People do not follow through with suicidal plans because they talk about suicide, they follow through because they feel alone and abandoned.

Final Thought: Most people think of suicide as passive and harming the individual only. In my experience suicide can be a very aggressive act. When someone is thinking, "They will miss me when I am gone!" or "This will show them!", these are aggressive thoughts. They are an attack on those that survive. Learn everything you can about suicide and challenge all your prejudices.

Question 163   Section: Clinical-Diagnostic

The correct answer is A
Korsakoff's syndrome goes by many names (Korsakoff's dementia, Korsakov's syndrome, Korsakoff's psychosis, or amnesic-confabulatory syndrome). It is a neurological disorder caused by the lack of thiamine (vitamin B1) in the brain. Its onset is linked to chronic alcohol abuse and/or severe malnutrition. (Alcohol has a lot of calories and chronic alcoholics can often get there calorie needs met by drinking, however, there are no vitamins and nutrients in alcohol, so eventually the person will suffer from severe nutrition.) The syndrome gets its name from the neuropsychiatrist who popularized the theory, Sergei Korsakoff.

The six major symptoms of Korsakoff's syndrome are 1) anterograde amnesia, 2) retrograde amnesia 3) severe memory loss 4) confabulation 5) meager content in conversation 6) lack of insight and apathy.

Unfortunately Korsakoff's involves neuron loss and damage to neurons. It then progresses to gliosis which damages to supporting cells of the central nervous system and can culminate into bleeding in the dorsomedial nucleus or anterior group of the thalamus (a very important brain organelle).

The damage is generally permanent and Thiamine treatment may help some, however it is more likely that the patient will need chronic care and a supportive living environment for the remainder of their life.

B is INCORRECT
Tardive Dyskinesia is characterized by repetitive, involuntary, purposeless movements, such as grimacing, tongue protrusion, lip smacking, puckering and pursing of the lips, and rapid eye blinking. Rapid movements of the extremities may also occur. The patient may also exhibit impaired movements of the fingers. People with Tardive Dyskinesia have difficulty not moving.

C is INCORRECT
Psychogenic fugue is an older term from the (DSM-IV Dissociative Disorders 300.13), and is a rare psychiatric disorder characterized by reversible amnesia for personal identity, including the memories, personality and other identifying characteristics of individuality. The state can be short-lived (hours to days), but can also last months or longer.
A type of psychogenic fugue is known as "dissociative fugue" which usually involves unplanned travel or wandering, and can result in the patient establishing a new identity. The amnesia remains for the period of the fugue state, but upon recovery, all

memories from the fugue state are usually integrated, into the overall memory.

D is INCORRECT
Alzheimer's disease is a newer name for a series of disorders which used to be called Dementia. Technically, the formal name of Alzheimer's is Senile Dementia of the Alzheimer's Type. It gets its name from the person who first described the symptoms, German psychiatrist and neuropathologist, Alois Alzheimer.

Question 164   Section: Clinical

The correct answer is B
Schizophrenia is a medical condition, which affects the brain. While we do not know its cause, and there is no cure, we do know (through MRI technology) there are significant changes in neuronal activity and there is often a significant loss of neurons. It is accepted, in the field, generally, that schizophrenia is the product of a disease process, or multiple disease processes and is not the result of internal psychological conflicts.

A is INCORRECT (Something you would want to focus on)
Anything you can do to preserve or maintain present levels of functioning is very important. Given the meager information presented in the question we have to make several assumptions. First, the client is not hospitalized, therefore they are living in the community. Second, they are functional enough they do not require hospitalization. Our goal should always be toward client self-determination and providing services in the least restrictive environment.

C is INCORRECT (Something you would want to focus on)
Any time you can orient a client to their present reality, whether they suffer from schizophrenia or another malady, you are

helping. A client who is reality focused can make better decisions regarding their life and future.

D is INCORRECT (Something you would want to focus on)
Working with adaptive behavior and helping the client make the behavior more adaptive is extremely important. Start where they are and lead them forward.

Question 165   Section: Clinical

The correct answer is C
The client has just used you as a movie screen and projected her mother onto you and is now transferring her emotions and desires onto the projection of her mother. As a therapist, you must withdraw the screen so the projection fails and therefore the transference is unsuccessful. This will cause the manipulation to fail and you should see the client attempt to use other mechanisms. Remember, the client is using this mechanism (set of behaviors) because it is very functional for getting their needs met. You have to assume that they are in therapy because they are running into situations where there old mechanisms no longer work as well, if at all. This is the time to explore and learn to use new mechanisms.

A is INCORRECT
Displacement is the mechanism whereby the user tries to reduce anxiety by "dumping" their feelings for one person (usually someone who has more power than them) onto another person (usually someone with less power than them.)

B is INCORRECT
A counter-transference reaction is identical in nature to a transference reaction, EXCEPT, it is the THERAPIST who projects and transfers feelings onto the CLIENT. Only the therapist can counter-transfer, and unless you are very aware

[148]

of what you are doing and are well grounded in psychoanalytic theory, counter-transference is usually BAD.

D is INCORRECT
Sublimation is an ego defense mechanism where a client has strong feelings on a specific issue and instead of expressing them, pulls them back inside themselves and uses the "ego" energy associated with the issue to power some other issue. This can be a very positive experience or it can be a very negative one. If you have strong feelings of being persecuted and treated unjustly, and you become an advocate for the less fortunate, channeling your "ego energy" into helping them battle injustice, this would probably be a positive example of sublimation.

Question 166   Section: Clinical

The correct answer is A
From age 6 to 12 a child is learning "methods of interacting" and "competence at interacting with others." This requires they learn to cope with their emotions. During this stage of development the goal is to create and develop new skills and knowledge. If we are allowed to do this, we develop a sense of "industry" or competence. Part of this stage is the development of control over our emotions, especially when dealing with other people. If the child fails to learn how to resolve feelings, they can develop a sense of inadequacy and inferiority. This will almost certainly damage self-esteem and competence. The parents are interfering with his ability to learn how to handle his emotions. Without an external outlet, he is likely to compensate for this lack of training in the form of internalized anxiety and fear.

B is INCORRECT

Eating disorders follow a similar path but there is no indication that there is a problem with food. It is possible, if this were a female instead of a male, they might begin to exercise control over themselves and their family, by controlling their food intact and /or binging and purging.

C is INCORRECT
Psychomotor problems are not usually associated with a compensation mechanism at this age. If you see psychomotor issues, it would be best to get a medical evaluation, preferably from a neurologist, immediately.

D is INCORRECT
Given the data in the question, this would not seem to be a problem, however, if this were to continue unabated, you might certainly begin to see this type of behavior by age 12 or 13. This boy will eventually learn to compensate for having their emotions squashed, but it will probably be a "non-productive" form of compensation.

Question 167   Section: Clinical

The correct answer is D
His approach is very intellectualized and rational. Alcoholism is a very complex illness that does not lend itself well to rationalization. Most alcoholics can rationalize their behavior or understand it as wrong, however, it is not often helpful to initial recovery. The reasons for his wife's alcohol problems could be physical/genetic, behavioral, psychological or a combination of all three. What is clear is he has taken on a co-dependent role and would benefit from working on codependent issues. You might also explore his familial background regarding alcohol abuse by his parents.

A is INCORRECT

His approach is a manifestation of denial and a refusal to see the complexity of alcohol abuse and addiction.

B is INCORRECT
This would probably not be appropriate for the initial stages of therapy. There are many issues, which would need to be met in order to deal with this specific issue.

C is INCORRECT
The "dance" between the ALCOHOLIC and the CO-DEPENDENT is very complex, subtle and reinforcing in ways that are almost never apparent. Both parties are getting needs met and both have agendas, whether understood of hidden. Alcoholism almost never "goes away" and his defense mechanisms could be adequate to last him the rest of his life without a change. An excellent text for understand the complexities of the alcoholic-codependent relationship is Claude Steiner's, "Games Alcoholics Play"

Question 168   Section: Clinical

The correct answer is B
Alcohol and drug addiction are extremely complex situations. One of the primary issues is life structure or lack of it. When a client is homeless or unemployed, they are lacking in structure. Boundaries, which are normally weak and unhealthy in substance abusing clients, are minimal or non-existent in this situation. There is no reason to look forward to a different day" and no concrete reason "Not to use."

A is INCORRECT
A concurrent anxiety disorder may well cause some problems with their addiction, however, it can be dealt with in treatment and does not necessarily correlate to a poor prognosis.

C is INCORRECT

Age does not correlate with poor prognosis. If anything, common sense would indicate that age would probably correlate with successful treatment. One of the tenets of substance abuse counseling is that you treat when you can and you treat every time someone comes back. It is not unusual for the addict to "fall off the wagon". Once they do and they come back to treatment, you pick up where they left off. They have a greater chance to absorb the lessons of treatment.

D is INCORRECT

It is a major mistake to diagnose or try to treat a personality disorder during an addiction. The basic concepts of addiction would indicate weak boundaries and poor ego strength. These are the hallmarks of both the addict and the individual with a personality disorder. Treat the addiction first and the "personality disorder" may go away, because it was never there to begin with.

Question 169   Section: Clinical

The correct answer is B

Cognitive behavioral therapy (CBT) is a psychotherapy whose aim is to solve problems of dysfunctional emotions, behaviors and thoughts through a systematic and goal-oriented procedure operating in the present. Empirical evidence exists that CBT is effective for treating a variety of problems, including mood, anxiety, personality, eating, substance abuse, and psychotic disorders. Treatment often consists of specific, technique-driven, brief, direct, and time-limited treatments for specific psychological disorders. It is useful in individual therapy and group treatment.

A is INCORRECT

Treatment's goal is to reduce the need for illegal drugs. There are many forms of treatment.

C is INCORRECT
This technique moves into the realm of insight-oriented therapy. This is usually done with a psychodynamic approach.

D is INCORRECT
This is generally done as a replacement maintenance therapy and its overall purpose is to reduce and eliminates the use of illegal drugs, as well as avoiding the criminality associated with drugs. When used as a treatment method for injectable drugs it reduces the transmission of infectious diseases and allows the user to gain health. This type of drug treatment is currently in use in the United States in the use of Methadone to treat Heroin, Morphine, Oxycontin and other opiate abuse.

Question 170 Section: Clinical

The correct answer is C
Of the numerous different Tricyclic medications current available all have an overdose possibility of increased cardiac toxicity. Of all of the TCA's, two of them (Elavil and Dothiepin) account for 81.6% of all the deaths by TCA overdose. When compared to all other drugs, TCA's are responsible for 34.14 deaths from overdose per one million prescriptions.

A is INCORRECT
SSRI's; selective serotonin reuptake inhibitors account for 2.02 deaths from overdose per one million prescriptions.

B is INCORRECT
MAOI's; monoamine oxidase inhibitors account for 13.48 deaths from overdose per one million prescriptions.

D is INCORRECT
Atypicals (Atypical antipsychotics) account for 6.19 deaths from overdose per one million prescriptions.

Reference
British MEdical Journal. 1995 Jan 28;310(6974):221-4.
Relative mortality from overdose of antidepressants.
Henry JA, Alexander CA, Sener EK.

Question 171 Section: Psychotherapy

The correct answer is D

During the initial phases of treatment, your client is likely to feel anger at the system and some hostility towards you as the treatment provider. Just because the justice system has recognized that your client has a problem does not mean that your client has recognized his problem. It would be unlikely that your client's behavior reached a level high enough to get the attention of the justice system without your client having a problem.

A is INCORRECT
Your feelings may well play a part in the initial phase of treatment. They should not. As you are only human, your feelings might interfere. If they do, talk it out with your clinical supervisor.

B is INCORRECT
Everyone manipulates. It is human nature. Addicts attempt to manipulate more because they have a greater tendency to lie to themselves and therefore will lie to others. The disease of addiction fosters lying. As a counselor, you should expect it and then NOT take it personally.

C is INCORRECT

In court ordered treatment, the lack of local resources will not be likely to cause major problems during the initial phase of treatment. As the client begins to own their recovery and the response to their addiction process, then resource scarcity will play a larger part.

Question 172 Section: Ethics

The correct answer is A

This is a clear example of what ethics professionals call the "slippery slope". The chances of you accepting a cup of coffee as a token gesture will probably have no impact on your relationship with the client. But, you have just crossed a boundary, no matter how small, and the relationship has changed in ways that you can not predict. You do not know what "buying a cup of coffee means to the client"! In some cultures, providing food and drink is very important and sets up very clear roles. What happens the next time the client meets you and wants a cup of coffee but only has enough money for themselves. They then decide to forgo the coffee rather than embarrass themselves by not being able to but you one. Alternatively, they say, "Hey, I want a cup of coffee and I am broke today, since I got last time, how about you getting them this time?" Simple things can get complicated very fast when you do not maintain clear boundaries. Remember, boundaries are nothing more than rules you create about how to interact with other people. Make your rules and do not violate them and you will be much happier as a therapist.

B is INCORRECT

Nothing is "Just a ..." All human behavior is rooted in needs. The client knows some of these needs and some are unknown and unconscious. Sharing food and drink is a rather intimate gesture. It is often a gesture among equals or among persons trying to start a relationship based on equality. The relationship between you and your client is never equal and never will be.

C is INCORRECT
This is an acceptable answer but not the BEST answer. By walking down to the cafeteria with them, they may perceive the relationship as more than therapist-client. If it is not a behavior you would do in your office with a client, then do not do it outside of your office.

D is INCORRECT
The moment you accept this offer, you have begun to change the boundaries of the relationship in very subtle ways. Whether you ultimately pay or not.

Question 173 Section: Ethics

The correct answer is C
This answer is the BEST answer given the choices and information given, however, information can only be released for specific reasons. Some of these reasons are: the client is being investigated for a crime involving sexual abuse or physical abuse of a child, elderly person, or a disabled person. Also, remember, you are never obligated to release any specific information to law enforcement, outside the boundaries of child/elder/disabled abuse without a court order. If you have any questions, always consult an attorney.

A is INCORRECT
Without informed consent, you cannot release to anyone. The rules regarding attorney-client privilege, and whether the information you have released falls under this protection is far too complicated for you to determine. If the client's lawyer wants information, get informed consent for the client before releasing it.

B is INCORRECT
NEVER…There is NO better explanation

D is INCORRECT
Definitely not! Just because you are married, and even if she is a clinician as well, you are not allowed to discuss your cases with your spouse.

Clinical Pearl: In the mid 90's my wife and I worked for the same private practice. I completed an assessment on a family; mom, dad and two sisters; and began seeing the youngest sister in individual therapy. I also saw the mom and dad occasionally in relation to the issues the youngest daughter was struggling with. Mom and dad told me they had gotten another therapist to see the older daughter. As per our ethics, I never questioned this. Three months after I began sessions, I was watching the 11 PM news with my wife and the face of my client, the youngest daughter, came on the news in relation to a serious crime having been committed. As I sat in shock my wife got up and said, "I need to call her mother and see how she is doing." I was confused, "Why would you call her mother? How do you even know the name of her mother?" My wife replied, "Because I am seeing the older daughter in therapy." To which I replied, "Funny you should mention that…"

My wife and I saw two different children from the same family in the same private practice and never knew the other was involved with the family. Just because you share a life, does not mean you need to share your work.

Question 174 Section: Ethics

The correct answer is D

This falls back on two very simple ethical concepts. The first – a Therapist-Client relationship is inherently one of different power levels. The therapist has more power and control than the client. The relationship is NEVER one of equals. The second – Once a client, ALWAYS a client. This is a boundary issue that you must adopt if you are to practice clinically. There are no exceptions. You can talk yourself into any situation you want and you can convince yourself that you are doing what is best or "there could be no harm", but, the truth is the possibility of harm exists.

A is INCORRECT
A written contract does not wipe away the concept of a dual relationship.

B is INCORRECT
Your feelings of a lack of an exploitive situation do not TRUMP the ethical code

C is INCORRECT
A dual relationship is a dual relationship, regardless of what you choice to discuss or avoid.

Clinical Note: I know these answers sound BLACK & WHITE...but boundaries need to be very clear. You are interacting with emotionally vulnerable people. You are simply a therapist, not a guru, sage or anointed person. You need boundaries...your client needs you to have boundaries.

Question 175 Section: Psychotherapy

The correct answer is B
Deceitful interactions and intentional destructiveness are both indicators that the family system would not be successful in family therapy. Family therapy requires commitment to change

and an overarching goal to make the group better than an individual. The pattern of deliberate destructiveness and deceitfulness are dynamics that an individual uses to maintain control in a pathological environment. These are "ID" based responses. This constellation would generally indicate there is no "SUPER-EGO" functioning of note in the family and therefore no shared purpose.

A is INCORRECT
The constant violation of interpersonal boundaries is a great place to start in family therapy. Families have many types of boundaries and many ways to mark their space. Interpersonal boundary violations indicate a system that needs "resetting" and "retraining". This situation is ripe for a family therapy approach.

C is INCORRECT
All families keep secrets. When the pattern become so pervasive it appears to dominate the clinical picture, it should be treated like a boundary issue. This situation is amenable to family therapy.

D is INCORRECT
Just because some members of the family have no desire to participate, if they show up they will probably benefit. The external pressure by the family will probably pull them into the therapeutic process.

Clinical Note: Family therapy is probably one of the toughest forms of therapy known to social work. Due to standard communication diagramming, you need to focus on so many variables in order to be successful, it is sometimes mindboggling. Social Work Programs offer a course in family therapy. You should definitely take it before attempting family therapy. But, if you want to be successful, you should also take several courses in the Marriage and Family Therapy program at your university. It also helps if you are slightly older and have your own family. There are unique issues to raising a family that will make you much more sensitive to a family's needs. If you wish to do family therapy, get "bunches" of training at every opportunity.

Question 176 Section: Psychotherapy

The correct answer is A

Enmeshment had a tendency to develop poor boundaries between people. It fosters a "poor ego strength" which can result in blurring between roles and responsibilities. This "blurring" between roles can be very devastating to a family.

According to Judith L. Herman in her 1981 book "Father-Daughter Incest." Published by Harvard University Press. She determined a number of 'markers' which would lead the therapist to believe there was a possibility of incest. Her study included 40 victims of father-daughter incest and 20 victims of non-contact sexual abuse.

She discovered that "incestuous families were conventional to a fault. Most were churchgoing and financially stable. They maintained a facade of respectability that helped hide the sexual abuse. The fathers' authority in the families was absolute, often asserted by force. Half of the fathers were habitually violent, but never enough to send a family member to the hospital. Their sexual assaults were usually planned in advance. The men were feared within the family but impressed outsiders as sympathetic, even admirable. In the presence of superior authority, they were ingratiating, deferential, even meek. They were hard-working, competent, and often very successful. Of the 40 fathers, 31 were the sole support of their families. Sex roles were rigidly defined. Mother and sisters were considered inferior to father and brothers. The incestuous fathers exercised minute control over the women's lives, often discouraging social contacts and keeping them secluded in the home. Most of the mothers were full-time housewives; six did some part-time work, and three had full-time jobs.

B is INCORRECT
Attitudes of permissiveness do not correlate highly with incest.

C is INCORRECT
Permeable boundaries and extreme chaos actually appear to correlate negative with incest. The incestuous family tends to be controlled, with rigid boundaries. Chaos seems to be the antithesis of incest.

D is INCORRECT
High conflict relationships tend to be negatively correlated with incest. This seems appropriate, as the severe violation which occurs in incest would require control and secrecy to maintain. A high conflict relationship would have a tendency to violate any secrecy and locus of control.

Question 177 Section: Psychotherapy

The correct answer is C
The client clearly suffers from a Major Depressive Disorder and the voices indicate some psychotic features are present. Remember, hearing voices or seeing things which do not exist are the hallmark of psychosis.
According to the DSM-IV:

> A) a person who suffers from major depressive disorder must either have a depressed mood or a loss of interest or pleasure in daily activities consistently for at least a two week period.

B) This mood must represent a change from the person's normal mood; social, occupational, educational or other important functioning must also be negatively impaired by the change in mood.

C) Major depressive disorder cannot be diagnosed if a person has a history of manic, hypomanic, or mixed episodes (e.g., a bipolar disorder) or if the depressed mood is better accounted for by schizoaffective disorder and is not superimposed on schizophrenia, schizophreniform disorder, delusional disorder or psychotic disorder.

D) Further, the symptoms are not better accounted for by bereavement (i.e., after the loss of a loved one) and the symptoms persist for longer than two months or are characterized by marked functional impairment, morbid preoccupation with worthlessness, suicidal ideation, psychotic symptoms, or psychomotor retardation.

This disorder is characterized by the presence of the majority of these symptoms:

1) Depressed mood most of the day, nearly every day, as indicated by either subjective report (e.g., feels sad or empty) or observation made by others (e.g., appears tearful).
2) Markedly diminished interest or pleasure in all, or almost all, activities most of the day, nearly every day
3) Significant weight loss when not dieting or weight gain (e.g., a change of more than 5 of body weight in a month), or decrease or increase in appetite nearly every day.
4) Insomnia or hypersomnia nearly every day

5) Psychomotor agitation or retardation nearly every day

6) Fatigue or loss of energy nearly every day

7) Feelings of worthlessness or excessive or inappropriate guilt nearly every day

8) Diminished ability to think or concentrate, or indecisiveness, nearly every day

9) Recurrent thoughts of death (not just fear of dying), recurrent suicidal ideation without a specific plan, or a suicide attempt or a specific plan for committing suicide.

A is INCORRECT

The Depressive disorder NOS category includes disorders with depressive features that do not meet the criteria for Major Depressive Disorder, Dysthymic disorder, Adjustment Disorder with Depressed Mood or Adjustment Disorder with Mixed Anxiety and Depressed Mood. Sometimes depressive symptoms can present as part of an Anxiety Disorder Not otherwise Specified. Examples include:

1) Premenstrual Dysphoric Disorder: in most menstrual cycles during the past years, (e.g., markedly depressed mood, marked anxiety, marked affective liability, decreased interest in activities) regularly occurred during the onset of menses). These symptoms must be severe enough to markedly interfere with work, school, or usual activities and be entirely absent for at least 1 week post menses.

2) Minor depressive disorder :episodes of at at least 2 weeks of depressive symptoms but with fewer than the five items required for Major Depressive Disorder.

3) Recurrent brief depressive disorder: depressive episodes lasting from 2 days up to 2 weeks, occurring at least once a month for 12 months(not associated with the menstrual cycle)

4) Post psychotic depressive Disorder of schizophrenia :a Major Depressive Episode that occurs during the residual phase of schizophrenia.

5) A Major Depressive Episode superimposed on Delusional Disorder, Psychotic Disorder Not Otherwise Specified, or the active phase of Schizophrenia.

Situations in which the clinician has concluded that a depressive disorder is present but is unable to determine whether it is primary, due to a general medical condition, or substance induced.

http://en.wikipedia.org/wiki/Depressive_Disorder_Not_Otherwise_Specified

B is INCORRECT
The client clearly suffers from a Major Depressive Disorder, but the voices indicate a psychotic component which is not addressed in this diagnosis.

D is INCORRECT
The alcohol use occurred after the onset of the depression and became worse after the onset of the auditory hallucinations. The alcohol creates problems, but, was not the trigger or precursor to the problems.

Question 178

The correct answer is D
By far, the most serious potential for damage to children in substance abusing environments is neglect, physical and sexual abuse.

A is INCORRECT
These are not highly correlated with this family environment

B is INCORRECT
There have been no specific causal links in the research. If a person is "more prone" to develop Schizophrenia or Bipolar

Disorder may have increased problems due to the higher level of overall stress, however, no current correlation exists.

C is INCORRECT
Unfortunately, we have very little data on the causes of social phobia and panic attacks. They may be environment, genetic, or a mix of these and other things as well.

Question 179   Section: Psychotherapy

The correct answer is B
Both Substance Use/Abuse diagnoses and Mental Health issues are coded on Axis I. Only Mental Retardation and Personality Disorders are coded on Axis II. When a person suffers from a substance use/abuse disorder and a mental health diagnosis, they are said to have a dual (two) diagnosis and treatment becomes much trickier, because the entanglement of the two categories need to be teased out and sometimes you need to focus on the substance use first, and other times the mental health issues. This type of client is why you must get extra training in substance abuse issues.

A is INCORRECT
Neither of these issues would be coded on Axis II

C is INCORRECT
All Diagnoses are Multi-axial. They must cover all five axes.

D is INCORRECT
The DSM-IV-TR requires axial diagnosis.

Question 180   Section: Diagnosis and Assessment.

The correct answer is D
The purpose of the "Draw-a-Person" test is to assist professionals in inferring children's cognitive developmental

levels with little or no influence of other factors such as language barriers or special needs. Any other uses of the test are merely projective and are not endorsed by the first creator.

Test administration involves the administrator requesting children to complete three individual drawings on separate pieces of paper. Children are asked to draw a man, a woman, and themselves. No further instructions are given and the child is free to make the drawing in whichever way he/she would like. There is no right or wrong type of drawing, although the child must make a drawing of a whole person each time - i.e. head to feet, not just the face. The test has no time limit; however, children rarely take longer than about 10 or 15 minutes to complete all three drawings. Harris's book (1963) provides scoring scales which are used to examine and score the child's drawings. The test is completely non-invasive and non-threatening to children, which is part of its appeal.

To evaluate intelligence, the test administrator uses the Draw-a-Person: QSS (Quantitative Scoring System). This system analyzes fourteen different aspects of the drawings (such as specific body parts and clothing) for various criteria, including presence or absence, detail, and proportion. In all, there are 64 scoring items for each drawing. A separate standard score is recorded for each drawing, and a total score for all three. The use of a nonverbal, nonthreatening task to evaluate intelligence is intended to eliminate possible sources of bias by reducing variables like primary language, verbal skills, communication disabilities, and sensitivity to working under pressure. However, test results can be influenced by previous drawing experience, a factor that may account for the tendency of middle-class children to score higher on this test than lower-class children, who often have fewer opportunities to draw.
Reference: http://en.wikipedia.org/wiki/Draw-A-Person_Test

A is INCORRECT

Fine and gross motor function is best evaluated by an Occupational Therapist. This is usually not a social work function and you may be overstepping common practice, which could cause ethical issues.

B is INCORRECT
There would be no need to evaluate children's personality structures at this age. Personality is not fully developed and is malleable at this age.

C is INCORRECT
This test would not assess these issues. Some people have used it for this, however, it is not agreed upon to be tested or validated for it.

Question 181   **Section: Psychotherapy**

The correct answer is D
Your worker is suffering from compassion fatigue and is under tremendous stress. It may be totally related to the job or to other issues in her life; however, it is still a problem. Her productivity will decrease and you should expect to see problems with her judgment and scheduling. The initial method of addressing this issue is to give the worker time off and refer for stress counseling. The fact that this worker may need to change jobs or work in a different area of social work should also be considered.

A is INCORRECT
Counter-transference is a projection during therapy. The projection is from the therapist to the client. It is usually considered to be unhealthy and can be damaging to the therapist-client relationship as well as having the potential to create a dual relationship

B is INCORRECT

This worker may be depressed. The depression may have made her more susceptible to compassion fatigue, or may be a part of it. Regardless, the primary symptoms presented by the worker indicate burn-out, stress overload and compassion fatigue.

C is INCORRECT

There is no indication of projection occurring in the situation described by the question.

Remember, projection is a psychological defense mechanism where a person subconsciously denies his or her own attributes, thoughts, and emotions, which are then ascribed to the outside world, usually to other people. Thus, projection involves imagining or projecting the belief that others originate those feelings.

Projection reduces anxiety by allowing the expression of the unwanted unconscious impulses or desires without letting the conscious mind recognize them.

An example of this behavior might be blaming another for self failure. The mind may avoid the discomfort of consciously admitting personal faults by keeping those feelings unconscious, and by redirecting libidinal satisfaction by attaching, or "projecting," those same faults onto another person or object.

http://en.wikipedia.org/wiki/Psychological_projection

Question 182   Section: Psychotherapy

The correct answer is A

The Rogerian centered therapist uses current life events and reflects information back to the client in a "life-affirming manner." They are interested in the 'here-and-now' and will assist the client in 'being heard' so they can release the issues they are struggling with and be able to cope better and bring new and less problematic issues into their sphere of consciousness.

B is INCORRECT
Cognitive behavioral therapy (CBT) is a psychotherapeutic approach. CBT aims to solve problems concerning dysfunctional emotions, behaviors and cognitions through a goal-oriented, systematic procedure in the present.
The particular therapeutic techniques vary within the different approaches of CBT according to the particular kind of problem issues, but commonly may include keeping a diary of significant events and associated feelings, thoughts and behaviors; questioning and testing cognitions, assumptions, evaluations and beliefs that might be unhelpful and unrealistic; gradually facing activities which may have been avoided; and trying out new ways of behaving and reacting. Relaxation, mindfulness and distraction techniques are also commonly included. Cognitive behavioral therapy is often also used in conjunction with mood stabilizing medications to treat conditions like bipolar disorder.

http://en.wikipedia.org/wiki/Cognitive_behavioral_therapy

C is INCORRECT
The psychodynamic approach is interested in gathering information about current behavior and past experience to determine issues of developmental importance in the past and how to determine the impact of past issues on the present system.

D is INCORRECT
The multicultural approach is an eclectic system of many disciplines which focus on the role gender, culture, sexual-orientation and societal impacts affect the life of the client.

Question 183   **Section: Behavior**

The correct answer is B
Statistics are hard to come by and this appears to have roots both in the physical and the cultural. In general, adolescent males are more likely to act-out with aggression. This is probably related to the surge in testosterone (a male hormone) which comes around the early teen years.

A is INCORRECT

In general, girls are more prone to sexually acting out than boys. There appears to be multiple cultural and physiological issues involved in this answer, many of which are still being researched. Consider this a general interpretation of the data available.

C is INCORRECT
The data on this is very confusing. Some studies show girls more than guys and other studies show more equality between them (girl and guys run away at the same rate.)

D is INCORRECT
Once again the data is to muddles on this to be definitive. It would not be possible to say either sex has a higher prevalence rate.

Question 184   **Section: Behavior**

The correct answer is C
In psychoanalytic theory, the superego is a personality construct, which internalized the role of the parent. It can be viewed as the "parent inside your head" which helps you make decision which take into account the needs or feeling of others. It is believed to be created from having external parenting forces applied to the child during growth. The lack of this personality structure causes impulsive behavior, which does not take into consideration, the feeling of others.

A is INCORRECT

Ego functioning is simply the "adult role" during interactions.

B is INCORRECT
While the formulation of a conduct disorder may well be caused by a lack of a structured family system, the system is not a personality structure.

D is INCORRECT
Much like the answer to B, lack of an authoritative figure may help create an underdeveloped SUPEREGO structure; it is not a personality structure. The three Freudian Personality Structures are ID, EGO, and SUPEREGO.

Question 185   Section: Diagnosis

The correct answer is D
While it is age-appropriate behavior for children between the ages of four and six or possibly as late as seven to enter into a room nude in order to evoke some excitement, the fact that the child was found in a closet, indicates that they are interested in hiding their activity. The age of the child, the fact they were found in a closet with another child of the same age, and the fact that both children were naked, would lead you to consider that this is a sexually acting out behavior that has occurred because the child has been victimized. You would want to assess the child for possible sexual abuse victimization. If you were to get enough information to suspect victimization then you should report the incident to your local department of social services.

A is INCORRECT
An oppositional defiant disorder may possibly be diagnosed as early as age eight, it would require a lengthy list of behaviors which are problematic for childhood socialization.

B is INCORRECT
A conduct disorder is usually diagnosed in early to middle teenage years. A conduct disorder has marked examples of inappropriate, violent, and predatory behaviors.

C is INCORRECT
Attention deficit hyperactivity disorder is not generally associated with sexually acting out behaviors. The fact of the matter is, the sexually acting out behavior needs to be your issue of primary focus.

Question 186   **Section: Psychotherapy**

The correct answer is C
Displacement shifts sexual or aggressive impulses to a more acceptable or less threatening target.   This allows the redirection of emotions to a safer outlet and also allows the separation of emotions from real objects. The redirection of the intense emotion toward someone or something that is less offensive and/or less threatening, with the benefit of avoiding the issue directly is very powerful. In this situation, she has displaced the sexual feelings she has for her ex-partner onto the new man in her life. It is safe to place them on him, while it is unsafe (due to rejection and emotional abandonment) to place her sexual feelings on her ex-partner.

A is INCORRECT
Distortion is the gross reshaping of external reality to meet internal needs. It is one of the pathological defense mechanisms. If a client is using this mechanism, you should be alert for severe pathology.

B is INCORRECT
Projection is a primitive form of paranoia. Projection also reduces anxiety by allowing the expression of the undesirable impulses or desires without accepting conscious awareness of them. It also allows the client to attribute his or her own unacknowledged, unacceptable and/or unwanted thoughts and emotions to someone else.

D is INCORRECT
Intellectualization is a form of isolation, which allows the client to concentrate on the intellectual aspects of a situation in order to distance themselves from the associated anxiety-provoking

emotions. They will use the mechanism to separate emotions from ideas; entertain desires and wishes in a formal and affectively bland manner in order to fail or refuse to act upon them avoiding unacceptable emotions by focusing on the intellectual aspects. This is a very difficult defense mechanism to counter in therapy.

Question 187   **Section: Psychotherapy**

The correct answer is D

In Gestalt Therapy, unexpressed guilt is viewed as unfinished business, which will cause the client to be unable to achieve a holistic, self-organizing tendency. In the gestalt perspective, the whole is greater than the sum of the parts. Unfinished business would be equated to focusing on a specific part of your life and being unable to integrate the rest.

Gestalt has two theoretical principles, which lead to two more methodologies, which it views as methodological principles. The Two theoretical principles are 1) Principle of Totality (The conscious experience is considered globally as it takes into account all of the physical and mental aspects of the individual, at the same time) and 2) the Principle of psychophysical isomorphism, which stated the existence of a correlation between conscious experience and cerebral activity.

From these two principles the two methodological principles are born. They are 1) Phenomenon Experimental Analysis – (from the Totality Principle, any psychological research should take as a starting point phenomena and not be solely focused on sensory qualities.) and 2) the Biotic Experiment – where the norm was experimenting in natural situations and under real conditions, that could be reproduces with greater fidelity in a habitual manner by the client.

This left Gestalt systems with four key principles.

1) Emergence, the process of complex pattern formation from simpler rules. It is demonstrated by the perception of the Dog Picture, which depicts a Dalmatian dog sniffing the ground in the shade of overhanging trees. The dog is not recognized by first identifying its parts (feet, ears, nose, tail, etc.), and then inferring the dog from those component parts.

2) Reification, the constructive or generative aspect of perception, by which the experienced percept contains more explicit spatial information than the sensory stimulus on which it is based.

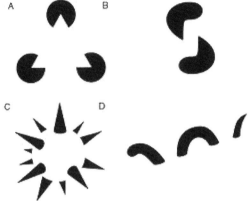

3) Multistability, the tendency of ambiguous perceptual experiences to pop back and forth unstably between two or more alternative interpretations. This is seen for example in the Necker cube, and in Rubin's Figure/Vase illusion.

4) Invariance, a property of perception whereby simple geometrical objects are recognized independent of rotation, translation, and scale; as well as several other variations such as elastic deformations, different lighting, and different component features

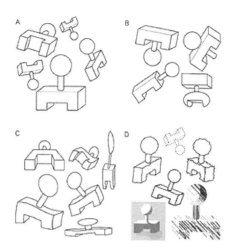

A is INCORRECT
Dysfunctional is too broad a term to accurately describe the situation.

B is INCORRECT
Unfinished business is never considered normal.

C is INCORRECT
Neurotic is an old term used by the psychoanalysts which has fallen out of favor with modern cognitive behavioral principles.

Question 188   **Section: Psychotherapy**

The correct answer is D
He meets the diagnostic criteria for an Antisocial Personality Disorder. He also meets the criteria for a conduct disorder, however he is over 18 now and the behavior has not stopped. A review of the diagnostic criteria follows:

(A)There is a pervasive pattern of disregard for and violation of the rights of others occurring since age 15 years, as indicated by three (or more) of the following:
(1) failure to conform to social norms with respect to lawful behaviors as indicated by repeatedly performing acts that are grounds for arrest (2) deceitfulness, as indicated by repeated lying, use of aliases, or conning others for personal profit or pleasure (3) impulsivity or failure to plan ahead (4) irritability and aggressiveness, as indicated by repeated physical fights or assaults (5) reckless disregard for safety of self or others (6) consistent irresponsibility, as indicated by repeated failure to sustain consistent work behavior or honor financial obligations (7) lack of remorse, as indicated by being indifferent to or rationalizing having hurt, mistreated, or stolen from another

B. The individual is at least age 18 years.

C. There is evidence of Conduct Disorder with onset before age 15 years.

D. The occurrence of antisocial behavior is not exclusively during the course of Schizophrenia or a Manic Episode.

A is INCORRECT
While he does meet the criteria for a conduct disorder, he has passed the age of 18 and the Antisocial PD is a more appropriate diagnosis. The criteria for a conduct disorder is:
(A) A repetitive and persistent pattern of behavior in which the basic rights of others or major age-appropriate societal norms or rules are violated, as manifested by the presence of three (or more) of the following criteria in the past 12 months, with at least one criterion present in the past 6 months:
> **Aggression to people and animals**
> (1) often bullies, threatens, or intimidates others (2) often initiates physical fights (3) has used a weapon that can cause serious physical harm to others (e.g., abat, brick, broken bottle, knife, gun) (4) has been physically cruel to people (5) has been physically cruel to animals (6) has stolen while confronting a victim (e.g., mugging,

purse snatching, extortion, armed robbery) (7) has forced someone into sexual activity

Destruction of property

(8) has deliberately engaged in fire setting with the intention of causing serious damage (9) has deliberately destroyed others' property (other than by fire setting)

Deceitfulness or theft

(10) has broken into someone else's house, building, or car (11) often lies to obtain goods or favors or to avoid obligations (i.e., "cons" others) (12) has stolen items of nontrivial value without confronting a victim (e.g., shoplifting, but without breaking and entering; forgery)

Serious violations of rules

(13) often stays out at night despite parental prohibitions, beginning before age 13 years (14) has run away from home overnight at least twice while living in parental or parental surrogate home (or once without returning for a lengthy period) (15) is often truant from school, beginning before age 13 years

B. The disturbance in behavior causes clinically significant impairment in social, academic, or occupational functioning.

C. If the individual is age 18 years or older, criteria are not met for Antisocial Personality Disorder.

Specify type based on age at onset:

Childhood-Onset Type: onset of at least one criterion characteristic of Conduct Disorder prior to age 10 years

Adolescent-Onset Type: absence of any criteria characteristic of Conduct Disorder prior to age 10 years

Specify severity:

Mild: few if any conduct problems in excess of those required to make the diagnosis and conduct problems cause only minor harm to others

Moderate: number of conduct problems and effect on others intermediate between "mild" and "severe"

Severe: many conduct problems in excess of those required to make the diagnosis or conduct problems cause considerable harm to others

B is INCORRECT
The behavior is to severe for an oppositional defiant disorder.
Review the criteria below.
A pattern of negativistic, hostile, and defiant behavior lasting at
least 6 months, during which four (or more) of the following are
present:
>(1) often loses temper (2) often argues with adults
>(3) often actively defies or refuses to comply with adults'
>requests or rules (4) often deliberately annoys people
>(5) often blames others for his or her mistakes or
>misbehavior (6) is often touchy or easily annoyed by
>others
>(7) is often angry and resentful (8) is often spiteful or
>vindictive
>>Note: Consider a criterion met only if the
>>behavior occurs more frequently than is typically
>>observed in individuals of comparable age and
>>developmental level.

B. The disturbance in behavior causes clinically significant
impairment in social, academic, or occupational functioning.
C. The behaviors do not occur exclusively during the course of
a Psychotic or Mood Disorder.
D. Criteria are not met for Conduct Disorder, and, if the
individual is age 18 years or older, criteria are not met for
Antisocial Personality Disorder.

C is INCORRECT
Narcissistic Personality Disorder has an entirely different flavor.
The criteria follow:
DSM-IV-TR 301.81 (in Axis II Cluster B) as: A pervasive pattern
of grandiosity (in fantasy or behavior), need for admiration, and
lack of empathy, beginning by early adulthood and present in a
variety of contexts,
>as indicated by five (or more) of the following:
>(1) Has a grandiose sense of self-importance (e.g.,
>exaggerates achievements and talents, expects to be
>recognized as superior without commensurate
>achievements) (2) Is preoccupied with fantasies of
>unlimited success, power, brilliance, beauty, or ideal

love (3) Believes that he or she is "special" and unique and can only be understood by, or should associate with, other special or high-status people (or institutions) (4) Requires excessive admiration (5) Has a sense of entitlement, i.e., unreasonable expectations of especially favorable treatment or automatic compliance with his or her expectations (6) Is interpersonally exploitative, i.e., takes advantage of others to achieve his or her own ends (7) Lacks empathy: is unwilling to recognize or identify with the feelings and needs of others (8) Is often envious of others or believes others are envious of him or her (9) Shows arrogant, haughty behaviors or attitudes

Question 189   Section: Psychotherapy

The correct answer is A
The Anchoring Bias is the common human tendency to rely too heavily, or "anchor," on one piece of information or one trait when making decisions. The client is more than their diagnosis and both sets of diagnoses may be wrong, skewed of inappropriate.

B is INCORRECT
The Attentional Bias is the implicit cognitive bias defined as the tendency of emotionally dominant stimuli in one's environment to preferentially draw and hold attention.

C is INCORRECT
The Bandwagon Bias is the tendency to do (or believe) things because many other people do (or believe) the same. Related to group-think and herd behavior.

D is INCORRECT
The Blind Spot Bias is the tendency to see oneself as less biased than other people.

    Personal Note: It is my belief that given the expanded caseloads and lack of staff we, as social workers, have had to cope with over the past decade, it is very easy to become "sloppy" in our diagnosis. This can be related to lack of time to correctly diagnose or just plain exhaustion. You should always come to your own diagnosis.

Question 190   Section: Psychotherapy

The correct answer is C
Normalcy bias – the refusal to plan for, or react to a disaster, which has never happened before.

A is INCORRECT
Negativity bias – the tendency to pay more attention and give more weight to negative than positive experiences or other kinds of information.

B is INCORRECT
Neglect of probability – the tendency to completely disregard probability when making a decision under uncertainty

D is INCORRECT
Omission bias – the tendency to judge harmful actions as worse, or less moral, than equally harmful omissions (inactions).

Question 191 Section: Diagnosis

The correct answer is D
While the precursor behaviors can be seen in early to late teenage years, it would be diagnosed as a Conduct Disorder. The DSM has an express prohibition for assigning a diagnosis of ASPD prior to the age of 18.
Antisocial personality disorder is characterized by a long-standing pattern of a disregard for other people's rights, often crossing the line and violating those rights.

Individuals with Antisocial Personality Disorder frequently lack empathy and tend to be callous, cynical, and contemptuous of the feelings, rights, and sufferings of others. They may have an inflated and arrogant self-appraisal (e.g., feel that ordinary work is beneath them or lack a realistic concern about their current problems or their future) and may be excessively opinionated, self-assured, or cocky. They may display a glib, superficial charm and can be quite voluble and verbally facile (e.g., using technical terms or jargon that might impress someone who is unfamiliar with the topic). These individuals may also be irresponsible and exploitative in their sexual relationships.

Symptoms of Antisocial Personality Disorder
Antisocial personality disorder is diagnosed when a person's pattern of antisocial behavior has occurred since age 15 (although only adults 18 years or older can be diagnosed with this disorder) and consists of the majority of these symptoms:
- Failure to conform to social norms with respect to lawful behaviors as indicated by repeatedly performing acts that are grounds for arrest
- Deceitfulness, as indicated by repeated lying, use of aliases, or conning others for personal profit or pleasure
- Impulsivity or failure to plan ahead
- Irritability and aggressiveness, as indicated by repeated physical fights or assaults
- Reckless disregard for safety of self or others
- Consistent irresponsibility, as indicated by repeated failure to sustain consistent work behavior or honor financial obligations
- Lack of remorse, as indicated by being indifferent to or rationalizing having hurt, mistreated, or stolen from another
  Reference: http://psychcentral.com/disorders/sx7.htm

A is INCORRECT

The diagnostic criteria for Childhood Disintegrative Disorder is presented below:

A. Apparently normal development for at least the first 2 years after birth as manifested by the presence of age-appropriate verbal and nonverbal communication, social relationships, play, and adaptive behavior.

[181]

B. Clinically significant loss of previously
   acquired skills (before age 10 years) in at least
   two of the following areas:
   (1) expressive or receptive language
   (2) social skills or adaptive behavior
   (3) bowel or bladder control
   (4) play
   (5) motor skills

C. Abnormalities of functioning in at least two of the following
areas:
   (1) qualitative impairment in social interaction
       (e.g., impairment in nonverbal behaviors,
       failure to develop peer relationships, lack
       of social or emotional reciprocity)

   (2) qualitative impairments in communication
       (e.g., delay or lack of spoken language,
       inability to initiate or sustain a
       conversation, stereotyped and repetitive
       use of language, lack of varied make-
       believe play)

   (3) restricted, repetitive, and stereotyped
       patterns of behavior, interests, and
       activities, including motor stereotypies and
       mannerisms

D. The disturbance is not better accounted for by another specific
Pervasive Developmental Disorder or by Schizophrenia.

B is INCORRECT
In children with this Pervasive Developmental Disorder there is
substantial delay in communication and social interaction
associated with development of "restricted, repetitive and
stereotyped" behavior, interests, and activities.

Diagnostic criteria for 299.00 Autistic Disorder

A. A total of six (or more) items from (1), (2), and (3), with at least two from (1), and one each from (2) and (3):

(1) qualitative impairment in social interaction, as manifested by at least two of the following:
(a) marked impairment in the use of multiple nonverbal behaviors such as eye-to-eye gaze, facial expression, body postures, and gestures to regulate social interaction
(b) failure to develop peer relationships appropriate to developmental level
(c) a lack of spontaneous seeking to share enjoyment, interests, or achievements with other people (e.g., by a lack of showing, bringing, or pointing out objects of interest)
(d) lack of social or emotional reciprocity

(2) qualitative impairments in communication as manifested by at least one of the following:
(a) delay in, or total lack of, the development of spoken language (not accompanied by an attempt to compensate through alternative modes of communication such as gesture or mime)
(b) in individuals with adequate speech, marked impairment in the ability to initiate or sustain a conversation with others
(c) stereotyped and repetitive use of language or idiosyncratic language
(d) lack of varied, spontaneous make-believe play or social imitative play appropriate to developmental level

(3) restricted repetitive and stereotyped patterns of behavior, interests, and activities, as manifested by at least one of the following:

[183]

(a) encompassing preoccupation with one or more stereotyped and restricted patterns of interest that is abnormal either in intensity or focus
(b) apparently inflexible adherence to specific, nonfunctional routines or rituals
(c) stereotyped and repetitive motor mannerisms (e.g., hand or finger flapping or twisting, or complex whole-body movements)
(d) persistent preoccupation with parts of objects

B. Delays or abnormal functioning in at least one of the following areas, with onset prior to age 3 years: (1) social interaction, (2) language as used in social communication, or (3) symbolic or imaginative play.

C. The disturbance is not better accounted for by Rett's Disorder or Childhood Disintegrative Disorder.

C is INCORRECT
Children with this mental disorder, display repetitive nonfunctional movements that can result in bodily injury or interfere with normal functioning.

Diagnostic criteria for 307.3 Stereotypic Movement Disorder
A. Repetitive, seemingly driven, and nonfunctional motor behavior (e.g., hand shaking or waving, body rocking, head banging, mouthing of objects, self-biting, picking at skin or bodily orifices, hitting own body).

B. The behavior markedly interferes with normal activities or results in self-inflicted bodily injury that requires medical treatment (or would result in an injury if preventive measures were not used).

C. If Mental Retardation is present, the stereotypic or self-injurious behavior is of sufficient severity to become a focus of treatment.

D. The behavior is not better accounted for by a compulsion (as in Obsessive-Compulsive Disorder), a tic (as in Tic Disorder), a stereotypy that is part of a Pervasive Developmental Disorder, or hair pulling (as in Trichotillomania).

E. The behavior is not due to the direct physiological effects of a substance or a general medical condition.

F. The behavior persists for 4 weeks or longer. Specify if: With Self-Injurious Behavior: if the behavior results in bodily damage that requires specific treatment (or that would result in bodily damage if protective measures were not used)
Ref:
http://www.behavenet.com/capsules/disorders/autistic.htm

Question 192   Section: Diagnosis

The correct answer is C
The Global Assessment of Functioning (GAF) is a numeric scale (0 through 100) used by mental health clinicians and physicians to subjectively rate the social, occupational, and psychological functioning of adults, e.g., how well or adaptively one is meeting various problems-in-living. The scale is presented and described in the DSM-IV-TR on page 34. The score is often given as a range, as outlined below:
91 - 100 Superior functioning in a wide range of activities, life's problems never seem to get out of hand, is sought out by others because of his or her many positive qualities. No symptoms.

81 - 90 Absent or minimal symptoms (e.g., mild anxiety before an exam), good functioning in all areas, interested and involved in a wide range of activities, socially effective, generally satisfied with life, no more than everyday problems or concerns (e.g., an occasional argument with family members).

71 - 80 If symptoms are present, they are transient and expectable reactions to psychosocial stressors (e.g., difficulty concentrating after family argument); no more than slight impairment in social, occupational, or school functioning (e.g., temporarily falling behind in schoolwork).

61 - 70 Some mild symptoms (e.g., depressed mood and mild insomnia) OR some difficulty in social, occupational, or school functioning (e.g., occasional truancy, or theft within the household), but generally functioning pretty well, has some meaningful interpersonal relationships.

51 - 60 Moderate symptoms (e.g., flat affect and circumstantial speech, occasional panic attacks) OR moderate difficulty in social, occupational, or school functioning (e.g., few friends, conflicts with peers or co-workers).

41 - 50 Serious symptoms (e.g., suicidal ideation, severe obsessional rituals, frequent shoplifting) OR any serious impairment in social, occupational, or school functioning (e.g., no friends, unable to keep a job).

31 - 40 Some impairment in reality testing or communication (e.g., speech is at times illogical, obscure, or irrelevant) OR major impairment in several areas, such as work or school, family relations, judgment, thinking, or mood (e.g., depressed man avoids friends, neglects family, and is unable to work; child frequently beats up younger children, is defiant at home, and is failing at school).

21 - 30 Behavior is considerably influenced by delusions or hallucinations OR serious impairment, in communication or judgment (e.g., sometimes incoherent, acts grossly inappropriately, suicidal preoccupation) OR inability to function in almost all

areas (e.g., stays in bed all day, no job, home, or friends)

11 - 20 Some danger of hurting self or others (e.g., suicide attempts without clear expectation of death; frequently violent; manic excitement) OR occasionally fails to maintain minimal personal hygiene (e.g., smears feces) OR gross impairment in communication (e.g., largely incoherent or mute).

1 - 10 Persistent danger of severely hurting self or others (e.g., recurrent violence) OR persistent inability to maintain minimal personal hygiene OR serious suicidal act with clear expectation of death.

A is INCORRECT
This is coded on AXIS IV

B is INCORRECT
Provisional Diagnosis is coded on the AXIS it would go on if it was not a provisional diagnosis

D is INCORRECT

Question 193   Section: Diagnosis

The correct answer is B
According to Freud's psychoanalytic theory of personality, the superego is the component of personality composed of our internalized ideals that we have acquired from our parents and from society. The superego works to suppress the urges of the id and tries to make the ego behave morally, rather than realistically.
http://psychology.about.com/od/sindex/g/def_superego.htm

A is INCORRECT
According to Freud, the ego is part of personality that mediates the demands of the id, the superego and reality. The ego prevents us from acting on our basic urges (created by the id), but also works to achieve a balance with our moral and idealistic standards (created by the superego). While the ego

operates in both the preconscious and conscious, it's strong ties to the id means that it also operates in the unconscious. The ego operates based on the reality principle, which works to satisfy the id's desires in a manner that is realistic and socially appropriate. For example, if a person cuts you off in traffic, the ego prevents you from chasing down the car and physically attacking the offending driver. The ego allows us to see that this response would be socially unacceptable, but it also allows us to know that there are other more appropriate means of venting our frustration.
http://psychology.about.com/od/eindex/g/def_ego.htm

C is INCORRECT
The id is the only component of personality that is present from birth. This aspect of personality is entirely unconscious and includes of the instinctive and primitive behaviors. According to Freud, the id is the source of all psychic energy, making it the primary component of personality.
The id is driven by the pleasure principle, which strives for immediate gratification of all desires, wants, and needs. If these needs are not satisfied immediately, the result is a state anxiety or tension. For example, an increase in hunger or thirst should produce an immediate attempt to eat or drink. The id is very important early in life, because it ensures that an infant's needs are met. If the infant is hungry or uncomfortable, he or she will cry until the demands of the id are met.
However, immediately satisfying these needs is not always realistic or even possible. If we were ruled entirely by the pleasure principle, we might find ourselves grabbing things we want out of other people's hands to satisfy our own cravings. This sort of behavior would be both disruptive and socially unacceptable. According to Freud, the id tries to resolve the tension created by the pleasure principle through the primary process, which involves forming a mental image of the desired object as a way of satisfying the need.
http://psychology.about.com/od/theoriesofpersonality/a/persona lityelem.htm

D is INCORRECT

A term used by in psychoanalytic theory to describe the energy created by the survival and sexual instincts. According to Sigmund Freud, the libido is part of the id and is the driving force of all behavior.

The way in which libido is expressed depends upon the stage of development a person is in. According to Freud, children develop through a series of psychosexual stages. At each stage, the libido is focused on a specific area. When handled successfully, the child moves to the next stage of development and eventually grows into a healthy successful adult.

In some cases, the focus on a person's libidinal energy may remain fixed at an earlier stage of development in what Freud referred to as fixation. When this happens, the libido's energy may be too tied to this developmental stage and the person will remain "stuck" in this stage until the conflict is resolved.

For example, the first stage of Freud 's theory of psychosexual development is the oral stage. During this time, a child's libido is centered on the mouth so activities such as eating, sucking and drinking are important. If an oral fixation occurs, an adult's libidinal energy will remain focused on this stage , which might result in problems such as nail biting, drinking, smoking and other habits.

Freud also believed that each individual only had so much libido energy. Because the amount of energy available is limited, he suggested that different mental processes compete for what is available. For example, Freud suggested that the act of repression, or keeping memories out of conscious awareness, requires a tremendous amount of psychic energy. Any mental process that required so much energy to maintain had an effect on the mind's ability to function normally.

While the term libido has taken on an overtly sexual meaning in today's world, to Freud it represented all psychic energy not just sexual energy.

http://psychology.about.com/od/lindex/g/def_libido.htm

Question 194 Section: Diagnosis

The correct answer is D
The primary purpose of the DSM is to assess the client according to recognizable behaviors and symptoms as well as information gathered from the client and other collaterals.

A is INCORRECT
Given the wide variety of theoretical underpinnings utilized by our profession, there is no specific way to determine the "BEST" approach to treatment. As all clients are individual and respond differently, what may work for one person, may not work for another person. We do know that certain disorders respond better to specific kinds of treatment. For instance, Grief and Mourning responds better to group therapy, and Borderline Personality Disorder responds well to Dialectic Behavior Therapy.

B is INCORRECT
Mapping the etiology of a disorder may help us understand where it first developed and what stressors or life events have influenced it, however, it is not a function of the DSM.

C is INCORRECT
Evaluating a prior diagnosis comes from gathering information and reworking a diagnosis. The DSM is not specifically designed to assist in the evaluation of prior professional work.

Question 195   Section: Diagnosis

The Correct answer is D
Moderate Mental retardation is represented with an IQ range between 35-49.

A is INCORRECT
Borderline intellectual functioning is a categorization of intelligence wherein a person has below average cognitive ability (an IQ of 71–85), but the deficit is not as severe as mental retardation (70 or below). This is technically a cognitive impairment.

Clients in this range have a relatively normal expression of affect for their age, though their ability to think abstractly is rather limited. They tend to reason in a more concrete manner. They are usually able to function day to day without assistance, including holding down a simple job and the basic responsibilities of maintaining an apartment.

B is INCORRECT
Autism is a disorder of neural development characterized by impaired social interaction and communication, and by restricted and repetitive behavior. These signs all begin before a child is three years old. Autism affects information processing in the brain by altering how nerve cells and their synapses connect and organize. Autism is a spectrum disorder that does not necessarily correlate with mental retardation.

C is INCORRECT
Mild mental retardation indicates a person with an IQ range of 50-69

THE IQ SCALES ARE

Class	IQ
Profound mental retardation	Below 20
Severe mental retardation	20–34
Moderate mental retardation	35–49
Mild mental retardation	50–69
Borderline intellectual functioning	70–84

Question 196   Section: Diagnosis

The Correct answer is B
As a child develops, the process of internal monitoring sharpens and grows. This is the development of the superego. It is considered to be the controller of the human personality and allows the individual to judge things as "right" or "wrong". When a person has an under-developed or mis-developed superego, they are more likely to be impulsive and ego-

centered. They will want to meet their needs first, often without regard to the needs or wants of others. This impulsivity and "ME-centeredness" shows itself in many of the criteria of the Conduct Disorder.

A is INCORRECT

The function of the EGO is to moderate between internal impulses of the ID and with the help of the SUPEREGO, allow the client to interact with the world. This is the realm in which all of the ego-defense mechanisms can be used.

C is INCORRECT
An authoritarian parent is one who values control and power over discussion and cooperation. While you might think that imposing strict power and control over a child would assist the development of the internal moral control mechanism (Superego), it could actually hinder it if the child is not allowed to focus on and cope with his own internal controls.

D is INCORRECT
A rigid family structure is one with many boundaries and expectations. It may or may not be conducive to superego development, depending on the personality traits of the child.

Question 197   Section: Diagnosis

The correct answer is C
This is one of the Freudian stages of Psychosexual development.
"Fixation" is the Freudian term for problems with a stage. In this stage fixation can cause sexual unfulfillment, frigidity, impotence, and unsatisfactory relationships

A is INCORRECT
This stage is known as the Oral stage. Freud believed oral fixation might
result in a passive, gullible, immature, and manipulative personality.

B is INCORRECT
This stage is known as the Anal stage. Fixation at this stage can take 2 separate paths. Retentive fixation might be associated with obsessive organization or excessive neatness. Explusive fixation might be associated with reckless, careless, defiant, disorganized, and coprophiliac behavior.

D is INCORRECT
This stage is known as the Phallic stage. The major barrier to overcome at this age is the Oedipus complex (in boys and girls) according to Sigmund Freud.

Question 198   Section: Ethics

The correct answer is B
According to the NASW Code of Ethics, Section 1.08(a) :
Social workers should provide clients with reasonable access to records concerning the clients. Social workers who are concerned that clients' access to their records could cause serious misunderstanding or harm to the client should provide assistance in interpreting the records and consultation with the client regarding the records. Social workers should limit clients' access to their records, or portions of their records, only in exceptional circumstances when there is compelling evidence that such access would cause serious harm to the client. Both clients' requests and the rationale for withholding some or all of the record should be documented in clients' files

A is INCORRECT
There is no need to contact an attorney at this stage. You could seek legal assistance from NASW, but knowledge of your ethical code would probably be better.

C is INCORRECT
You cannot simply refuse to release the documentation, and fail to follow-up with any other action.
D is INCORRECT
If you are concerned the content of the record may cause the client a problem or that the content would need interpretation

by a professional to be properly understood, you can not release the record.

Question 199   Section: Diagnosis

The correct answer is D
In 2000, the American Psychiatric Association revised the PTSD diagnostic criteria in the fourth edition of its Diagnostic and Statistical Manual of Mental Disorders (DSM-IV-TR)(1). The diagnostic criteria (A-F) are specified below.
Diagnostic criteria for PTSD include a history of exposure to a traumatic event meeting two criteria and symptoms from each of three symptom clusters: intrusive recollections, avoidant/numbing symptoms, and hyper-arousal symptoms. A fifth criterion concerns duration of symptoms and a sixth assesses functioning.

Criterion A: stressor
The person has been exposed to a traumatic event in which both of the following have been present:
The person has experienced, witnessed, or been confronted with an event or events that involve actual or threatened death or serious injury, or a threat to the physical integrity of oneself or others.
The person's response involved intense fear, helplessness, or horror. Note: in children, it may be expressed instead by disorganized or agitated behavior.

Criterion B: intrusive recollection
The traumatic event is persistently re-experienced in at least one of the following ways:
- Recurrent and intrusive distressing recollections of the event, including images, thoughts, or perceptions. Note: in young children, repetitive play may occur in which themes or aspects of the trauma are expressed.
- Recurrent distressing dreams of the event. Note: in children, there may be frightening dreams without recognizable content

- Acting or feeling as if the traumatic event were recurring (includes a sense of reliving the experience, illusions, hallucinations, and dissociative flashback episodes, including those that occur upon awakening or when intoxicated). Note: in children, trauma-specific reenactment may occur.
- Intense psychological distress at exposure to internal or external cues that symbolize or resemble an aspect of the traumatic event.
- Physiologic reactivity upon exposure to internal or external cues that symbolize or resemble an aspect of the traumatic event

Criterion C: avoidant/numbing
Persistent avoidance of stimuli associated with the trauma and numbing of general responsiveness (not present before the trauma), as indicated by at least three of the following:
- Efforts to avoid thoughts, feelings, or conversations associated with the trauma
- Efforts to avoid activities, places, or people that arouse recollections of the trauma
- Inability to recall an important aspect of the trauma
- Markedly diminished interest or participation in significant activities
- Feeling of detachment or estrangement from others
- Restricted range of affect (e.g., unable to have loving feelings)
- Sense of foreshortened future (e.g., does not expect to have a career, marriage, children, or a normal life span)

Criterion D: hyper-arousal
Persistent symptoms of increasing arousal (not present before the trauma), indicated by at least two of the following:

- Difficulty falling or staying asleep
- Irritability or outbursts of anger
- Difficulty concentrating

- Hyper-vigilance
- Exaggerated startle response
-

Criterion E: duration
Duration of the disturbance (symptoms in B, C, and D) is more than one month.

Criterion F: functional significance
- The disturbance causes clinically significant distress or impairment in social, occupational, or other important areas of functioning.

Specify if:
- Acute: if duration of symptoms is less than three months
- Chronic: if duration of symptoms is three months or more

Specify if:
With or Without delay onset: Onset of symptoms at least six months after the stressor

> American Psychiatric Association. (2000). Diagnostic and statistical manual of mental disorders (Revised 4th ed.). Washington, DC: Author.

A is INCORRECT
A psychotic break describes a term used for an occasion when a person is experiencing an episode of acute psychosis. It could be for the first time, or after a significant period when the panic issue was in remission.

Environmental triggers, such as losing a loved one, are also known to be the precursor stressor prior to a panic attack. Some drugs have been associated with psychotic breaks. These include LSD, dextromethorphan (in higher doses), PCP, and opiates (mainly from experiencing withdrawal symptoms). There are other things can also cause temporary psychosis. Symptoms of psychotic breaks vary greatly, usually depending on the circumstances of diagnosis or any contributory substance ingested. Symptoms can range from harmless, sometimes unnoticed delusions, to violent outbursts and major depression.

B is INCORRECT

Panic attacks are periods of intense fear or apprehension that have a sudden onset[and of relatively brief duration. Panic attacks usually begin abruptly, reach a peak within 10 minutes, and subside over the next several hours. Often those afflicted will experience significant *anticipatory anxiety* between attacks, especially in situations where attacks have previously occurred. The effects of a panic attack vary.. Many who experience a panic attack for the first time, fear they are having a heart attack or a nervous breakdown. Repeated panic attacks are considered a syndrome of panic disorder.

Screening tools like Panic Disorder Severity Scale can be used to detect possible cases of disorder, and suggest the need for a formal diagnostic assessment.

DSM-IV Diagnostic Criteria for Panic Attack

A discrete period of intense fear or discomfort, in which four (or more) of the following symptoms developed abruptly and reached a peak within 10 minutes:

- Palpitations, or accelerated heart rate
- Sweating
- Trembling or shaking
- Sensations of shortness of breath or smothering
- Feeling of choking
- Chest pain or discomfort
- Nausea or abdominal distress
- Feeling dizzy, unsteady, lightheaded, or faint
- De-realization (feelings of unreality) or depersonalization (being detached from oneself)
- Fear of losing control or going insane
- Sense of impending death
- Paresthesias (numbness or tingling sensations)
- Chills or hot flashes

C is INCORRECT

An adjustment disorder is a psychological response to an identifiable stressor or group of stressors that cause significant emotional or behavioral symptoms that do not meet criteria for anxiety disorder, PTSD, or acute stress disorder. The condition is different from anxiety disorder because the anxiety disorder lacks the presence of a stressor, or post-traumatic stress disorder and acute stress disorder, which are associated with a more intense stressor. The DSM-IV identifies 6 types of adjustment disorders classified by their clinical features. Adjustment disorder may also be acute or chronic, depending on whether it lasts more or less than six months.

The diagnostic criteria in the DSM-IV are

A. The development of emotional or behavioral symptoms in response to an identifiable stressor(s) occurring within three months of the onset of the stressor(s).

B. These symptoms or behaviors are clinically significant as evidenced by either of the following:

1. marked distress that is in excess of what would be expected from exposure to the stressor

2. significant impairment in social or occupational (academic) functioning

C. The stress-related disturbance does not meet the criteria for another specific Axis I disorder and is not merely an exacerbation of a preexisting Axis I or Axis II disorder.

D. The symptoms do not represent Bereavement.

E. Once the stressor (or its consequences) has terminated, the symptoms do not persist for more than an additional six months.

Specify if:

- Acute: if the disturbance lasts < 6 months
- Chronic: if the disturbance lasts ≥ 6 months

Question 200   Section: Assessment

The correct answer is C
Always try to understand what the client heard and how they interpreted it. Therapy and assessment requires both people to constantly assess meaning and content of speech. Before you can do anything else, you should try to get the client to explain how they interpreted the previous statements. This will not only allow clarification but will empower the client by placing them in a situation where they have something of value (their interpretation) and you are asking for their help.

A is INCORRECT
The written policy would be a good step, especially of it is translated into Spanish, however, it is not the FIRST thing you would want to do and would likely alienate the client.

B is INCORRECT
It is generally good not to ask a "Why" question before you know the client very well. A "Why" question requires a client to defend a position or explain something they might not be fully aware of. This course of action could cause rather serious problems.

D is INCORRECT
This would not be your NEXT BEST move. If you did not have a social worker fluent in Spanish, you would be risking not providing services to the client of having them drop through the cracks. You should also remember this is an assessment and does not necessarily mean you will be providing long-term services. You want to ascertain what the client heard and how they translated the information. It is easy to misinterpret information during assessments and therapy.